D0939488

From Colonialism
to
World Community

PRESBYTERIAN HISTORICAL SOCIETY PUBLICATIONS

1. *The Presbyterian Enterprise,* by M. W. Armstrong, L. A. Loetscher, and C. A. Anderson (Westminster Press, 1956; Paperback reprinted for P.H.S., 1963 & 1976)

*2. *Presbyterian Ministry in American Culture,* by E. A. Smith (Westminster Press, 1962)

3. *Journals of Charles Beatty, 1762–1769,* edited by Guy S. Klett (Pennsylvania State University Press, 1962)

*4. *Hoosier Zion, The Presbyterians in Early Indiana,* by L. C. Rudolph (Yale University Press, 1963)

*5. *Presbyterianism in New York State,* by Robert Hastings Nichols, edited and completed by James Hastings Nichols (Westminster Press, 1963)

6. *Scots Breed and Susquehanna,* by Hubertis M. Cummings (University of Pittsburgh Press, 1964)

*7. *Presbyterians and the Negro—A History,* by Andrew E. Murray (Presbyterian Historical Society, 1966)

8. *A Bibliography of American Presbyterianism During the Colonial Period,* by Leonard J. Trinterud (Presbyterian Historical Society, 1968)

9. *George Bourne and "The Book and Slavery Irreconcilable,"* by John W. Christie and Dwight L. Dumond (Historical Society of Delaware and Presbyterian Historical Society, 1969)

10. *The Skyline Synod: Presbyterianism in Colorado and Utah,* by Andrew E. Murray (Synod of Colorado/Utah, 1977)

11. *The Life and Writings of Francis Makemie,* edited by Boyd S. Schlenther (Presbyterian Historical Society, 1971)

12. *A Younger Church in Search of Maturity: Presbyterianism in Brazil from 1910 to 1959,* by Paul Pierson (Trinity University Press, 1974)

13. *Presbyterians in the South,* Vols. II and III, by Ernest Trice Thompson (John Knox Press, 1973)

14. *Ecumenical Testimony,* by John T. McNeill and James H. Nichols (Westminster Press, 1974)

15. *Iglesia Presbiteriana: A History of Presbyterians and Mexican Americans in the Southwest,* by R. Douglas Brackenridge and Francisco O. Garcia-Treto (Trinity University Press, 1974)

16. *The Rise and Decline of Education for Black Presbyterians,* by Inez M. Parker (Trinity University Press, 1977)

17. *Minutes of the Presbyterian Church in America, 1706–1788,* edited by Guy S. Klett (Presbyterian Historical Society, 1977)

18. *Eugene Carson Blake, Prophet with Portfolio,* by R. Douglas Brackenridge (Seabury Press, 1978)

19. *Prisoners of Hope: A Search for Mission 1815–1822,* by Marjorie Barnhart (Presbyterian Historical Society, 1980)

20. *From Colonialism to World Community: The Church's Pilgrimage,* by John Coventry Smith (Geneva Press, 1982)

*Out of print.

BX
9225
S534
A34

From Colonialism
to
World Community

THE CHURCH'S PILGRIMAGE

by
John Coventry Smith

THE GENEVA PRESS
Philadelphia

HIEBERT LIBRARY
Fresno Pacific College - M. B. Seminary
Fresno, Calif. 93702

20495

Copyright © 1982 John Coventry Smith

All rights reserved—no part of this book may be reproduced in any form without permission in writing from the publisher, except by a reviewer who wishes to quote brief passages in connection with a review in magazine or newspaper.

BOOK DESIGN BY DOROTHY ALDEN SMITH

First edition

Published by The Geneva Press ®
Philadelphia, Pennsylvania

PRINTED IN THE UNITED STATES OF AMERICA
9 8 7 6 5 4 3 2 1

Library of Congress Cataloging in Publication Data

Smith, John Coventry, 1903–
  From colonialism to world community.

  Includes index.
  1. Smith, John Coventry, 1903–   . 2. Presbyterian Church—Clergy—Biography.   3. Clergy—United States—Biography.   4. Missionaries—United States—Biography.   5. Missions.   6. Ecumenical movement.   7. Church and underdeveloped areas.   I. Title.
  BX9225.S534A34 1982   266'.5131'0924 [B]   82-12138
  ISBN 0-664-24452-1 (pbk.)

With thanks to God I dedicate this record
of our experience in the mission of the church
to Floy Bauder Smith: wife, listener, counselor,
and fellow missionary of the church in Japan
and in the United States

Contents

Foreword

AT THE TIME my wife, Floy Bauder Smith, and I began in Japan our careers as missionaries of the Presbyterian Church in the U.S.A., most thoughtful young missionaries of our generation were becoming aware that the modern missionary movement that had begun in Europe in the 1800s was entering a unique and exciting era. That movement had begun in the period of history that produced political colonialism, but colonialism was nearing its end; and the churches founded by missionaries were anxious to become independent along with their nations. These changes produced the growing pains of success and marked the end of an era in the world mission of the church. It was not the end of mission; rather the church and its missionaries were challenged by the need for profound change in what they were now doing and at the same time compelled to find and enter the ways by which the church would function in the new era.

The chapters of this book are not a complete history of twentieth-century changes in mission strategy but are an autobiographical approach reporting our experiences in the missionary and ecumenical movement. They are based on the records which we kept over the years from 1929 to 1970 concerning the things which we saw and heard.

I think that, by and large, we were led to face these changes with some considerable measure of success. The reader will have to be the judge. But we had an obligation to interpret to the American churches what we were doing. I can bear testimony that we tried to do this, but I also must confess that in large measure we failed. I can witness now to the fact that many Christians and their churches in the United States still think of church work in other lands as "our foreign mission" and have little conception of the world community of Christians that now exists. The mission now, however, belongs to this world community; and we must be aware of that fact as we profit from working together at a common and universal task.

If this book proves to be only a history on library shelves, I will have again failed. I am hoping that it will be an interesting and attractive story of the experiences of missionaries in our time. I therefore invite you to look over my shoulder at the events as we saw them, to share in our understanding of the problems we faced, and, I hope, to understand and participate in the changes that have come about. I believe that God has led and is leading us into an exciting new era in the mission of the church. I also believe that the new era can be as rewarding as the era that is passing, if only the church can enlarge its vision and find its place in the common task of the world Christian community, a place that God is preparing for us as we face the future.

A strong impetus to write this book came at the end of a dinner conversation with an old friend and colleague in ecumenical efforts, Bishop Lesslie Newbigin. As we parted, he said, "John, when are you going to make a record for us of your experiences in the missionary and ecumenical movement?" After he returned to Princeton, where he had been lecturing, he sent me a handwritten note telling me that he really meant it and I should get on with the job. The idea was immediately attractive. At the urgings of friends and family I had in the past started to write but always gave up after a few pages. I had never really wanted to write a history or an autobiography; but I now saw that there was a way I could record my involvement in the mission of the church, and the materials I needed were in the archives of the Presbyterian Historical Society in Philadelphia.

Before I could ask William Miller and Gerald Gillette of the Historical Society under what conditions I could use the files, they proposed that I join in an Oral History program, with Jerry interviewing me about significant events in the life of the church around the world. I then told them my own purpose and spent the next two years on an Oral History project that involved 25 two-hour interviews, which were taped and transcribed as research material. We estimated we had more than 500,000 words with 33 distinct chapters, and it was that material which provided the basis for the twelve chapters of this book.

I have always been glad that the Presbyterian Church had a policy of appointing both husband and wife as missionaries. Each had to meet the same basic qualifications, each was assigned a task, and each had the same vote in all meetings of missionaries. A wife could even get half of the common salary paid to her if she wished. So my wife Floy had a full share in these experiences; she made her contribution both as a missionary and later as a president of the Westchester Presbyterial. She also shared in the preparation of this book. I wrote drafts; she listened and commented. We were reasonably sure of publication when after nineteen years of Parkinsonism she passed away in September 1980. It is to her that I dedicate this book.

The final form of the book owes much to the editorial assistance of Dr. Scott Francis Brenner, and Scott and I made his wife Helen a reader and commentator. Mrs. Sue C. Knorr was our professional typist. It was my friend Clifford Earle who arranged my first contacts with the Presbyterian Historical Society.

And, of course, I owe much to my colleagues in the Presbyterian Church, and to other missionaries and leaders of national churches around the world with whom I have discussed the problems the churches face and what we ought to do about them. There is now a great company of intelligent and committed Christians, of every race and denomination, prepared to counsel together and accept the leading of the Holy Spirit as we move ahead in relation to one another. God bless us all.

I am very pleased that the Presbyterian Historical Society has officially designated this volume as a work in The Presbyterian Historical Society Publication Series, and that the Program Agency of The United Presbyterian Church U.S.A. has made possible its publication.

Chapter 1

A Personal Beginning

(Detroit, Tokyo, Sapporo, Wakayama, 1927–1934)

JUST INSIDE the front door of our apartment there is a bookcase filled to overflowing. On the very top there are more than a dozen mementoes from several places where we have lived or visited. The oldest one by far is a pencil box. The other day I began to wonder why I had kept it. Except for some pictures, it is the only memento of my childhood that I have. We have moved at least fourteen times since I received it, twice across the ocean by boat, and the box has always survived. It must have made a very great impression upon me.

I became a professing Christian at the age of nine in the United Presbyterian Church at East Mansfield, Ohio, where my father was pastor of that home mission church. I had been challenged by a sermon that he had preached concerning the cross and I asked him if I could become a communicant member of the church. After questioning me, he replied that I would have to be examined by the session. Father was the examiner and I satisfied the session. The one comment he made that I remember was, "You will have to be prepared to have people expect more of you now." Father was right.

After my father and mother had been graduated from Grove City College, and father had been graduated from Xenia Theological Seminary and worked to pay his college debts, both hoped to become foreign missionaries. However, father was then past thirty years of age and the Foreign Board in those days did not think a person of that age could learn a foreign language. A college classmate of theirs by the name of William Coventry became a missionary in Egypt, and when I was born they gave me his last name as my middle name.

My brother Walter was just one year younger than I, but we

started school together. He early had decided that he would be a farmer, following the example of our mother's father. At the time I remember I had no definite profession in mind. I was twelve or thirteen years old and in grammar school when Dr. Coventry, while on furlough from Egypt, visited us in Elyria, Ohio. I remember sitting beside him in our front room and listening to him talk of his work, including going from place to place on the Nile River in a boat called the *Ibis* that belonged to the Mission. He had doubtless brought gifts for all our family, including my sister Margaret, but I remember only the one he brought me, a pencil box from Jerusalem. It was made of olive wood and had the name Jerusalem beautifully imprinted on it. It was not long after this that I decided I was going to be a missionary and go to Egypt.

Like the pencil box, my decision to become a missionary survived, fulfilling my high school yearbook prophecies. At Muskingum College I was soon a member not only of the student YMCA but also of the Student Volunteer group, which consisted of those who were planning to become missionaries. Both of these groups of students had state and national organizations and through such contacts my vision broadened. I was a member of the college team that debated membership of the United States in the League of Nations. In both my junior and senior years I tried out for college orator, preparing an oration that combined my vision of peace in the world with missionary commitment. I placed third both times.

We elected our freshman president in January of our first year. I was nominated by Floy Bauder, a girl I did not know. I did not get around to asking her for a date until October of that year. We made up for lost time and were engaged the following February, both knowing that this meant we were committed to going abroad in Christian mission.

At Pittsburgh Seminary I continued my interest in the Student Volunteer Movement and in my senior year was the student chairman of the National Council of the SVM and was privileged to attend its quadrennial convention in Detroit. There were some five thousand students there in addition to the adult leadership. More important than anything else was the idea which was urged upon us that when we went out as missionaries to any country where the Christian church was established, we should go to work under the administration of that national church. I was fascinated with the idea and determined to try it when the time came. I remember reporting on the convention to a church in Pittsburgh and stressing this concept. At that time I did not imagine that this would lead to a dominant emphasis that would control our missionary activity and tend to shape the course of Christian mission.

Both Floy and I were graduated in 1928, she from college and I from seminary. We were both accepted by the Board of Foreign Missions of the United Presbyterian Church of North America for service in Egypt. I was ordained, and we were married. But the Board had no funds that year to send us. After I had spent a year as pastor of two small churches outside Beaver, Pennsylvania, the Four Mile U.P. Church and the Fairview Reformed Presbyterian Church, the Board still had no money, so with its blessing we applied to the Board of the Presbyterian Church in the U.S.A. and were assigned to Japan. After we were appointed and before we left, my mother told me for the first time that she and father had prayed before I was born that I would be a missionary.

We were three days on the train to Seattle and then two weeks on the ship to Yokohama. The denominational change was not difficult for us. Our own denomination was conservative but not fundamentalist and we already had friends from the SVM in other denominations with whom we would be studying in language school, but we knew no Presbyterians in Japan. When we landed at Yokohama on November 1, 1929, there was no one to meet us. An Evangelical United Brethren missionary by the name of Paul Mayer was there to meet two churchmen of his denomination. He also welcomed and advised us. We checked our baggage, went by train to Tokyo with a young Japanese pastor who was introduced to us by Dr. Mayer, and then by taxi to Meiji Gakuin, a school where Presbyterian missionaries were teaching. After one false start we arrived on the doorstep of Willis Lamott's residence. The Japanese girl who answered the door called Mrs. Lamott. I told her I was John Smith. She looked blank. I said, "I am John C. Smith." She still looked blank. Then I told her that Floy and I were new missionaries. It still took her a second or two to realize who we were. But we were at the right place. Her husband was the chairman of the Junior Missionary Committee of the Mission. They knew we had been appointed but the only word they had had about our coming was a cable that ended,

"Smiths sailing November." And we had arrived on the very first day of that month.

After the first few moments the Lamotts gave us a royal welcome. We stayed with them for five or six days, including Floy's birthday, celebrated with a beautiful cake. Soon we moved to the home of Dr. and Mrs. Henry Stegeman on the other side of the campus at Meiji Gakuin, which was a boys high school and college supported in part by both Dutch Reformed and Presbyterian boards.

We attended the School of Japanese Language and Culture, an interdenominational school quartered across Tokyo in the YMCA. We were busy, for we had arrived six weeks late for the school term and had some catching up to do with the help of a tutor. In addition, in the spring our first child would be born, John Coventry, Jr.

Coming from rural Pennsylvania we were surprised, even then, at the facilities that Japan had. Small towns had paved streets, large primary schools, and electric lights. Few people had private cars but taxis were always available at modest rates. Running water was good but there were no sewerage systems. Human manure was collected and spread on the fields. Most of all we were surprised by the crowds of people on the trains and on the streets.

Howard and Ruth Hannaford were also teaching at Meiji Gakuin and became our official advisers. Howard introduced me to the local Japanese churches and both of us attended the Union Church, which had an English service on Sunday afternoon. There were several hundred thousand Christians in Japan then and most mainline Protestant churches were represented along with the Roman Catholic and the Orthodox churches.

Willis Lamott and Howard Hannaford were both on the Executive Committee of the Presbyterian Mission and I began to learn from them. I am surprised as I look back that we had never had any courses at seminary in what we call missiology, the theory and practice of mission. In time it would be discovered that church history out of a book was not adequate. I had conversations with Willis and Howard and then with fellow students at the language school, some of whom had been at Detroit. They had not been quite as much impressed as I was with *the idea of administration by the national churches of the work of missionaries*. The platform speakers, John R. Mott,

Robert E. Speer, and John A. Mackay, all spoke of the importance of the national church and stopped there. Perhaps the
application to the work of missionaries had come from the
student discussion groups, in which there were many foreign
students who were studying in American colleges. In any case I
was still learning as rapidly as possible and not yet ready
vigorously to propose new things when I did not yet know the
old things.

In the spring I attended my first Mission meeting. It was at
Gotemba, near Mt. Fuji. Every other year we met at Karuizawa,
a summer resort in the mountains. This first meeting was an
interesting learning process, as I talked to young Presbyterian
missionaries with more experience. I've always wondered why
we had Mission organizations. We were Presbyterians and it
would have seemed logical for us to start presbyteries and
include missionary concerns within those organizations. Maybe the fact that Presbyterians had first participated in foreign
missions through the American Board of Commissioners for
Foreign Missions, which was interdenominational and could
not be limited to a Presbyterian structure, was the reason.

Presbyterians believed they should establish self-governing,
self-supporting, and self-propagating churches, and that they
should be encouraged to join with other evangelical churches if
they wished. We were succeeding in some measure in Japan.
The church we had participated in establishing was Presbyterian in government but was the result of the efforts of the
missionaries from the Northern Presbyterian, Southern Presbyterian, Dutch Reformed, and Evangelical and Reformed
churches in the United States. Moreover, as in all Christian
churches in Japan, some of its first Christians were from the
body of *samurai*, or knights, who had served the *daimyo*, or
lords, in the feudal era and were no longer employed in the
central government established in the Meiji restoration. They
were courageous, proud, able, and respected. This all added
up to a church that rapidly became independent of missionary
supervision. Missionaries were members but not officers in the
church. They were still needed in schools and in pioneer
evangelism but not as "bosses."

But the organized Mission still continued. It had once been
all-powerful and it tended to retain all the power that was not
specifically given to the national church. Each American denomination had its own Mission, which not only handled the

personal problems of missionary support but made assignments of all missionaries, produced annual reports, granted
funds for budgets, and was the channel for all correspondence
with the denomination's American Board, even when it concerned the churches. For the missionaries, the Mission was
their power center. Very rarely did any Japanese attend Mission meetings. The Mission met annually and had an Executive
Committee of six with a chairman and a secretary. Missionaries
in separate geographical areas of the Mission were organized
into Stations which met once a month and on call.

There had been a major structure revision in the Japan
Mission in 1928 when Dr. Robert Speer and Dr. Hugh Kerr had
visited them. It was modeled after the Brazil Plan. In Brazil a
sizable part of the Presbyterian Church had withdrawn from
the main body in 1903, in part at least because of the continued
control of the presbyteries by the missionary members. Some
years later the Presbyterian main body in Brazil had literally
put their related missionaries at a distance from them. All
evangelism within the bounds of established presbyteries was
turned over to Brazilians and the missionaries had been given
new assignments on the frontier. The plan was that as established churches became strong enough to run their own
presbyteries the missionaries would move on to new territory.
This made the Mission a supervising body of new churches as
well as of all educational institutions except the seminaries. The
plan sounded good. It solved the problem of who was boss and
it worked for a time in a big country like Brazil where there was
room for everybody. But it was not a permanent solution. The
national church needed to be challenged to undertake the
evangelism of the entire nation and needed to supervise all the
work done for it in the nation.

It was soon evident that the Brazil Plan would not fit the
relatively small country of Japan. The presbyteries already
covered most of the nation. Subsidized churches were turned
over to the presbyteries, together with gradually reduced
subsidies; the evangelistic missionaries undertook new work,
but the work was always within the bounds of the present
presbyteries. In effect, the presbyteries and the Mission were
running on parallel lines without relation to each other. We
were bound to bump into each other, but we did not as yet
know that.

Our Presbyterian U.S.A. Mission had 65 missionaries. The

Nihon Kuristo Kyokai (The Church of Christ in Japan) had about 65,000 members and was the largest Protestant church in Japan. The Mission had established educational institutions as well, five high schools for girls, in one of which we shared with the Dutch Reformed; an interdenominational college for girls; and Meiji Gakuin, where we lived with our Dutch Reformed friends.

Gradual turning over of power to the Japanese was easier in these schools than in the church. Three of the schools already had Japanese principals, and boards of directors were in process of being established, to whom we would turn over the school property.

Missionaries were slowly being replaced on the boards by representatives of the alumni, by representatives of the natural constituency in the supportive community, and by representatives of the presbytery in which the schools were located. They were still being supported by the Mission with missionary faculty members and by small grants. This structure was one I was familiar with in the United States, but I was an evangelistic missionary and could not as yet envision the structure in which I would be involved.

In the summer of 1930 Floy, our baby, and I moved to Sapporo on the northern island of Hokkaido, which is off the coast of Siberia and 36 hours by train from Tokyo. We were to be assigned to Asahigawa, which is 80 miles north of Sapporo, but we were obliged to spend our second year as language students in Sapporo. Here we had firsthand experience with the Japanese church. Sapporo was one of the places in Japan where the church was strong. It had an Imperial University which, by invitation of the government, had had as its first president a Dr. Clark from Amherst, Massachusetts, who was a committed Christian and whose Bible class produced a surprising number of Japanese Christian leaders. He had stayed only two years, but his last advice was still remembered. It was: "Boys, be ambitious." There were four churches in this city of 150,000 and the Nihon Kuristo Kyokai was the strongest. Its prominent pastor was Rev. Rinzo Onomura, now middle-aged and the leader of Hokkaido Presbytery. Although he had never lived outside Japan he was an ardent reader in Japanese, English, and German and an able preacher and theologian. We became good friends and he took me under his wing. He was already studying Dr. P. T. Forsyth of England, who was a forerunner of Karl Barth. Onomura was surprised that I did not know about Forsyth. Most of all he taught me about the church in Japan. I shared with him my dream that we evangelistic missionaries should work under the direction of the presbytery. He was in favor of it and taught me a great deal about the presbytery itself.

In the summer of 1931, Mission Meeting was in Karuizawa. A dozen or more of us first-term missionaries decided to meet occasionally to discuss our junior missionary problems. Sam Franklin was our leader. When we met apart from the time of Mission Meeting we invited an older missionary of our choice to meet with us. It proved to be a place where this talk about serving under the Japanese church could be aired and discussed with some measure of creativity.

One other thing we did that first year in Hokkaido. On my first trip to spy out the land I had met a group of students on the ferry between the islands. One of them who was trying out his English asked me what the central truth of Christianity was. I was not satisfied with the answer I gave. I had never had the question put just that way before. I began to study the New Testament almost every day, in addition to our language study. I soon found that I had the answer. The central truth of our faith is not a theological statement or an ethical truth. It is Jesus the Christ. I should have known that. My favorite sermon as I came to Japan was one on Jesus Christ. My text was from John, "We believe thou art Christ, the Holy One of God." I had not seen this as the center of all that we know in the Good News. Later in the 1930s C. H. Dodd's book on *The Apostolic Preaching* confirmed my conviction. Jesus Christ was what the apostles preached.

Junior missionaries were required to complete three years of language study before they were allowed to vote in either Mission or Station meetings. We stayed on in Sapporo at the suggestion of the Station for our second year there and our third year in Japan. Our tutor was a seminary student who was a Congregationalist. His denomination was experimenting with a plan for all missionaries to serve under the (Japanese) church, and we often discussed the progress of this plan at intervals between language study. There were now nine Presbyterian missionaries in Hokkaido Station: Three single ladies who were teaching at Northern Star girls school, another single lady who was retired, a couple back from furlough who were working in evangelism, and a single lady who had a kindergarten at the port city of Otaru. Floy and I were often a minority of two when this group discussed mission policy.

Life was not just language and Bible study along with Station meetings. We had snow on the ground from Thanksgiving to Easter and I did some cross-country skiing. We had social gatherings in the Station and with the foreign teachers at Hokkaido University. We welcomed visitors from abroad and even the Lindberghs stopped at a town on the northern tip of the island. And one evening we dressed up and attended a Heifetz concert along with several hundred other people.

Discussions with Japanese friends increased as our language improved. We sometimes talked about the Manchurian Incident of September 1931, which had begun to trouble the Japanese people. I sometimes preached in English with a Japanese translator at a small church on the edge of the city. In the spring I wrote a sermon in Japanese as part of my final examination and then preached it to the little congregation.

Onomura remained my closest Japanese friend. I have always remembered a story he told me about himself. The Japanese are accustomed to serve green tea with a cake or cookie. Onomura San never took the cake or cookie. I asked him about it. It seemed that early in his ministry in Sapporo he had a class of students from the university. Most of them were not Christians and he knew some sake-drinking and carousing went on over weekends. When he knew them well, he cautioned them about both drinking and smoking. Their reply was that since he never smoked tobacco or drank sake, he did not know enough about it to teach them. Onomura thought about that for a time and finally decided that he liked cake and cookies with his tea so much that giving that up might convince them. And so he had given them up for some twenty years. In an Oriental setting this made quite an impression. It also impressed me. Others thought him a bit eccentric and some called him "The Lion of the North." I have always thought he was a true example of the strength of the Japanese Christian minority.

I was visiting Asahigawa occasionally and getting acquainted with the work requirements we would be responding to when we moved in the summer, but toward the end of the winter of 1932 our son John was seriously ill. He weighed less at age two than he had at age one. Finally the doctors at Hokkaido

University advised us to go to a specialist at St. Luke's Hospital in Tokyo. We did so. His illness was diagnosed by Dr. Elliot as colitis. We rented a house for the summer at Karuizawa, where Dr. Elliot would also be, and we spent our first vacation as a family there. Finally we were advised to keep him out of the cold, snowy winter of Hokkaido for at least one year. The snow was often five feet deep and sometimes the temperature was more than 20 degrees below zero. The Mission committee agreed and stationed us back in Tokyo, where we occupied a furnished missionary residence and I substituted for another missionary who was on furlough and who had been teaching in the Meiji Gakuin high school. The course taught was English conversation and was interesting since I was able to try out some of the ideas about language teaching that I had learned in my own studies. We also had several student Bible classes in our home and one young businessmen's class which met at the YMCA. My supervisor was the dean of the high school, Dr. Senji Tsuru, who became a longtime family friend. The head teacher was also a minister who had a small suburban church which I attended on Sunday morning and where I preached once a month, at first in English with the pastor translating, and later in Japanese. Japanese sermons are longer than ours and at first the pastor had to add to my sermon. Later I learned to satisfy him. I also sang in a male quartet at the church and we had many friends there. The suburb was Senzoku, and we were to see many of these people again in subsequent years.

At the end of the year John was making progress but not yet gaining much weight. The doctor advised that we not return to Hokkaido, where exercise was limited for a three-year-old during the winter months of deep snow. We were reassigned by the Mission as evangelistic missionaries to Wakayama City, the capital city of the Province of Wakayama. We were forty miles from Osaka and on the Inland Sea. A sister hospital of St. Luke's was also at Osaka. Wakayama was about the same size as Sapporo. Our work was with students at a junior commercial college in the city. It also included a new church development at two points outside the city, Iwade and Minoshima. One community had 6,000 people and the other 13,000. No Christian work was being done in either of these places. We had a young Japanese associate by the name of Shiozuka working with us. He had just been graduated from the seminary in Tokyo. The Nihon Kuristo Kyokai in Wakayama City was smaller than the one in Sapporo, but it was a good church and the largest in the city. The others were Episcopal, Methodist, and Holiness. Our pastor was a good man but not the equal of Onomura Sensei. The greatest advantage was the fact that we were now in one of the largest presbyteries. It included Wakayama, Osaka, Kyoto, and Kobe. In its outlying towns and cities were located the majority of our evangelistic missionaries. There was no lack of stimulus or opportunity for discussion. The junior missionary meetings flourished and Japanese leadership was strong. We were still assigned by the Mission and reported to it, but we regularly consulted with the Naniwa Presbytery leaders and rejoiced in the new fellowship that had been established.

The student work at the college offered no problems in getting started. One of the younger elders at the church was a professor in the college and the adviser to the student YMCA. I soon had a Bible class for students both at our home and at the church. Getting started in Iwade and Minoshima was not easy. Shiozuka and I were fortunate in getting an invitation in Iwade from the manager of a textile mill to hold a series of nine or ten lectures in the mill's dormitory. We had about fifty people in the evening once a week and could use the facilities also for a Bible school for children on the afternoon of the same day. We were also able to go from house to house with a printed invitation to the Bible school. Eventually we had considerably more than fifty children enrolled.

By the time the lecture courses ended we had discovered three Christians through our calling, and they would secure for one day a week two rooms in a house where we could hold the Bible school and have a worship service. The Bible school diminished to some 20 or 25 and the worship service at first to 3 or 4, which gradually grew to 8 or 10. We continued our calling and invitations to the service. Sometimes we gave small tracts to interested people. Only occasionally were we turned away by people who thought we were beggars. We called separately, and I think that for both of us it was the hardest thing we ever did. But we did become known in the town and after a while children would greet us and sometimes sing a hymn we had taught them. Sometimes I would overhear one of them explaining to a friend that I was "Sumisu Sensei," the Japanese name for Teacher Smith.

One day we were especially impressed with the need for

what we were trying to do. We passed the town hall late in the afternoon and saw that a party was being held. It was for the officers of the town and the schoolteachers. No women were present from the town but they had imported geisha for the occasion. Later after dinner we saw some of the men arm in arm with the geisha going to the small hotel to spend the evening. Geisha are by no means all prostitutes, but there was little question this time.

Shiozuka and I never made a call for people to stand up and accept Jesus Christ. It was explicit in what we taught and was followed up later in private conversation. Later events proved that we were making progress.

Minoshima was a different situation. It was a fishing village beside the sea. There was one Christian, who was badly handicapped and could not walk. We were able to rent the Young Men's Association building, paying $2.50 a month for one afternoon and evening each week. This was not a Christian organization but was purely secular. We persisted in calling, though it continued to be difficult. I'm sure both of us were often tempted, after arriving on the train, just to stay in the station and take the next train back to Wakayama, but gradually children came, and a few adults. I had an English Bible class for the teachers in the high school. At first there were three young men who were the nucleus of the small group, meeting in the evening. We advertised a special meeting when the pastor from Wakayama would be with us. The hour arrived and no one came. We waited and waited but still there was no one and we took an early train back. The next week we were told that several did come later in the evening. Again, as in Iwade, it was two or three years before those first three asked for baptism.

Our junior missionary meetings discussed many problems. What about servants? What about private cars? What about economy? These were depression years. In Sapporo a man had been found dead in a trash box within two blocks of our house. What about the war in China? One year we studied a book by Tawney and in another we studied Reinhold Niebuhr's *Moral Man and Immoral Society*, and always on the side we discussed our own relationship with the Japanese church. Nor was it all discussion. One family in student work welcomed students and servants to eat with them at the family table. Another lived one year in a Japanese house in a village and became in truth a part of the community. None of us had private cars. Public transportation was available and we used it. Japanese who had private cars also had chauffeurs. We did not want to belong to that class.

Up to this time we had not felt much opposition in the Mission. We were discussing theory and caused no problem to the older group. Now the work that we did and the plans that we made were about to become a threat.

The Executive Committee of the Mission was itself concerned about improving the Mission's way of doing things. Sometime late in 1933 or early 1934 Willis Lamott, the Secretary of the Mission, brought a new plan for our discussion in Osaka. It was to locate more of our evangelistic missionaries in the Naniwa area so that all could plan together and be of help to one another. We considered it a move in the right direction but thought it could best be implemented in cooperation with and under the supervision of the Japanese church. In fact, to take this initiative by ourselves as the Japan Mission without the support of the Japanese church would only widen the gap between us.

Later in 1934 we had the last meeting of the junior missionary group before some of us went on furlough. I had been stimulated in 1932 in Sapporo by the visit of Dr. Sears, who was a member of the Laymen's Foreign Missions Inquiry Commission, a survey group that was financed by John D. Rockefeller, Jr. I think Sears was a Baptist and a minister. I was impressed by him and enjoyed the conversation. Later, in 1933 when the report of the Laymen's Commission came out, I reviewed it for a Station meeting in Tokyo. At the time I was not much concerned about its theology but much interested in what it said about relationships with the indigenous churches. The report quoted Dr. Sears at this point on Japan. He said he had come prepared to support the missionary group in Japan, but after talking with leaders of the churches and with missionaries he reluctantly decided that by reason of a psychological situation in the relationship between the churches and the missionaries, the number of missionaries should be reduced. (Was this the first instance where a moratorium on missionaries was suggested?) In any case, in 1934 the Depression was reducing the number of missionaries, and we were convinced from actual experience that we could do some things that would change the psychological situation. The Eugene Barnards, the

Henry Bovenkerks, the Sam Franklins, Winburn Thomas (not yet married), and the Smiths, along with three or four single women missionaries, were unanimous that we wanted to try. I had been the chairman of that meeting and was authorized to write fully to the chairman of the Mission Evangelism Committee and report our opinion.

It was one of the longest letters I have ever written. I reported that we were informally consulting the church leaders about our work but we still felt awkward in engaging in evangelism in villages and towns where there were few if any Christians, and doing it really in the name of an American Mission. It would be wholesome and inspiring if we could do it in the name of the Nihon Kuristo Kyokai.

We therefore proposed that the Japan Presbyterian Mission offer to the Nihon Kuristo Kyokai the services of all its evangelistic missionaries, together with their budgets, *now to be administered as a fully integrated part of the total evangelistic work of the Japanese church.*

We thought we had worn down the resistance of most of the educational missionaries. They would not be greatly affected anyway. We had a minimum of five older couples who we thought would oppose us, though two of them might be won over. The remaining three were outspoken opponents. One was among the oldest and was the best linguist in our Mission. Once he got some of us younger people together at Mission Meeting and said something like this: "You do not understand the weakness of the Japanese. They never will be able to do things as effectively as we do them. This last year I was building a low wall along our property in Tsu. I had selected the brick and then approached a mason who had been recommended to me. I took him out and showed how to lay the brick, then left for my own work. That evening I discovered he had not done it well at all. The next morning I had him tear down what he had built and showed him again what I wanted. That evening the wall was as bad as before. So the next morning I took him out and kicked over the wall. Then I showed him again, and he did it well. This illustrates the problem you will have in working with the Japanese church." This also indicated the reason why we were still dealing with a bad psychological situation. We were not yet confident we would win.

The year 1934 was a busy one before our going on furlough. It was our first full year in Wakayama. We were involved in policy problems. But when we got to Karuizawa early in July, Dr. Elliot examined our boy, John, and reported he weighed as much and was as tall as a four-year-old should be. To add to that good news, our second child, Louise Adele, was born on July 23. As one of our friends said, "Now you have all the kinds there are." In September we were back in Wakayama for the tail end of a typhoon which blew off part of our roof. By the time we got the repairs done we were ready for our furlough and sailed the last of November from Kobe. The sea was rough along the coast up to Yokohama and all of us, except our four-month-old Louise, were seasick. But Willis Lamott came down from Tokyo to see us off on the long journey home and reported that the Evangelistic Committee had recommended our proposal to the Executive Committee, which had then adopted it unanimously as their own and would recommend it to the Mission. Later the Japan Presbyterian Mission adopted it with one or two dissenting votes.

None of us younger missionaries were members of the Executive Committee which supervised the Secretary's correspondence with New York, but certainly Willis had kept them informed about what was brewing. I realize now that we must have been perceived as a strong force by the Executive Committee and by the Board. They would have had to be armed with very good reasons to resist thirteen people about to complete their first terms and become the nucleus of the missionary force of the future.

Later, when I was settled at Hartford Seminary on my furlough study, I wrote to Dr. Cleland B. McAfee, who, after being Moderator of the General Assembly and a member of the Board of Foreign Missions for many years, was now our Secretary for the Far East. I suggested that I might go to see him, and we met in his home for lunch. He did not question me when I told him some of our experiences and how hopeful we were for the future. I am sure, however, that we were not the only group of young missionaries who were thinking this way, and apparently the authorities had decided to encourage some experiments in this direction.

We knew this was only the beginning in Japan. The next steps would be in implementing the plan, and this would take time. We were not aware then that this step would lead to others until the Christian mission began in a serious way to slough off the influence of colonialism. Japan would prove to be one of the easiest countries in which to do this. After all, Japan was a free country, whereas the great majority of countries where Presbyterian missionaries were at work were still under colonial governments.

Chapter 2

Attitudes Are Changed, Sometimes

(Hartford, 1935; Wakayama, Tokyo, 1936–1940)

FLOY AND I had expected to study for a year in Edinburgh on our way to Japan in 1929. We changed our minds when we knew that the baby was on the way. It would be better to get settled and then have the baby than to cross the ocean, have the baby, and then cross another ocean or two before we got settled. At least that was the doctor's advice, and we had followed it. Now, going on furlough in 1934, we had another decision to make. Should we go to Edinburgh as planned, on the scholarship I had from Pittsburgh Seminary, or should we go to the Kennedy School of Missions, which was permitted for a missionary on the terms of the scholarship. We decided on Hartford, Connecticut, where the Kennedy School was located. With two grandchildren our parents did not know, we wanted to be near them, and we wanted to get acquainted with the Presbyterian Church in the U.S.A., which we had joined two months prior to our sailing for Japan.

We got home for Christmas and a round of visits with families. Floy's parents had an upstairs apartment we could use. Floy and the children stayed there while I went to Hartford for the second semester. After a long summer we both went to Hartford with the children and stayed in a student apartment for the fall semester.

By this time we knew what we wanted out of furlough study. (1) We wanted a general updating of our theological background. (2) We wanted to reconcile my interest in the social aspects of Christianity and the basic elements of our faith. (3) We wanted to know more about Buddhism, the prevailing religion in Japan. Finally, it was necessary for me to produce a thesis as a requirement for the scholarship and for a Master of Theology degree from Pittsburgh Seminary.

In most things we succeeded even beyond our hopes. Hartford was part of the answer, but the fact that our Japanese experience had taught us what the things were that we wanted to study also played a great part. We would strongly advise that postgraduate study come after some mission experience. It tends then to focus the study on the things that have become important.

William Barr became my first teacher. He was my roommate, a missionary from India of the Evangelical and Reformed Church. He had a wife and children in St. Louis. He taught me to play bridge and as a team we played younger students. This knowledge became very providential indeed in 1942 in the Yokohama internment camp.

The Kennedy School of Missions was a part of the Hartford Seminary Foundation. I was registered in the School of Missions but my courses were largely in the seminary itself. Our theology professor was Herbert Farmer of England, who was temporarily at Hartford before going back to Westminster College in Cambridge to take John Oman's chair. Farmer was a quiet but brilliant theologian. His lectures were carefully prepared and read, sometimes only a sentence or a paragraph at a time, with his personal interjections along the way. He allowed plenty of time for questions and discussion. This was not theology out of a book but out of the life experience of a Christian telling us about his own beliefs in his own words. I had never had such an experience before. My seminary training at Pittsburgh had given me a good foundation, especially in English Bible under Dr. James G. Hunt and in homiletics under Dr. W. R. Wilson. But now I was doing graduate study and I liked it.

Hornell Hart was professor of sociology before going to Duke University. He was dealing with the Christian ethical elements in sociology and using concrete examples. I remember writing a paper for him on the differences between Reinhold Niebuhr and Kirby Page in the peace movement in the United States. We studied extrasensory perception, not out of a book, but by hearing Dr. J. B. Rhine himself tell about his experiments.

Douglas Mackenzie was teaching a seminar for graduate students. He had retired as president of Hartford. The seminar was two hours long each week in his home, where we always ended with tea. The first semester we studied Kant and the second Spinoza. I had to read most of our assignments two or three times, but it was an exciting experience, again because he was openly sharing his own personal conclusions with students that he loved. His last class with us was also his last class ever. He died on a trip to Africa within a few weeks.

We had one class on mission policy that was almost a complete failure. It was taught by the Dean and he confessed his notes were twenty-five years old. He was wise enough to let the dozen or so missionaries on furlough simply talk together about policy. We had no exam and no term paper. But a course in psychology under Daniel Fleming more than made up for it. He was teaching at Union Seminary in New York but came one day a week for a two-hour course. He taught us to use the psychological categories of inferiority and superiority complexes in evaluating experiences we had or observed while abroad. The one book I remember was John Heinrich's *The Psychology of a Suppressed People*, written out of his experiences in Northern India and Pakistan. His principles still help me understand the "prostration of spirit" that affects suppressed people in all parts of the world. One comment Fleming drew from me one day I will always remember. For the next assignment he asked us each to be ready to tell what we would preach about if we had but one chance to speak to an American audience. I stopped at the door to tell him I did not need to wait a week to know what I would say. It would be, "You will need to reduce your standard of living." That was nearly fifty years ago and I was expressing my reaction to the affluence of America compared to the poverty of most of the rest of the world.

I took one course in contemporary theology. Because I had already studied the textbook used, I was given special assignments. One was to review Karl Barth's commentary on *Romans* for the class. I remember mentioning two things. One was the statement that the world of man and the world of God are completely different and do not overlap. They are *tangent* at one point, the resurrection of Jesus Christ. I could understand the emphasis here. The other was that the world of man is like an amount which is placed within a parenthesis in algebra, $(a - b)$. God has placed an eternal minus sign in front of this world making it $-(a - b)$. I could understand this if it were hyperbole, but I could not follow him if he meant that working within the parenthesis to improve the world resulted only in making things worse, $-(a + b)$. We turned to a German student in the class who had studied under Barth and asked him what Barth would say. He replied that Barth would probably insist that it would make things worse.

I had chosen "Early Buddhist Ethics" for my master's thesis. Japanese Buddhism was Mahayana Buddhism, which came later. But to understand what came later one had to understand the original, which was Hinayana. I could study Mahayana later in Japan. In fact, Dr. Karl Reischauer had written the basic book on Mahayana Buddhism and he was our colleague in Japan. I was especially interested in the ethical part of my thesis. For me the problem of Hinayana is the problem of ethics without an eternal dimension. In fact, Gautama Buddha taught his disciples that he did not assert or deny the eternal. It simply was not important or profitable for day-to-day living. At least in the study of Buddhist ethics I had found part of my answer. How different from the Christian belief in God—a God essential for everyday living.

My greatest experience at Hartford, however, was at an extracurricular event. The Student Volunteer Movement held a conference in the spring and Dr. John Mackay was the main speaker. At that time he was the Latin American Secretary of the Presbyterian Foreign Board. He spoke three times. At the third service his text was from Job, "The morning stars sang together." The context indicates that this occurred at Creation, and Dr. Mackay took off from there. His conclusion was that the Creator intended that all creation should work together, including mankind. Christians were intended to work toward this goal. It hit me where I was and I felt that I was walking on air for several days. I still think this was the single most significant sermon that I have ever heard. It answered my question of how faith in God is related to my participation in society.

We did not get acquainted with many individual Presbyterian churches on our furlough. We attended the First Presbyterian Church in Hartford but we also often went to vespers at a Congregational church. I spoke at the New England Synod and preached several times at Thompsonville, where the church was vacant. I heard George Buttrick preach at Madison Avenue on Palm Sunday and I attended the General Assembly in Cincinnati as an advisory delegate from the Japan Mission.

This was the Assembly that refused to seat Carl McIntire as a commissioner because he and others continued to be members of the Independent Presbyterian Board of Foreign Missions. I knew little of the controversy but I was convinced that anyone who repeatedly accused Robert E. Speer, the Secretary of the Assembly's Board, of being a heretic did not belong as a voting member of the Assembly.

I did see the staff of the Foreign Board in action. Sam and Dorothy Franklin were studying at Union Seminary in New York. Sam wrote me that they were in trouble and were appearing before a staff committee of the Board. I telephoned Dr. Cleland McAfee and got permission to attend the meeting. Sam had been sent to New Rochelle to preach on the day of their Every Member Canvass and at the service distributed a statement that he and his students in Kyoto had drawn up about the economic situation. The trustees of the church promptly protested to the Board. Dr. William Schell, the Home Base Secretary, presented the problem. McAfee, Mackay, Speer, and Franklin Mack, the Youth Secretary, were there. We talked for about two hours. I realize now that with people like J. Gresham Machen and Carl McIntire breathing down their necks they had to take this seriously.

No decision was reached; this was only a hearing. Sam apologized for distributing the paper on that particular occasion but asserted the paper contained what he believed on the subject. Speer said one could discuss such things with his family before the fire in the evening but not in a sermon on Sunday morning. Mackay said that he still met for Bible study with a group of liberal Peruvians in New York who were "persona non grata" in their own country. Si Mack confessed that as a staff member he agreed with Sam. Schell was most uncompromising. McAfee said he would try to work this out. He had been Sam's professor and friend at McCormick Theological Seminary.

Six months later when we saw Sam and Dorothy at the station in New York on our way back to Pittsburgh and then to Japan, Sam confided to me that he had told McAfee that if he could talk with some of the Board members and if some agreed that he represented them, he would go back. McAfee was to make the arrangements. When the time came, the Franklin children had been ill and McAfee assumed that they could not come. By that time Sam had an offer from Sherwood Eddy to head up a farm project in Mississippi. McAfee advised him to take it.

All was not lost. Sam worked with Sherwood Eddy, finished his Ph.D., and went into the chaplaincy in World War II. Then he was asked to go back to Japan with the Board as full-time professor at Tokyo Union Theological Seminary, where he served for more than twenty years in the field of social ethics, also helping in new church development.

We left Hartford with a master's degree but with much more that was excellent preparation for what we faced in Japan. We had made new friends. One was Bill Orr, who later became a professor at Pittsburgh Seminary. Another was a professor at the Christian Reformed Seminary in Grand Rapids, where I preached the baccalaureate sermon the year I was Moderator. And then there was Alford Carleton, who was a Congregational missionary in the Middle East and who later became the Secretary of the American Board of Commissioners for Foreign Missions. We were fast friends and were often together in the National Council of Churches and the World Council of Churches, and in our common tasks in misson.

Wakayama, 1936–1939

After a brief visit with our families in the Pittsburgh area, we went again by train and boat to Yokohama and then to Kobe. This time friends met us at the boat and in two or three hours we were back in our home in Wakayama. The outstanding thing I remember was that Winburn Thomas rode up to Osaka with us and asked me to be his best man at his wedding. He was filling in for Sam Franklin in student work at Kyoto and now was engaged to be married to Fuji Yamamoto, an American of Japanese parentage who was teaching at Doshisha University. The wedding was to be in the summer. We were very happy for both of them.

The next day, February 27, 1936, we learned that on the day before, soldiers, under the leadership of young officers, had attacked the Prime Minister's residence and almost succeeded in taking over the government. The soldiers surrendered only after the Emperor, on the advice of his senior officials, appealed personally to the officers. A new government had to be formed, but this was becoming increasingly difficult. The Japanese constitution provided that only an Army man could be War Minister and only a Navy officer could be Navy Minister. The Navy posed no problem; they were less militant. But the Army could veto a government by refusing to recommend a War Minister. There was no proof that the high officers in the Army had approved the attempt at a coup, but the young officers received only a minor reprimand. The Army contended that if the political parties in the Diet did not do justice to Japan's defense needs, they could not restrain the young officers. A compromise was reached, but the threat to civilian democratic government remained. Up to this time Japan's twentieth-century government had been modeled very much after that of Great Britain.

We soon found that Shiozuka had been doing well while we were gone and that we could take up our relationships with Iwade and Minoshima, as well as in Wakayama itself, with little change.

The most important aspect of our second term was the implementation of the new policy of relationship with the church which was adopted by the Japan Mission as we were leaving on furlough. Nihon Kuristo Kyokai had accepted the offer of evangelistic missionaries within the church administration. At the national level there was an overall committee that consisted of both Japanese and missionaries. The real administration was done at the presbytery level. We were in the largest presbytery, the one with the largest engagement in evangelistic work. Missionaries became members of the presbytery with one vote rotated with every five members, the same vote that Japanese members had who were not pastors of self-supporting churches. The right to judge our ministerial standing was still with our presbytery in the United States but Naniwa Presbytery had the right to invite us to Japan and to send us home. Our work was joined with all the other evangelistic programs of the presbytery and was administered by a committee of six, which usually included Moderator Kuwada, Stated Clerk Iijima, Henry Bovenkerk, and myself. We had monthly meetings. We made assignments, approved budgets, and met problems of missionaries in new church development under the presbytery. We missionaries never met ahead of time to plan strategy. The six of us took up the agenda item by item without previous consultation. We trusted each other. It was one of the richest experiences of our lives. The plan had provided the structure but the plan would not have worked without the trust that undergirded our attitude in the meetings.

I remember being asked by Darley Downs, the director of the language school, to speak to the new students the year we were in Tokyo in 1932–33. I told them I hoped Darley would forgive me if I did not place language as the first requirement for the new missionary. I could place it second *and* third *and* fourth. But something else was first. It was the attitude of the missionary toward persons of another color and culture, the willingness to work under their direction and to make contributions to the whole. This need was especially true for Westerners who had unconsciously absorbed attitudes of superiority toward less economically developed countries. We would need all the grace that God could give us if we were to effectively change this.

It seemed to come easy for us in Naniwa Presbytery, probably because we had prepared for it but also because there was then less bitterness there than in some other parts of the church. I was to learn of the bitterness later. This experience was to instill confidence that we could overcome tougher problems.

Tommy and Fuji had chosen July as the month of their marriage. There was still a hurdle. A wife had to qualify for missionary appointment with the Board. Fuji was a committed Christian, she had her M.A. from a good university in California, and she was an American citizen. The missionaries who knew her had recommended her to the Board and the Mission Executive Committee had backed it up. But still the Board hesitated. They did not say yes, but neither did they say no. Dr. Hereford, a missionary on furlough in the South, traveled to New York to assure them we were in favor of it. But a substitute in the office for Dr. McAfee wrote to Tommy that some of them advised that Tommy should take a short furlough and "find a white girl." None of the rest of us knew about that then, but Tommy and Fuji did. Finally Tommy wrote to the Board that they were getting married on July 14. If Fuji was appointed as a missionary, well and good, but if she was not, the letter was also to be regarded as his resignation. The appointment did not come through before the marriage, but it finally came through.

I began preaching again in Japanese and soon was able to

take full charge of a service at either Iwade or Minoshima. We could then be given a further assignment. The Presbytery Committee gave us Gobo, a town of some 15,000 farther down the coast beyond Minoshima. Gobo had had an evangelist at one time but the work had been closed for at least five years. We found one Christian who was still active and others who still knew something about the Christian faith. Shiozuka took major responsibility at Gobo, and after a summer with a seminary student, Shiozuka and his family moved to Gobo. Before the second year was over the presbytery organized this group that was now 15 baptized Christians into a congregation on its way to becoming a full member of presbytery. This kind of new church development was what we hoped and worked for at the other two assignments, Iwade and Minoshima. In fact, this was the goal of an evangelistic missionary.

In Pittsburgh Seminary we had been required to memorize our sermons that we preached to the faculty. That made for careful preparation, but also for rather stilted delivery. At the Four Mile U.P. Church I departed from that practice, outlined carefully, practiced the delivery once or twice, and then spoke extemporaneously. But when it came to Japanese, I had to go back to memorizing after writing the full manuscript. I dictated to Shiozuka in as good Japanese as I could muster. He then dictated it back to me with the corrections he had made. I wrote it in Japanese, using the syllabic kana along with the kanji (ideographs) which I was learning. Then I went to the attic in Wakayama and repeated it every hour on the hour until I could say it. I always carried my manuscript in my pocket but never used it in the service. Then one night in Iwade I forgot the wording in the middle of a sermon. I was determined not to read, so after a minute I continued, preaching extemporaneously but including phrases and sentences that I could remember. From that time on this was the way I preached, always writing carefully but abandoning my manuscript, except for quotations.

It was interesting to watch the growth of our work as part of the work of presbytery. For example, in Gobo when financial matters came up I found that I was of little use to them as an adviser. But the congregation's attitude toward the decisions of our Japanese presbytery committee led to their acceptance, even if they were the same as I had advised.

There were thirteen ministers of our church in Wakayama

Province. Two were missionaries. Besides myself, the other was Ernest Chapman, who was at the other end of the prefecture in Shingu. In 1937 the thirteen of us had a retreat at Shingu with studies and speeches and some public meetings. I remember that I preached one evening and led the Bible study one day. I used the Old Testament, a practice that was rare in the Japanese church, and this led to a discussion about the place of the Old Testament in the Christian faith.

In Wakayama itself there had been a change of pastors. Ishikawa was now the Secretary of the Nihon Kuristo Kyokai for its work outside Japan among Japanese communities in Korea, Manchuria, and China.

Okada Masao succeeded him. He was younger, only two years older than I, and he was made of the same cloth as my friend Onomura in Hokkaido. He was candid, blunt, and sometimes quick tempered, but pure gold in commitment and loyalty. He had served in Tokyo after graduation and was a *deshi* (disciple) of Takakura, who was the president of the seminary. Okada was Barthian in theology, preached long sermons, and sometimes was difficult to understand. But he was as open as he was blunt, and he was willing to learn. In his first year, church attendance increased by 50 percent and program and budget were in proportion.

As a fellow member of Presbytery, Okada took a deep interest in what we were doing outside Wakayama. In 1938 we held a conference in Wakayama, not just for the ministers but for all the churches in our province. On Friday the ministers met for a retreat. On Saturday, 91 Christians had studies and discussions as well as inspirational addresses. On Sunday the visiting ministers preached in the local churches. It had been organized on the basis of my budget but it ended up having almost as much budget support from the Wakayama congregation. The people from the smaller churches were strengthened by associating with those from stronger churches, and the stronger churches began to see that they had a mission to help those who were weaker.

We were no longer junior missionaries, but we held one last meeting at the Bovenkerks' in Tsu. We had a chance to compare our experiences under the new policy. There was confidence and trust in most instances, and misunderstandings were cleared up. That same year, 1937, I was asked to report to the interdenominational Japan Missionary Fellowship on why we had come back to Japan after our first furlough. I took the occasion to tell something of our experience and to emphasize the fact that the psychological situation could be changed and missionaries could work under the church.

That the psychological situation had changed was evidenced in another incident. Okada had come to Wakayama from Tokyo. When I first talked to him about our work in Wakayama he told me bluntly that the younger pastors in Tokyo did not believe that there was any need for missionaries. I was not surprised, for I had heard a little about that. I simply told him what we were doing and that there was no one else on the scene to do it. Several months passed and we were involved together in the work as I have already indicated. Then Leroy Dodds, a missionary to India who was becoming a Board Secretary, visited us in Wakayama and had lunch in our home with Okada. I had not warned him at all but he asked Okada what he thought missionaries could do in Japan. Okada told him of his first reply to me and then said that now he had changed his mind, that if missionaries could work with the church as we were working, there was need for them.

Dr. Robert E. Speer and Dr. Cleland B. McAfee had retired from the Board of Foreign Missions at approximately the same time, and in 1937 two new men had been added to the staff. Leroy Dodds became Secretary for India; Dr. Charles Leber of Scranton, Pennsylvania, became Secretary for the Far East. In 1937 they both attended our Mission meeting and we were impressed. Dodds understood us from his past experience and Leber could inspire us and the church with his messages.

Also at the 1937 Mission meeting some of the younger missionaries became members of important committees. I was elected to the Executive Committee and Bovenkerk and I were given the task of relating our Mission to the Southern Presbyterians, especially to Chuo (Central) Seminary. We were to be involved with this for the next *four years*.

Our Northern Presbyterian position in relationship with the Nihon Kuristo Kyokai (Nikki for short) was not always shared by the other Missions related to the same church. This was particularly true with the Southern Presbyterians, whose work was largely in the area of Naniwa Presbytery. When we were received into the membership of Naniwa in 1936, the Southern Presbyterians were not. The obvious reason for this failure was the fact that they did not fully cooperate with the church. Once at a general synod meeting in Tokyo, Dr. Tada, the moderator, asked the Southern Presbyterians why they did not cooperate more fully with the Nikki Church. Dr. William McElwain, who had studied on furlough under J. Gresham Machen, replied, "We do not accept the creed of the church." Tada asked, "Do you believe the statements it makes?" (It was the Apostles' Creed, plus additional articles on the Bible, the church, and the work of the Holy Spirit.) McElwain replied, "Yes." Tada asked, "Then what is the matter with it?" McElwain's reply was, "It is not enough." Tada asked, "What more do you want?" McElwain responded: "We believe that the whole counsel of God is contained in the Westminster Confession. Until that is made the confession of the Japanese church, we cannot cooperate fully with you." We Northern Presbyterians at the time also had as our creed the Westminster Confession but did not believe we should impose all of it on the Nikki Church. The basic elements they already had. Let them add to it as the Holy Spirit led them. (Insisting on the Westminster Confession would have opened the door to the Dutch Reformed and the German Reformed insisting on their confession, and we would have been importing our foreign differences into the life of the church in Japan.)

The Southern Presbyterians had come to Japan after the Nihon Kuristo Kyokai and its institutions had been established. They joined forces with the other Reformed churches in this Japanese church, but with reservations. They participated in the Meiji Gakuin Seminary where the other Missions were, but at the turn of the century they objected to a textbook used by Prof. Uemura Masahisa. It lacked a full system of theology but Prof. Uemura was supplementing it with his own lectures. The objection was carried all the way to New York and the textbook was withdrawn. But the Southern Presbyterians also wanted Uemura dismissed. He was retained and the Southern Mission withdrew and formed their own seminary in Kobe. This was Chuo (Central) Theological Seminary.

We Northern Presbyterians got involved in Chuo because in the early 1900s we had a Bible school in Osaka, started by the Cumberland Presbyterians. Under pressure from the missionaries in that area the Bible school had merged with Chuo. The Southern Presbyterians made the condition that they would always have a proportion of 3 to 2 on the faculty and on the board of this new seminary, which was not officially related to the church, although it prepared ministers for the church.

It was about thirty years later that Bovenkerk and I came into the picture, but our opposite numbers on the faculty and on the board were another McElwain and another Moore, sons of men who had objected to Uemura years before. They were good men but they were chips off the old blocks.

This explains the problems we faced at Chuo. It also is a basic explanation of the bitterness between missionaries and church in Tokyo, for after the Southern Presbyterians had withdrawn from Meiji Gakuin, then Prof. Uemura also withdrew, joined Japanese friends, and formed his own Japan Theological Seminary which was then closely related to the Nikki Church and had no missionary professors or any other Mission support. Dr. Uemura was a very able man, pastor of the largest Nikki church in Tokyo, editor of the *Fukuin Shimpo* (Gospel News), which for years was the church's leading publication. The Japan Seminary grew and soon was larger than either the one at Meiji Gakuin or the one at Kobe. It is not surprising that it asserted its Japanese character and was at times antimissionary. Its history explained many things for me, including the beginning of the psychological situation. Just before we arrived in Japan, the Meiji Gakuin Seminary was absorbed by the Japan Seminary and Dr. Reischauer, from Meiji Gakuin, joined the combined faculty. It was said, however, that he would be the last missionary on the faculty. Onomura, in Hokkaido, and Takakura, the new president, were both devout disciples of Uemura, and Okada was a disciple of Takakura. Between them I was exposed to the strengths of their position and sometimes to its bitterness. Looking back we could realize the divisive significance of the three seminaries where there had been one.

When Heinie Bovenkerk and I came to the board at Chuo we filled the two places reserved for our Mission. There were now seven members, two of them *Japanese, elected by the Missions and not by the synod.*

Dr. Fulton, Southern Presbyterian missionary, who was seventy-four and president of the seminary, died in 1938 at Karuizawa. Dr. Fulton's death meant that we had to elect a new president. This issue brought about our first confrontation. The first nominating committee's proposal was voted down. The second nominating committee consisted of Moderator Kuwada of Naniwa Presbytery, Lardner Moore, and myself. Lardner began by saying, "Now we have an opportunity to raise the banner of Orthodoxy in the Japanese church by electing Will McElwain." On the other hand, we began by suggesting a Japanese president. We compromised with a five-year term for Dr. Harry Myers, who was on the faculty and was a moderate Southern Presbyterian.

Heinie and I advocated that the Japanese members of the board might be increased by the Alumni electing one or two members. That was voted down. We also advocated that the two present members should be elected by the synod. We lost, but later, as the war drew near, Moore was appointed to draw up a statement that would satisfy us all. It proposed that the board, which was dominated by Southern Presbyterians, would nominate suitable people and then the synod could elect two from that number. I tried that out on one of the present Japanese members and he said the synod would not accept this. I wrote Lardner and told him what I had found out. I'll always remember his reply: "You have blown it for us. Maybe you intended to all along. If we do not get synod recognition now you will be solely to blame. You do not know how to get something from the Japanese when you know they do not want to give it." It took several days before I could answer that. Then I wrote: "I did not know I was being used to deceive the Japanese. If that is the case, I will resign." I happened to be taking my turn as chairman of the board that year. Lardner had sent his letter to all the board members. I did likewise, and that brought the chairman of the Southern Presbyterian Mission to see me. We spent almost two hours together. Finally he said: "I think I now understand you. You trust the Japanese Christians and we don't."

Will McElwain would not have said it that way. I've heard him say: "It is not a question of trusting their honesty or sincerity. They say and do what they believe. I do not trust their Christian judgment as to what is right."

Some time later I had word from Kobe that the Southern Presbyterians were proposing to close the relationship with us and move closer to the Machen group. It had all been decided and we need not have a board meeting. We refused and called a board meeting. Heinie and I were there and we closed out our relationship with what dignity we could muster.

We had tried but we had failed for our purpose. But in any case, through this extended process our Japanese friends in the church and ourselves had been drawn closer together and had established channels of trust.

In the late 1930s nationalist tension increased in Japan but, at least in the first years, it did not seriously hamper our work in Wakayama prefecture. It became difficult to make new friends but we could still work among old friends. Iwade and Gobo were no problem. The Christian witness had been there long enough to be familiar. Swarms of children still came to Bible school at Iwade and they were well behaved. Minoshima was becoming a different matter. Children came but they were more unruly. The high school principal said he hated to see me coming to visit some of his teachers who were in my Bible class. The Buddhist priest advised his people to boycott the tombstone maker who had been baptized. The newspaper editor took one swat at me, but it did not hurt much. He hit harder after I was gone. Baptisms still occurred.

Our being able to do this freely in most places may have been largely due to the work that Dr. J. B. Hail had done as a pioneer missionary in the prefecture. He was a Cumberland Presbyterian missionary. In the early 1900s the Cumberland Presbyterians had work in Naniwa and their Mission was the "West Mission." U.S.A. Presbyterians were the "East Mission," centering in Tokyo-Yokohama. The union of the two churches in the United States occurred in 1906. Dr. Hail, the Wakayama missionary, had been the last Moderator of the Cumberland Presbyterian Church in the United States before the union.

In Wakayama, Dr. Hail traveled up and down the prefecture, mostly on foot, wearing straw sandals as Japanese farmers did. He retired to a home in Wakayama City which he deeded to the church. For years after his death, they remembered him at Easter with a church service held early in the morning at his grave. There were many stories about "Hairu Sensei." The one I remember best was told me by a Mr. Suzuki, who at one time was his associate.

Before the days of railroads and buses they would set out on foot along the road that led them into the mountains. They carried little luggage, except for a large *bento* (lunch) that Mrs. Hail had packed carefully for them. Once Suzuki complained that the *bento* was too heavy to carry up the mountain road. He wanted to throw it away, there surely would be a lunchroom at the top of the mountain. But Hail said no, and then no again. They got to the top and there was a marvelous view but no lunchroom. As they were eating their lunch by the side of the road Dr. Hail said, "The *bento* is like the Christian faith. As long as you carry it with you, it is a burden, but when it becomes part of you it is your strength."

Tokyo, 1939–1941

The 1938 Mission meeting was in May at Gotemba. The first day Dr. and Mrs. Reischauer took me for a walk. They told me that Tokyo Station was losing two missionary families. The Station must fill at least one of these positions and we were their first choice. Reischauer described the position as part time at Meiji Gakuin and part time in evangelism with the Tokyo Presbytery.

Floy and I now had seriously to consider this. I soon discovered that the 1934 Mission action which put evangelistic missionaries under the supervision of the church really had never been put into effect in Tokyo. All our missionaries in Tokyo were related in some way to institutions, most of them educational. They were responsible often to Japanese administration but not that of the presbytery. Many in the presbytery thought the missionary was not interested in evangelism. This was supported by the antimissionary spirit in the seminary which Okada had talked about. On the missionary side it was thought that the church was not interested in anything else but evangelism *(dendo)*.

We explored that summer what the Tokyo Presbytery invitation meant and found it was an authentic invitation and that six different suburbs around Tokyo were being considered for new church development. I also discovered that Okada had written to a seminary classmate who was the pastor of the Senzoku church and a member of the Presbytery Executive Committee, telling him of our working together and suggesting that it would be good for the work and for the presbytery if I should work with them. Members of the Senzoku church remembered us from 1933, and Kashiwai, the pastor, would become my adviser. I had a warm welcome from at least part of the presbytery and an official welcome I had never expected.

The action of 1934 had led to the forming of a cooperative committee in the Tokyo Presbytery, but the tasks they considered were mainly the individual missionary's personal projects and were on the fringes of the presbytery's concern. As a result of the 1934 action, *no individual missionary had joined the presbytery*. My accepting the presbytery's invitation would be the first breach in the wall that somehow had risen to separate us. It took several weeks for us to understand and believe this. Okada confirmed our conclusions. He hated to see us go but believed it was God's will. Okada also helped Naniwa Presbytery understand the situation. Floy and I came to believe that if we were to continue to try and change the psychological situation between Mission and Church, we could not refuse this invitation.

Then, to our amazement, we discovered that the Meiji Gakuin administration had never been consulted about my not being a full-time teacher. At first they were adamant. Lamott had gone back to the United States and Hannaford had not been there when this started. It had fallen through the cracks. The president now said I must teach *full time* but could give my *spare time* to the presbytery. This we could not accept. It would make the presbytery action a personal affair and not a mission assignment. That was not good enough. The decision finally was made by the Meiji Gakuin board, where several Japanese churchmen sat and where Heinie Bovenkerk and Karl Reischauer supported me. I was to teach fourteen hours in four days and the rest of my time was the presbytery's.

We were also disturbed by the attitude of most of the Tokyo missionaries about our evangelistic work. They questioned why I wanted a "preaching place." This was a thing of the past for missionaries. They now taught others to do it. I knew from experience that you could not teach others about things you were not committed to doing yourself. Such remarks made us even more determined to try for a change.

Our children were excited about the possibility of playmates on Meiji Gakuin campus and schoolmates at the American school in Tokyo. Floy and I were busy discarding and packing after five years in one house. We entertained friends and we had almost endless farewells at all the places where we were working and in all our Bible classes. We had to set the exact date and hour we would leave the Wakayama electric line station so our friends could see us off. We then made a list of our closest friends, had cards printed with our new address, hired a taxi for the day before we left and briefly visited the homes of our closest friends. According to Japanese custom we wore formal clothes—I in a morning coat with striped trousers, no less.

The farewell Sunday at the Wakayama church was the hardest for us. I preached that day, we had lunch, then there was more speaking and a prayer service. One woman in her prayer thanked God that I preached sermons she could understand. An elder, in his speech, said something I wish I could live up to. "Being with Smith Sensei is like being with the south wind; I feel warm and comfortable."

We were warmly welcomed in Tokyo and soon caught up with its faster pace. We remarked at that time that it was like catching up to Americans while we were on furlough. We scarcely got a word in edgewise at our first Station meetings. But things moved faster on other lines. My fourteen hours of teaching was scheduled on Mondays, Tuesdays, Thursdays, and Fridays. School started at 7:50 with physical exercises and a brief chapel service. We had a half hour for lunch and school was out at 2:30. After we got started I frequently had a Bible class after school.

The first week a pastor by the name of Goshi, who had a church nearby and was also a professor in the Japan Theological Seminary, called to invite me to presbytery, which met the following week. There I would be received by transfer from Naniwa. Howard Hannaford was also joining, as well as four or five others, among them our old friend Henry Stegeman of the Dutch Reformed Church. Did my coming prompt their action? At least they had waited four or five years to do it until I came along.

We were cordially welcomed at presbytery. The new members included some young Japanese ministers. At the supper hour each new member had to speak briefly. I said I was glad to join along with young Japanese ministers. (I was thirty-six at the time.) I added that I was teaching four days a week at Meiji Gakuin but my services were available along with those of the Japanese young men, in whatever the presbytery wished me to do. The next day I had two invitations to start work with churches but the committee of presbytery would meet soon, and my assignment would be made then. Some time afterward, Henry Stegeman got me aside and said, "Don't you know you are undermining the dignity of the missionary?"

Teaching English conversation at the high school level was the least popular assignment for missionaries at Meiji Gakuin.

I had experience enough to know how to do it and I also considered it the most important missionary task at the school. At that time even junior colleges in Japan were preparatory for professional school. Decisions as to professions were made in high school. One went from high school into science, medicine, business, or into the seminary. The decision to become a Christian was more often made in high school than in college. I was where I wanted to be.

By the end of April I was back on Sunday mornings at the Senzoku church, where Kashiwai was now the pastor. Many friends remembered us and both Kashiwai and I counted on making this suburban church the basis of starting another church farther out from the center of Tokyo. He was chairman of the committee that would make the decision for the presbytery and act as an advisory committee for me. We still had a great deal of exploring to do before we decided on a location.

The first of May I preached for the first time at the special monthly chapel service of the high school to 1,000 boys and their teachers. I worked pretty hard on that one. A fellow teacher helped me smooth up my Japanese. We were a Christian school; a fair proportion of our students came from Christian homes and the program gave expression to this. I also assisted with the student YMCA, went on trips with the students and identified myself as a member of the faculty. I was to preach two or three times a year at chapel. My Japanese was not as eloquent as that of some others and my vocabulary was rather limited, but I was assured that I was always understood and I was invited back.

The second week in July my friend Goshi, acting in his capacity as a professor in the Japan Theological Seminary, called me and said he would like to see me. I went the next day and he told me that the faculty of the seminary wanted to start a course in English Bible. The students themselves were requesting it because they had to use English commentaries and some might even study abroad. The faculty wanted me to teach the course and to teach it as I would teach English Bible courses in America. I replied that I would have to work hard to prepare but would do it—subject, of course, to the advice of those who had a claim on my time. He said the president of the seminary would talk to Dr. Hannaford about it.

Frankly, Floy and I were very much surprised. This was the school of Uemura and Takakura, often known for its antimissionary attitude, but both of these men were now dead and a change seemed possible. I consulted with my dean in the high school as well as Hannaford. Howard was a little dubious about Meiji Gakuin agreeing. Meiji had college courses to which these students could come across town to attend and I had said I would not teach more than 14 hours at Meiji. Dean Tsuru had the answer. Why not take the extra time from my assignment under the presbytery? There would be no objection to that on either side, and Meiji could share in the honor that had come to one of its teachers. My friends in the rest of the Mission congratulated me. I taught two upper classes the first year, and then the three upper classes after that.

Floy and I had met Dr. and Mrs. Karl Reischauer during language study and in 1932–33, and came to know them well. August Karl Reischauer was the Mission's scholar and also a good administrator. The Reischauers had been at Meiji Gakuin, but now lived on the campus of the Women's Christian College, which they had participated in founding. They had a daughter, Felicia, who could not speak or hear. Helen Reischauer had learned to communicate with her and then started the Oral School for the Deaf, the first of its kind in Japan. They had two sons, Robert and Edwin, both of whom got their A.B. degrees at Oberlin and their Ph.D. degrees at Harvard. Edwin Oldfather Reischauer (his middle name came from his mother) taught at Harvard and then, after the war, was for five years Ambassador to Japan from the United States. Bob taught at Princeton; he took a party of students to the Far East in the summer of 1937 and was killed by the Chinese bombing of Japanese-occupied Shanghai.

We are sure the Tokyo missionaries liked us, but they did not at first understand us. None of them had been in the junior missionary group that had struggled for change for five years. Their experience did not prepare them to face the problems of change which were now upon us. They had helped elect me to another three-year term on the six-member Executive Committee of the Mission, but I got little support for that first year, except from the Reischauers and later from Howard Hannaford.

After our furlough we bought a small piece of land and built a summer house at Karuizawa. It cost us $1,500, including land, house, and furnishings. During the summer of 1939 Okada was one of our guests. He was interested in what happened to us in Tokyo and we introduced him to the young missionary family that was being assigned to Wakayama.

Floy and I had served our time in the Sunday school and youth work in Karuizawa. Now that we owned a house we were members of the summer residents association. The great majority were Japanese and we made friends with Japanese from Tokyo that we would never have met otherwise.

Upon our return to Tokyo after the summer I started teaching in the Japan Seminary and had a place assigned in the teachers room. The professors were often prominent in the committees of both presbytery and synod. I soon agreed with Reischauer, who said that he learned more about Japan and the Japanese in the teachers room at the seminary than he learned anywhere else.

It was February before the committee recommended that we be assigned to Shinmaruko for new church development. It was a good place and justified Kashiwai's being careful. It was a suburb about forty-five minutes from us on an electric line and less than that from Senzoku. It had no churches of any kind. There were more than 5,000 people there, 1,200 in grammar school. There was a government girls high school of 600 students and a medical preparatory school of 400. The town was still growing, with many new houses going up.

We went to the seminary to get a recommendation for a man to work with me. I had money enough for rent and part-time salary for a student. However, they recommended a young man, Iwata, who was graduating in March. He was single, and his mother would come and live with him. He was by far their best man to work with children, and they felt he was made to order for this task. When I met him I found he could hold the attention of children and there was the possibility of him becoming a good preacher. I talked to Howard and then with the Station. They opposed me. I was not to employ a full-time man, for that meant that if the project failed, I could not drop him. Get a single student, and I could drop him when I wanted to. I was about as discouraged as I have ever been. I need not have been. When I talked to the young man himself, Iwata San, he said that money was no problem. He and other students wanted to earn their own way, *kaitaku dendo* (tentmaking ministry), if possible. He was already signed up to tutor some high school students and he would find more support. If I could pay the rent, his mother would keep house for him and bring a year's supply of rice from the country. Hurrah! I began to believe the early missionaries. They did not worry about the money. They trusted the Lord to provide.

We found a good house with three rooms that could be thrown together for services and we advertised a meeting for children one Saturday morning. Iwata had found three Christians in the town and we used them to distribute invitations on which parents could write the names and addresses of children and they could then use the invitations as tickets for the Saturday event. We had 65 children and Iwata was marvelous. He even distributed tissues for the children to blow their noses on if they needed to. He taught them songs, he used pictures he had made to illustrate Bible stories, and he entranced the children. Then he told them we would have a Sunday school if they wanted to come. They all wanted to. They set the hour of nine for the next morning and we had 55 children. The next Sunday we had 53 and we were on our way. We borrowed a small organ and we soon started an adult service. We started with 12 adults, fell to 8, and then went back up to 12 and 13. Once we had 17 when we had a special speaker on children's education. The Senzoku church furnished Bibles and hymnbooks and a Sunday school teacher. We got another by paying her carfare from a girls school in Yokohama. Iwata and I took turns preaching and I had the Communion services until he was ordained. We even bought some advertising space in the train station for a month so that all should know services were available. One woman walked some distance to tell us she had been praying ever since she moved to Shinmaruko that someone would open a Christian work there.

My experience at Meiji Gakuin led me to conclude that we needed another plan that would bring the Christian schools into vital relationship with the church. Boards of directors now had some presbytery representatives on them. They had Christian Japanese principals and teachers but the schools did not owe any accountability to the national church or even to the presbytery. We needed an Association of Christian Schools or a Department of Christian Education that would serve both the schools and the church and bring Christian educators together. But this had to wait until after the war.

In October 1939, synod met in Tokyo and we entertained Okada and also Heinie Bovenkerk. The latter was now the treasurer of our Mission and very busy. A pastor from Thailand was present also and wanted to visit Dr. Toyohiko Kagawa. I took him to the Sunday morning service. The church was crowded. Kagawa preached on the daily life of the Christian. He used many homely illustrations and got plenty of laughs. He preached for an hour and a half and kept us all listening closely. One of his illustrations was of the thankful heart that the Christian needs. He knew one old man, eighty-three years of age, who still did some street preaching and who distributed tracts for him when he preached in the old man's church. This man said that he was thankful even for the fact that he had his nose on his face right side up. If it had been the other way it would have caught the rain. As it was, it shed the rain from his mouth. The popularity of Kagawa and his ability to communicate with the common people in his preaching ought to have set an example for other ministers to follow, but there was little evidence that it did.

Kagawa was a graduate of Meiji Gakuin, but he made his reputation in Kobe where he worked in the slums, observing people and helping them. He was a writer of poems and of novels. These later became best sellers after being printed in serial form in newspapers. He was far and away the most popular preacher in the Christian community and in great demand. We met him first in Sapporo when he was holding meetings there in a secular auditorium and charging admission so that the crowds would be composed only of people who really wanted to hear. The churches used him to draw crowds to services, but the Japanese ministers regarded him as weak in theology. He was a member of the board at Meiji Gakuin and the missionaries had formed a Kagawa Fellowship to learn about him and to furnish support for him. He had grown up on the island of Shikoku, where he was baptized by a Southern Presbyterian missionary.

While Okada was with us I took him to preach for our Korean students. He did very well. One of my students at the seminary was an older Korean who took it upon himself to supply in some fashion a hostel for his fellows from Korea. There were literally hundreds, perhaps thousands, of them at school in Tokyo. Some of them had come to our door in Meiji Gakuin, sent by missionaries in Korea whom I had met while they were studying language in Japan. The seminary students helped. We got some money for him and he finally had a hostel for sixty students. At Sunday evening services there were considerably more.

In the process of teaching so many Bible classes I learned some things to do and not to do. I sought the students' convenience and then set a time to which we were committing ourselves. We stopped when the limit set was reached. Later we could start over again with a new limit. We did not try to cover too much in a lesson, but each had to answer at least one question on his reading. I also tried to drive home one or two points, using both English and Japanese to do it. For high school students I used the simplest of English translations, Goodspeed at that time. Other students might want another translation. I used the Revised Version in the seminary.

The Bible was and still is popular in Japan. During some years there were more Bibles sold in Japan than there were Christians. In 1981 I saw the exact figures of the Japan Bible Society. At that time there were 1,100,000 Christians and the Bible Society had sold 2,900,000 Bibles in the Japanese language during the preceding year. Only the United States and India sold more Bibles than Japan. In Japan, the Bible is regarded as a major part of Western culture. Parents want their children to know about it.

We were busy in the summer of 1940. The YMCA at Meiji Gakuin had a relationship to the national YMCA. It had occurred to me in the spring of 1940 that we ought to have a Meiji Gakuin camp during the summer. We could obtain the use of a Y camp for the purpose if there was adequate interest. We got an estimate of cost from those who had had experience and then I talked to the dean and he sent me to the president and he agreed. We soon had thirty boys signed up for a week in the summer and found three faculty members able and willing to stay the whole week. The camp was on the seashore and we combined bathing, hiking, and study, after the model of the Hi-Y camps that I had grown up with in the United States. I came down from Karuizawa for the whole time and shared in everything as one of the teachers.

When I got back from the seashore to Karuizawa I was invited on very short notice to take the three devotional periods at the annual meeting of the Japan Fellowship of Christian Missionaries. They had invited a man from China and at the last minute he could not come. I had three 45-minute periods, prepared three addresses in three days, and then began getting each one ready to give a day at a time. I survived. The fact that we all were quite aware down deep inside ourselves that the war was spreading in Europe and might come our way gave weight to everything I said. I preached on "Being as a Basis for Doing," on "Repentance and Forgiveness," and on "Jesus Christ."

By the time I had a semester or more at the seminary and felt at home in the classes, I began to say more to the students and to speak freely about things that I thought needed saying. For example, I began trying to emphasize that Jesus was a teacher who used everyday illustrations and "the common people heard him gladly." This was contrary to the ordinary conception of the task of the *sensei* in Japan. *Bokushi* (shepherd) was often used for pastor in Japan, but the more common term was *sensei* (teacher) and it had the background of the Chinese word which really meant scholar. Many pastors believed that they had to be scholarly to the point of not being entirely understood in order to hold the respect of their congregations. Takakura, the president of the seminary, was dead now and he had been succeeded by Murata, who was a good administrator but not a scholar. Takakura's influence still persisted. For example, he was accustomed to preaching with his eyes closed, literally closing his eyes for ten or fifteen minutes at a time, and some of the students and young pastors did that too. When I would insist to the students that the way they preached was very important, some would not believe me, insisting that the only thing that mattered was *what* you preached.

Being in the Japan Theological Seminary also inspired me to want to study the theology of Uemura and Takakura and Kuwada, the latter being in succession in the Theological Trio of the Nihon Kuristo Kyokai. Dr. Kuwada was professor of systematic theology when I was at the seminary. Later, after the formation of the United Church, he became the president of Tokyo Union Theological Seminary.

Early in 1941 international tension led the Meiji Gakuin board to reduce the amount of missionary teaching. I still taught at the Japan Seminary and preached once a month at Shinmaruko. Now I accepted the invitation to be chairman of the board at Tokyo Union Church and preach once a month. Also I taught one day a week at a private English conversation school whose principal was a Karuizawa friend. The money I received for this made it possible for me to employ Iwata San for two mornings a week, and we began systematically to study Japanese theology. Murata and Kuwada at the seminary were very much interested in this. We read and made notes on selected issues of Dr. Uemura's *Fukuin Shimpo* (Gospel News). Then we read and made notes on Dr. Takakura's book "Orthodox Theology" and prepared to do some work on Dr. Kuwada's "Outline of Theology," a recent book of more than four hundred pages.

The notes that I made on Uemura and Takakura were later taken from my baggage by the Yokohama police and I never saw them again. But one paper that escaped them was a one-page summary of his theological position which Dr. Kuwada wrote for me just before I left. This statement appears below and illustrates my thesis that Japanese theologians were freely choosing for themselves the elements of Western theology which they thought met their needs, and they were remarkably able in this. This had to be the first major step in preparation for any significant unique contribution that Japanese theologians would be able to make in the future.

NOTES ON MY THEOLOGICAL VIEWPOINT (1941)
H. Kuwada

During the earlier period of my theological study, I received the influence of such writers as Schleiermacher, Ritschl, Herrmann, and John Baillie, but somehow I could not satisfy with these theologians. Later, I got some important suggestions from Otto's "Das Heilige." Then about ten years ago I came under the influence of K. Barth and other dialectical theologians and accepted some basic viewpoints of their theology.

Therefore, I may call myself a Barthian, although I do not like this term, but Barthian in a wider sense and not in a narrower sense at all. I have learned not only from Barth, but also from many other writers, such as Calvin, Kierkegaard, Brunner, Gogarten, Bultmann, Heim, Tillich, Forsyth, and Denney.

My own theological viewpoint is to recognise the significance of the Special Revelation of God in Christ, and to emphasise both the Scripture and the Church. *To hear the Word of God from the Scripture in the Church*—some such is my theological standpoint. I do not agree with the fundamentalists in the view of the Scripture. Although I recognise the Bible as the norm of faith and doctrine, I also recognise the need and results of scientific study of it. And then I believe and emphasise the point that the place of the living Christians is the

Church. The living and actual Christianity is the Church. On this point I am perhaps different from both the fundamentalists and the mystics. In the fundamentalists, I think, Christianity is considered very much as matter of doctrines, while I think the Christian faith as living. The mystics recognise Christianity as the present and living faith, but they consider it mainly as an inner life and do not recognise the actual, concrete, and social side of the Christian faith. I think that Christianity is not only mystical, but also actual and concrete. I believe in the living Christ and the Holy Spirit, the present and living activity of God, but this, not in the sense of mysticism, but connected with the faith of the *Church* as the Body of Christ. The Church, hidden and visible, is the actual place where the Holy Spirit dwells. Thus I hear the word of God of the *Scripture* in the *Church*.

My attitude towards life and this world is included in the three words, faith in God, love to Neighbors, and hope for the eschatological fulfilment. I believe that the Christian should live in this world not from naturalistic or merely humanistic viewpoint, but most fundamentally in the faith in God. This faith in God must be manifested in the actual life and become love to men. Thus we Christians must recognise the *meaning of the activities* in the *present world*, family, economic activity, state, civilization, and most of all, activity of the Christian Church. But the activity in the present age does not mean for us the end in itself, but witness, prayer, discipline to the fulfilment. Merely ethical Christianity, which has not eschatology, does not give the real power to the present world, but falls at last to secularism and worldliness. Both eschatology and Ethics are important for true Christian life.

The position of the Present Writer—Professor of Christian Theology, Nippon Shingakko. Author of such books as "The Outline of the Christian Theology," "The Essence of Christianity," "Dialectical Theology," "Understanding of Theology"; translator of the Japanese edition of Barth's "Credo."

Chapter 3

On the Way to War

(Tokyo, 1940–1941)

ON MAY 10, 1940, "Hinkei" met at our house. "Hinkei" was the Japanese name of the book review fellowship to which I belonged and which met eight or nine times a year. There were twelve of us for dinner, but I do not remember the book reviewed that night. I do remember that we were immersed in trying to understand the radio report that had just come informing us that the Phoney War was now a real one and that the Germans had broken into France and there was nothing to stop them. We wondered: if France fell, would England be able to resist? And what about the relationship of all this to Japan? The Axis powers, Germany and Italy, had not yet brought Japan close to war but we knew that a victorious Germany would increase the probability.

We had lived with the possibility of war in the dim distance since the Manchurian Incident of September 1931. Onomura and I had often talked about it. My businessmen's Bible class in Tokyo in 1932–33 had sometimes focused its discussion on the possibility of war. Being again in Tokyo was a stimulus to think about Japan's politics and its conflict with China. We learned to understand something of the struggle that went on between the civilian government and the military. Japan was less than seventy years out of military feudalism. Civilians were in control of the political system under the Emperor but the military spirit was carried on by the Army and Navy. Military officers might not be descendants of the samurai, but if not, they still could maintain the tradition. They had won a war with China in the late nineteenth century and another with Russia at the turn of the century. Even if the civilian political parties ruled, the military still had a peculiarly strong place in the government.

Civilians and military leaders alike dreamed of Japan becoming a great world power, much like Great Britain. Japan also was an island nation with little in natural resources except its people. Its future must lie in controlling the natural resources in its part of the world, just as England controlled the resources of its colonies. Japan's business leaders believed this could be done by economic advancement over a long period of time. The military preferred more immediate action. The Navy especially resented the naval treaty of the 1920s, negotiated by civilians, which limited Japan to a ratio of 3 to 5 as over against both Britain and the United States. In the rural areas of Japan there was little opportunity for young men to advance and many of them sought their future in the military services. They were convinced they could not wait for the long civilian process.

Moreover, the natural resources in Japan's part of the world were already controlled by Western powers: The Netherlands had such control in Indonesia, the United States in the Philippines, England in Hong Kong and Singapore, and France in Indochina. China itself was divided into spheres of influence reserved for the great powers. In its war with China, Japan had taken a place among the great powers in China. As a result of its war with Russia, Japan had ousted Russia from a part of China and added that to its own. In the meantime, Japan had also annexed Korea as a buffer between itself and Russia. To the military the future was clear. Force must play a large part in making the imperial dream possible. They could not wait for slower economic penetration.

In the early 1930s the issue was still being debated openly in Japan, both in the Diet and in the newspapers. At that time I was a convinced pacifist and found it easier to argue from that standpoint against Japan's policy than to enter into the more difficult arguments about power politics, which involved all of us together in Asia.

We have already referred to the greeting that we got as we returned to Japan from our first furlough in February 1936, on the day that young officers tried to seize the government in Tokyo and almost succeeded.

Early in 1937 the Japanese took advantage of trouble near Peking itself and finally landed troops in Shanghai in order, as they said, to "protect our interests." Fighting at Nanking followed this. War was not declared, but for practical purposes it was war. China's bombing of the Japanese occupation of Shanghai led to the death of Bob Reischauer. Also that same summer Searle Bates, a Disciples professor in Nanking Seminary, came to Karuizawa and we arranged a meeting of both Americans and Japanese to hear him tell of how some Japanese soldiers had raped and otherwise mistreated Chinese civilians.

The Manchurian Incident in 1931 had not caused a stir among the people one way or another. The Peking Incident did. In some places Peking had struck first out of frustration at Japan's encroachment. This was used in Japan to arouse the people. Soldiers were called up and seen off at the railroad stations. Blackouts were held and the general level of involvement of all people was raised. The pressure of the military on the civilian government was also greater. A leader of a political party could no longer hope to be Prime Minister. Nonparty elder statesmen were chosen, but they were still civilians. We had not reached the level of military government.

Wakayama was a port city for the embarkation of troops bound for China. The city government encouraged people to turn out and see them off. This was usually on Sunday morning. Someone suggested that the church services be called off. We had a ministers meeting. I was the only foreigner and kept quiet. The first issue was quickly settled. We would not dismiss the church services but in them would pray for the boys. All agreed. Then one man said, "We have begun to pray for a Japanese victory." Our pastor, Okada, said: "We don't. We pray that God's will may be done." The first pastor replied, "That's the same thing." Okada responded: "No, it's not the same thing. God's will may be done even if Japan is destroyed." There was silence, but no trouble followed Okada's statement.

Another incident was more delicate and involved us. There were two English teachers at the Junior College who were foreigners. One was an American newcomer by the name of Nugent, who was just my age. One day the newspapers in Wakayama and Osaka carried his picture and an interview with him in which he said he was a staunch friend of Japan and was writing to his friends in America explaining the justice of Japan's action in China. The son of his cook had been called up by the Army and needed a Japanese sword, since he was an officer. Nugent had bought a sword for him and was promising to care for his family while he was gone. This was quite a subject of conversation among us who knew him. It became serious when the police officer who was carrying responsibility for all foreigners came to ask me if I was writing to my friends as Nugent was writing to his. I said I sometimes could explain Japan's actions to my friends, but if I did so, I would also have to say there were some things I could not agree with. He then said, "What are those things?" I put him off and then he wanted me to take time and write them down for him. While I was considering that, I was strongly advised by my Japanese friends to forget it. Fortunately I was not pressed by the police. After the war I saw Nugent in Tokyo. He was on MacArthur's staff in charge of some phase of Japanese education, and had the rank of colonel.

In addition to the clash between the civilian government and the military, there were other struggles going on in Japan. I am not an authority on them, but I have read John Toland's book *The Rising Sun*, which was written after the war and after hundreds of interviews with people in Japan, and I believe it gives a reasonably accurate picture.

The Emperor was acting on the advice of elder statesmen, former prime ministers, and others close to the throne. In general they were favorable to civilian government and opposed to the military. But in reality they had no power, except the power of ideas, and even this power was being eroded. There were also some groups that now began to propose an out-and-out fascist government. Their thesis was that in time of crisis, civilian political parties were not adequate, and the country must turn to the true patriots with their unquestioned loyalty to the Emperor. The Emperor himself had given the people the right to vote. It was time now for the suffrage to be given back to the Emperor so that he could act on the advice of these true advisers. This was fascism with a Japanese twist. We were not there yet, but we were on the way. Sometime in 1937 I wrote my parents that I thought we might have three more years before we were excluded from service in Japan. I was almost exactly right.

When we moved to Tokyo in 1939 we found the tension was easier than in Wakayama. We were operating in a larger context and were more often in the Christian community. But in July we had a new experience. Let me tell it just as I recorded it on July 5, 1939:

I was finishing my letters up here in my study and the fifth-year boys were having military practice on the playground below me. We have two military officers attached to the school to give military instruction. They are appointed by the government and are subject to school supervision. One of these fifth-year boys did something wrong and the chief officer ran halfway across the playground, hit him in the back of the head, then in the front, and then proceeded to punch him in the face for all he was worth. I was out of the chair and down the stairs as fast as I could go. Floy was in the hall on the second floor and called me, but I did not stop. I did not mean to use force but I was going to walk calmly into the fracas when I got there. Fortunately, it was over. The boy was going into the school building and the officer was back teaching. Some of the boys were talking about it, but none except the military men among the teachers had seen it. I knew the boy and knew he had not willingly done anything wrong.

Floy and I did not know what to do. We did not want to take it to the dean of the high school or to the president of the whole school. If they had to handle it, it might cause a great deal of trouble, and still my conscience would not let the thing rest. After four or five days we decided the thing to do was to talk to the officer himself. I talked to Howard Hannaford about it and he thought the officer would not understand what I meant. However, I decided to go ahead. Friday morning I left the house for chapel meaning to seek an opportunity. We have morning calisthenics first and as the boys went into chapel I stayed behind and so did the officer. But I lost my nerve. After chapel I was delayed for a bit and the boys had gone to their classes when I came out. I did not have first class and started across the playground on my way home, and there was the officer all by himself about ten feet from where I was to pass. The Lord was giving me another chance. That time I could not pass it up. We had always been friendly in our greetings to one another, although we had never talked before. This time I stopped and after a bit I asked if he would mind if I said something to him. He said to go ahead. I then said that I was simply a teacher in the school and had no authority at all. However, as one teacher to another I wanted to say that I had seen him punish the boy. I did not know what the custom was in the Army, but in a Christian school I did not think we ought to use such measures. I told him I was not going to the school authorities but had come directly to him. He is a very fiery fellow but he did not flare up. He said he was sorry for it and that he had been wrong. The boy was to blame, he said, for it was the third time the same mistake had been made and some example had to be set. However, he had used the wrong method. He thanked me for telling him and I left him. We still speak to each other very pleasantly. [At this late date I wonder if the officer thought that he had met "the south wind."]

Now that I had done it, I did report informally to my friend, Dean Tsuru, what I had done so my side of the story would be known if it ever came up. If I had talked with Tsuru first he would have had to take responsibility for me.

At the end of the summer of 1939 the chief subject of discussion was Germany's nonaggression pact with Russia. Some of us had thought about the possibility, but the Japanese people seemed to be taken completely by surprise. Japan had a pact with Germany, and Russia was Japan's political enemy. Now Germany was implying that it would not come to Japan's assistance if Russia should attack Japan. In some of the newspapers Germany was being called "a viper."

In the middle of October 1939, our American Ambassador made quite a stir. Joseph Clark Grew was an able man and known as a good friend of Japan. This time he told how it was: that America did understand Japan's actions in China and did not like them. America would be true to its treaty commitments there. The Japanese must recognize that that is unchangeable. We of the Christian community hoped this statement might do some good.

In October a missionary friend was jailed in Kyoto. He was the representative of the Student Christian Movement in the Far East, and was arrested as he was boarding a boat in Kobe. His wife and children were allowed to go on to Shanghai. He also was eventually released.

In 1940, when Germany's potential victory in Europe was recognized in Japan, the Japanese leaders had to think what then might happen to the Dutch, French, and English colonies in their part of the world. A German victory could mean German control there also, if Japan by that time were not fighting at Germany's side. When Germany later broke its nonaggression pact with Russia and began to win there also, the fear of a German neighbor in Siberia entered the area of Japan's concern. Japanese military planners must have thought that Japan, if it did not hurry, was increasingly likely to be left out of a German victory. At the same time, Grew's speech had reminded Japan that it must consider the United States as a possible enemy if it joined in the struggle. But to stay out might mean the postponement for a long time of Japan's dream of acquiring resources in its part of the world. The problem now entered the area at the highest level. Everyone was concerned about Japan's future in the world. Japan's next step was to move farther into China and to threaten Indochina. If spheres of influence were to be shuffled, Japan wanted to move from strength.

On August 3, 1940, I wrote to my parents about my speaking to the Japan Fellowship of Christian Missionaries and said: "My manuscripts are still at the police office. They wanted them because the four detectives who had heard me could not follow me as I spoke. They have delayed returning them. One detective came yesterday to say they had not completed reading them. They were in longhand and you folks know they might be difficult."

On August 25 I wrote again: "If this letter seems scrambled it is because we cannot get our minds off the situation here in Japan." Then I proceeded to list several things that were happening:

1. An English reporter commits suicide, is suspected as a spy and that sets off a spy scare.
2. All political parties are dissolved and one single party is established. Moderates try to contain it but radicals also have a new avenue of expression. [The political party was patterned after the successful model in Germany.]
3. The Salvation Army and the Episcopal Church are attacked as foreign, with headquarters in England and foreign heads in Japan. The Salvation Army General and foreign Episcopal bishops may have to leave, and maybe

other missionaries of these groups also. Maybe they cannot even go to church.

4. There are rumors about others affected, especially mission schools in fortified areas, such as Kyushu and Shimonoseki. There are new regulations for others also.

5. The government is permitting, and perhaps authorizing, that pressure be brought to bear for the churches to form one united church. The Congregationalists and the Methodists have already discussed it and others seem about to join them. Later they will approach the Presbyterians.

In the letter I commented on two things: the focus on the English who have colonies in Asia, and the spy scare intended to unify the Japanese around the new central one-party government.

I ended the letter by commenting: "If pressure is brought to bear upon our church because of the presence of missionaries, then I think I am in favor of resigning from the church. . . . Our connection with the church would be severed and they would then stand on a clear religious issue rather than defend themselves as being groups influenced by foreigners." I also hoped we would be treated differently because we were not in official positions in our church. In both these hopes we were soon disillusioned. In the eyes of the government, missionaries in Japan and their churches were inseparable, no matter what the relationship was.

During all this Reischauer was in America and Hannaford was in China. I was acting as the chairman of the Executive Committee. I was glad to see Hannaford back in Japan in the middle of September.

September also marked a great event in our family: Louise started going to school. John had started at the American school the year before, after studying three years with his mother in Wakayama. Now Louise went with him every morning on the bus. She was excited but handled herself very well. The music teacher at school did not want to take a six-year-old, but after she heard Louise play she accepted her. Louise could hold her own when teased. I wrote: "There is a boy in John's class who is with our children coming home on the bus. He began teasing Louise and one day as he left he said, 'Goodbye, sweetheart.' So now Louise calls him 'sweetheart' and tells him she is going to kiss him. Now he runs whenever she comes near. She told Floy that she really would not kiss him."

On September 27 we had a meeting at our house of missionaries and presbytery representatives. We were informed that recommendations to the synod meeting in October would include one that the Nihon Kuristo Kyokai join the Union of Protestant churches on condition that:

1. All Protestant churches join;
2. The Apostles' Creed plus an evangelical statement be adopted as the creed;
3. A nonepiscopal church government be agreed upon.

We were then informed that one of the recommendations was that all missionaries sever their relationships with the church. This was the recommendation of extremists in the new party and would have to be acted on by the synod. We were being informed ahead of time. Schools would not be affected by this. I would still teach at Meiji Gakuin and at the Japan Seminary, but Shinmaruko would be off limits for me.

Synod met in Tokyo October 10–17. Action was taken on church union with the above conditions added. Synod appointed a committee of fourteen to participate in the negotiations. Some of these were professors in the seminary.

The chairman of the National Christian Council was Bishop Abe of the Methodist Church. The recommendation concerning missionaries had been prepared after consultation with him. On October 9 I discovered that the day before, under the instruction of their bishop, the Methodist Church had limited the activities of their missionaries but had kept them in the church. Howard and I kept the communications open, and the synod appointed another committee to explore the possibilities of keeping them in the churches and then to act on a plan that would be the same as in the other churches. In November, synod's special committee reported that missionaries could stay in the church. The only change for me was that at Shinmaruko, Iwata would be in charge and I would assist him. This was really a gain for us, for it meant that whatever happened to me, the project would go on under the presbytery.

We did not have time to catch our breath before another difficulty arose from a different direction. On October 17 rumors were flying about that the U.S. Government was advising people to go home. There was no such advice in Tokyo, but evidently American consuls in Korea and China had been given some leeway in giving advice in their areas. Our Board in New York counseled caution but not alarm. We agreed, but there were some who were jittery. Heinie Bovenkerk and I made some tentative plans just in case. Some missionaries of other denominations were going already. I wrote: "November 1st I took over as acting pastor of Tokyo Union Church. That first Sunday the scheduled preacher took sick on Sunday morning. I was reached just an hour before the service and prepared to preach on the way to the church. I did not have to do that again."

On November 20 the Board in New York cabled: "Situation unchanged; however strongly advise mission plan immediate furloughs children, mothers accompanying children, first class fares if necessary." I contacted Heinie in Osaka that night and he started getting reservations. It turned out that part of our families could not get reservations until January 20. In the meantime the Board clarified its cable and indicated that maybe they had been pushed by the U.S. Government. The cable ended: "Indicate partial withdrawal understanding Board desires maintain maximum effective staff for continued service." We agreed with this advice.

Floy and I proposed to the other families where wives with children were going that they join us in a letter to the Board explaining that we all wanted to stay if possible but were making reservations for January 20. We hoped there might be a change, however, and therefore requested that the Board cable us through Hannaford by January 8 indicating any change, and if there was no change, repeating exactly the wording of the first cable. (January 8 was the last date when we could still cancel the reservations, and the exact wording was necessary lest some of us begin to debate why any changes were made.) The Bovenkerks, Barnards, Martins, and ourselves followed this plan along with the DeMagdts of the Reformed Church. We hoped against hope that the five or six weeks would change things, but we began preparing. On January 8 the cable was the same.

The Board's cable also encouraged borderline health cases to go. At the same time it sought to maintain a working force. Men also could have gone at their own request and some did. I was very proud of Floy. Going home with small children was going to be tough, especially when there was a possibility of war and my furlough would not normally be due until February 1943. But we had gone through this step by step both in thought and prayer and agreed that our Christian witness led us to make this decision. Our Japanese friends never advised us to go. Our continued presence must have been an embarrassment to some but they never said so. On the other hand, there was strong advice to stay. Dr. Kagawa said openly that if missionaries were sent from America, of course they should go home. But if they were sent from heaven, they should stay. We were not planning to stay if war seemed sure. We had explored that and rejected it. But we were not yet ready to run.

On December 8 we received twenty-five new members at the Tokyo Union Church. Most were affiliated members with their long-time membership somewhere outside Japan, but two were by confession of faith and one by adult baptism. It was the first adult baptism Union Church had had in living memory. I also worked out a form for the reception of affiliated members. Lamott had suggested it once before, but no one had done it.

We had our first Christmas at Shinmaruko. The 25th was a Saturday and we had our children's Christmas then. The next day we had a Communion service and the reception of the first members Shinmaruko ever had. Three came by letter and one by baptism. I had examined the candidate for baptism earlier in the week and now conducted the service with Iwata preaching. I did not go every Sunday, but went a good share of the time and preached once a month.

We had time to think through what things we would send with Floy and what things I would keep. I kept some books, our Karuizawa china, and some silverware and bedding. We sold the piano but kept our furniture on the chance we would be back. Floy took all our best china and silverware, along with our Japanese treasures and some of my books. We had packers for everything and had no damage on the trip. Louise wanted to go, but John was not so sure.

The *Kamakura Maru* sailed from Yokohama for San Francisco on January 23, 1941. It carried five mothers and thirteen children who were very dear to our Mission. Husbands and fathers were down to see them off. It was a traumatic experience. One man could not stay to watch. Heinie and I went clear to the end of the pier and watched and waved as long as we could see. Floy had Hester's youngest in her arms, for Hester was carrying their fourth child, who would be born in Michigan.

At Meiji Gakuin, John DeMagdt moved in with me and brought his cook, Hosoi San, with him. He and I had a sale which she conducted, somewhat like a garage sale. Anything we had that was made of cotton, wool, or leather was salable, even if it was well worn.

After Japan's further push into China and its threat to Indochina had produced a predictable U.S. protest, negotiations were begun in Washington which might lead to some settlement that would contain Japan. They went slowly. Japan at times sent additional people to these negotiations and one of them sailed on the same ship with our families. He was Admiral Nomura, a retired Navy officer who was considered a moderate. His presence gave additional assurance that the ship would reach its destination.

For the two weeks of the trip the ship was in touch with Japan by radio and we could send telegrams to one another at Japanese rates. They had a touch of seasickness, but otherwise all went well. The Board had people to meet them in San Francisco and they were on the train for Chicago that night. Families met them there and brought them home. For Floy and the children that was Ellwood City, Pennsylvania, where her parents lived. They soon rented a small house on the rear of the lot where her Uncle John and her Aunt Nannie lived. It was about two hundred yards from her parents' home and less than two blocks from her brother's. She was able to unpack our things, settle into a home, and get the children into school. She then began to wait. Hers was the hardest job, especially after the war began. Everyone who observed Floy during the months of decision in Japan and life with the children at home invariably remarked on her courage, her faith, and her ability to go ahead and do the things that were necessary. Howard Hannaford called her a heroine.

The Methodists handled their problem of possible evacuation differently. They sent their chief executive for foreign missions and one of their bishops out to confer with missionaries, pastors, and some political leaders for a period of three weeks. On the ship back to America they reached a decision and cabled back when they landed that all Methodist missionaries should leave Japan. Most were gone in a few weeks and all by summer. The report they made, as reported by the press, was at points astounding. In one article, our own Presbyterian paper reported: "Delay in leaving Japan may mean imprisonment or death." . . . "The exodus of foreign missionaries is almost complete." . . . "Japan is now in the exact likeness of the Nazi form." . . . "The vast accumulation of mission property is being taken over by the government." . . . "If a Japanese Christian is seen shaking hands with a departing missionary or teacher, the click of a camera tells that his picture is being taken and his name secured to be given to the secret police as a suspected traitor, to be kept under surveillance." I wrote an answer to that article, for the bishop was telling my friends that that was what I was facing. I also helped Ted Walser of the Fellowship of Reconciliation write a letter to the U.S. Government urging full cooperation with Japanese peace representatives. Forty-two Americans signed the document, including an Embassy official.

With the Methodist evacuation the Presbyterians became the largest remaining group, although our numbers also gradually decreased. The Reischauers had to leave on their doctor's orders because of his bleeding ulcer. Fathers of the children that were gone began also to leave. Some were jittery and unduly scared. The duties of those who stayed increased. I became the chairman of the Executive Committee and also taught ten classes in the college department of Meiji Gakuin, with reduced hours in high school. The pressures made others of us more nervous and irritable than usual.

The Nihon Kuristo Kyokai took seriously both its responsibility now in the church union negotiations and for the missionaries that remained. The leadership of the union movement had been in the hands of the chairman of the National Christian Council. He was under pressure to move fast by eager beavers both in politics and in the churches. The decision of the Presbyterians to join slowed things up. They were the largest single group and needed to be satisfied. There was the question of the decision on the creed. We insisted on a creed and found that the Lutherans supported us. The others were not much concerned. Finally one day in the committee one said, "All right, you write the creed and we will take it." The reply was, "That is the matter with you, you do not really believe we need a creed." The tentative solution came to be a kind of federation with a general organization and purpose but each group keeping some authority and some distinctive beliefs.

There was also the question of leadership. They had accepted the Presbyterian proposal that there would be no bishop. The government people were tired of talking to the heads of thirty-three denominations and wanted one person who could represent them all and who could be held accountable. The Japanese name for him was "Torisha" and had no religious significance. He was to be elected by the church. The first nominating committee failed to find an acceptable person. The second nominating committee had our old friend Onomura from Hokkaido as chairman and succeeded in having Tomita, a Presbyterian pastor, nominated and elected. So the latecomer Presbyterians now headed the process. It was rank partisanship in one sense, but it was also good statesmanship. It protected the interests of those who had not been easily caught up in the momentum of the crisis. We knew Tomita as the chairman of the board at Meiji Gakuin. He was a "rock." He reminded me of Darley Downs's comment on a previous occasion. Darley was a Congregationalist, but he said, "If it comes to resistance unto blood, the Presbyterians will be there."

Of course no missionary was anywhere near the committee on church union. I got my taste of the discussion in the Japan Seminary faculty room. Later in 1941, I was also present at a retreat which the leaders of our church had near Tokyo to talk and pray about their problems and the threatening war which might overtake us all. Mrs. Tamaki Uemura, the daughter of Prof. Uemura, the famous first theological leader, who was a minister in her own right, was one of the leaders in this meeting.

Goshi was the chairman of the committee to care for us missionaries. From the first they told us that they were not in favor of our leaving and that they would tell us if they thought we ought to go. When the anti-spy movement threatened to close down all employment of Japanese by foreigners, all worked together to effect the transfer of money so that missionary projects had a chance of weathering the storm. When some schools got jittery, including Meiji Gakuin, this committee helped to settle the differences. When the economic freeze came in the summer of 1941 this group offered to help with money if we ran out. I was at this meeting at which Kagawa took leadership. He personally asked me to teach in his church.

I appreciated the offer very much but it would have meant giving up Shinmaruko, where I could still help.

I personally was committed to staying as long as possible as a personal witness to the universality of the gospel. Iwata shared this faith and we worked closely together. John DeMagdt left in the spring but I had a good house and a good cook, whose sister was living with her while she went to sewing school. I was teaching three courses in the Japan Seminary and had as many Bible classes as ever—at least six each week—in addition to my work at Shinmaruko and at Tokyo Union Church, and the Japanese theological studies I had begun.

The Paul Mayers joined me in our house in Karuizawa for the summer of 1941. We had sold the house back to the builder for the same price that we had paid for it and on condition that we could buy it back later. In August we met for two days as a Mission at Nogiri, a smaller summer resort on a lake some two hours from Karuizawa. With the support of Howard Hanna-ford and Heinie Bovenkerk, I proposed a modification in our policy. Under Board direction we were committed to keeping a workable nucleus of missionaries in Japan, no matter what. I proposed we continue the policy up to a point, but that we encourage each person now to make a tentative decision as to what he would do if a boat labeled by either government as an "evacuation ship" should be announced. The idea was resisted by some who believed that any such preparation somehow was a desertion of our hope for peace. The same group refused to register our missionary residence property with the American Embassy so that an official record of our ownership would be preserved. Howard and I got the Board to order us to do it and I made the final registration on December 1, 1941.

Japan's move into Indochina caused a break with the United States. That resulted in an economic boycott against Japan. Having no source of oil and iron of its own, Japan had been adding to its reserves from abroad. Now these reserves would begin to dwindle as they were used sparingly for daily needs. In the course of time Japan would not have enough to launch a war that would take it into Southeast Asia where oil was available. The United States was really saying with the boycott that Japan must soon decide to fight or to shut up.

Japan responded with an economic boycott of its own, which included freezing all monies owned by Americans in Japan. Heinie had anticipated this and had put cash in safes in Osaka

and Tokyo. By the end of the summer we still had two months'
supply left. The Board tried to send us money from Shanghai
but that failed. Japan's boycott was also on shipping. Mail was
scarce and at times we could not have left Japan if we had
wanted to. There were no ships. The two boycotts also aroused
feeling against Americans in Japan. We were better off in
Tokyo, but all our people were evacuated from Hokkaido and
we got shipping by way of Shanghai for them. We did the same
for the German Reformed people in Sendai. Some got back to
the United States from Shanghai; others got caught in the
Philippines. At one time the Board asked us to consider
moving temporarily to Shanghai or Manila but we decided
against it.

The Board did give some of us some encouragement. Terms
of service were reduced for separated families and my furlough
was now due on February 26, 1942, just six months away. That
date became a goal for our family.

In September of 1941 I wrote to Floy: "A week from Sunday
is World Wide Communion. In the notice that has gone out are
these words: 'It is most important when hate is on the march
and war is rampant in our world, that Christians everywhere
should maintain an unbroken fellowship. This fellowship in
Christ will stand out in contrast to our broken and disorganized
world. It will bear witness to a fellowship which can cross
frontiers of race, break through barriers of human prejudice,
and rise above the clash and conflict of warring nations.' You
and I have a chance to do something in this crisis that no one
else can do. And I think God is leading us to this work. I am
sure He will care for us until we can be together again."

A day or two before I conducted the World Wide Communion service at Shinmaruko, I wrote Floy again: "You wrote
that this has certainly made you realize the depth of our love.
That is true for me too. I love you and the children with all my
heart. Sometimes I am really sick because I cannot see you and
be with you. But I think also that one reason for the realization
of our love is that we are conscious of making a sacrifice
together for the sake of God's work. Because we live close to
God we are closer to each other. And if we were untrue to
God's leading we would be untrue to each other too. I pray
God all the time that He will take care of you all. I know He has
led us thus far and will lead us."

Dr. Tada, the perennial moderator of the synod, was the last chairman of the Chuo Seminary board. In the spring of 1941 he had worked out a compromise by which it could be related to the Japanese church. Heinie Bovenkerk and I were there and that night, after the meeting in Kobe, we got a taxi and took Dr. Tada down to the dock where he was taking a boat back to his home city. That night on the boat he had a heart attack and two days later he died at home. Without him the compromise at Chuo failed.

Heinie and I succeeded, however, in another Tada project which he had dreamed about. Early in 1941 an elder in Osaka who heard him preach proposed they raise money to send him to America to confer with his friends in the American church. This was taken up by the Japan National Christian Council and the deputation was enlarged. Heinie and I talked with Dr. Tada in his hotel in Tokyo some weeks before he was to go. He said he thought he might have trouble with other members of the delegation. He himself did not want to be drawn into politics and international relations. He wanted simply to talk with Christian friends and possibly to the General Assembly, about their Christian fellowship and how we must all seek to maintain that fellowship and try to contribute to solving our problems together. Now that he was gone, Heinie and I wrote a letter telling of his hopes. We sent the letter to Dr. Charles Leber at the Board in New York and he used it at the General Assembly. Later it was printed and circulated. The delegation did go and did establish a relationship which survived the war and was the basis for the first meeting of American and Japanese Christians in Japan after the war.

In the fall of 1941 we had a visitor at Meiji Gakuin and several of us talked with him over dinner. He was a well-known American reporter from San Francisco who had spent the last three months in Russia. He was convinced that Germany would win. Russia had the manpower and it might have the arms, he said, but it was immobilized by lack of transportation in the face of swift German tank attacks. Such reports could not help making the Japanese military decision urgent. If they waited, they would miss sharing the victory in their part of the world. I remember telling Ted Walser on Thanksgiving Day that the decision for or against war could well be made in the next few weeks.

Heinie and I both inquired about transportation. The best we could get was a boat to Shanghai in December. Then what seemed to be the "evacuation ship" was announced. The *Tatsuta Maru* was sailing the end of November to Los Angeles, in part to pick up some Japanese who were coming home from Panama. The date was postponed to December 2. We packed our things, got numerous permits from the government, made our last speeches, taught our last classes, and said good-by to our friends. But that begins another story.

Chapter 4

"The Same Tax of Suffering"
(1941–1942)

THE *Tatsuta Maru,* which sailed from Yokohama on December 2, 1941, was due to arrive in Los Angeles on December 14. It was taking the Great Circle route and thus would pass several hundred miles north of Hawaii. We have often been asked if the sailing of the ship at that time was a part of Japan's plan to deceive the United States. I have always answered that the sailing was legitimate in itself. There were Japanese in Panama to be picked up and both governments had cooperated in advertising the sailing and in encouraging their people to go. At the same time the Japanese carefully set the date of sailing so that the *Tatsuta* was both well on its way and still able to get back to Japan after the bombing of Pearl Harbor. The time of setting the date of sailing may well have marked the time that Japan finally decided to strike.

We had two December 7ths on board the *Tatsuta.* The first was on the Japanese side of the date line and was our Sunday. I preached at the service that morning. That evening at dinner we received a certificate from the ship's captain officially notifying us that he was bestowing on us an extra day. We had crossed the date line and the next day would also be December 7 for us and at Pearl Harbor.

Henry Bovenkerk and I had put our leaving Japan in the back of our minds and were concentrating on arriving in the United States. We had gotten some train schedules and made out the schedule for our arrival at home.

That second Sunday morning we had carefully written out the wording of the telegrams we would send our wives when we reached Los Angeles.

The *Tatsuta* turned around without any warning at 20 minutes to 12 noon. Some of the first-class passengers were playing deck tennis and one happened to glance back and saw the wake of the ship in the water as it circled. He dropped his hands and said, "My God." We second-class passengers had not heard of it, but at lunch someone reported that a first-class passenger had said we had turned around. We consulted several compasses but still could not believe it. After lunch I went to the first-class lounge and there read the announcement on the bulletin board. It was simply, "This boat is returning to Japan by government order." There were no other details and no reason was given. Heinie said that when I came back from first class they could tell what I had learned from the expression on my face. I was pretty close to tears but did not cry until after supper. We were a congenial crowd in the second class and we sat around and sang. Someone started, "There's a long, long trail a winding," and we all joined in. I for one could not finish it. It went too deep.

In spite of our disappointment, none of us thought it likely that war had started. Boats had turned around when the freeze on trade had gone into effect, and we supposed that it was most likely that a further break in relations had come but surely short of war. After the first blow we began making plans for getting out by way of Shanghai. We asked the purser if our baggage could be bonded so that we did not have to go through customs again. He gravely assured us it could be done. We had no news at all, for the ship's bulletin had ceased publication. The ship's people began painting the boat gray and at night we had air raid precautions with no lights showing. Thursday morning another passenger got two or three of us together and said his cabin boy had told him a tall story. The crew had heard on the radio that war had begun with America, that Pearl Harbor had been bombed and most of the American fleet sunk. We did not believe it but the next morning there were other stories that we thought could not be made up. When we shared that with other passengers they laughed at us. Saturday a Japanese plane came to meet us and escorted us for several hours. Sunday morning there were more planes and in the afternoon two destroyers. One went in front and one behind and we were taken through the net and minefield in the entrance of the harbor at Yokohama. Just after dusk we anchored well out in the bay.

Heinie had preached that Sunday morning and in the

afternoon we did two things. Mrs. John Hail of our Mission was on the ship and was sick with what proved to be cancer. We went to the purser and then to the doctor and asked that, if we could not go to our homes when we landed, they would see to it that Mrs. Hail was sent to a hospital. Then we repacked our baggage with the idea that we would take in our hand luggage enough things that could go with us if we were interned. We did not sleep any too well that night.

Monday morning, the 15th, we had breakfast as usual and during that time the ship was taken into dock.We were told to go to the smoking room to present our passports to the police. This was as usual. We went with Mrs. Hail to the first-class smoking room but Heinie and I were sent back to the second-class section. There were nine of us, all men. The police examined our passports as usual but this time they did not give them back to us. The man ahead of me wanted a receipt for his but was refused. When it came my turn I said that if Japan and America were at peace, they had no right to keep my passport, but if they were at war I wanted to know it. I got the reply that they could give no information but simply obey orders.

We were in the smoking room until 11 A.M. but soon discovered that we could not get out. When we wanted to go to the toilet a policeman went with us. A few minutes before 11:00 the cabin boys brought our hats and coats, and nothing else. We were then each assigned to one plainclothesman and marched off the boat, two by two. Each policeman held his prisoner by the arm. It was raining steadily and there was no one on the dock except a few stragglers and the wife of one of our nine men. She, a Japanese, was crying. We were put into waiting taxis and started across town. As we neared the edge of the city I asked my man where we were going, and he said, "The Kaihin Hotel." That is a famous seaside hotel in Kamaku-ra and was in the direction we were taking. However, we turned off toward the sea before we left Yokohama and stopped in front of a brown building at the seaside which had a new high board fence around it. We were taken into a hallway and confined for almost an hour. They began to search the first fellow and take everything he had. When I saw that, I was concerned about only one thing.

I had played tennis the summer before in Karuizawa with the grandson of Mikimoto, the pearl man. He was in the Tokyo store and the last of November I had gone to him and asked him to pick out the best necklace he would give me for what money I had. He went through several dozen necklaces and finally picked out one for Floy. It had cost me only $25 but it was worth a good bit more. I had kept it under lock and key on the boat and had taken it out and put it in my pocket on Monday morning. I did not want to give that up. I considered putting it around my neck while we were waiting but then thought that if it was discovered I would be in trouble. So I went through the examination and saw everything I possessed, except the clothes on my back, taken from me.

As the examination was finished we were taken into the next room, and we could catch glimpses of other bearded foreigners who were waiting for us in silence. When it came my turn I discovered that we were being taken through this room and down the stairs to the basement. By noon we were all there. It was a raw December day and there was no heat in the building. We finally were served a very poor lunch which only half of us could eat. Then an official came to tell us that we were to stay in this building but that there were no beds and no bedding. If we knew anybody in Yokohama, we could have a mattress and bedding brought. That was the beginning of our trouble, for seven of the nine of us were from outside Yokohama. I was able to give them the Meiji Gakuin Tokyo address and ask for bedding for three. Then finally we were brought newspapers which told of the opening of the war and of the Japanese victories. Thus we began very early to read between the lines and try to get at the truth behind the stories.

Toward evening we were greatly relieved when the police took us from the basement and put us in a small room off the larger room in which we had seen the other Yokohama foreigners. There were about twenty of them and we were not allowed to speak to them. After an even poorer supper we were each given two *futon* (quilts) and told to go to bed on the hardwood floor. We were still glad to get off the cement floor of the basement. We did not sleep much. We had no change of clothing, no razors, no neckties, no belts, no towels, no soap, and no toothbrushes. Fortunately we had a good foreign toilet. We continued in that situation for three days.

Then the bedding began to come in. On the fourth or fifth day Dr. Tsuru, the dean at Meiji Gakuin, and our cook, Hosoi San, came with bedding and toothbrushes. We were not permitted to meet them, but by going around the building we could catch sight of them. They had asked for our laundry and when they learned that we had no change of clothing they promised to bring some. In about ten days many of us were wearing Tsuru's underwear and Howard Hannaford's pajamas, shirts, and socks. They had furnished from our house mattresses for five people and pillows for three, and sheets had come from the Walsers in Tokyo. Hosoi San acted as the courier for these. Heinie and I wore scarves around our necks and let our beards grow.

The place where we were quartered was the Yokohama Amateur Boat Club. The first floor was the locker room with showers; the second floor was a tea room with an old English boat deck along three sides of it, where guests sat to watch the races. It had been taken over by a section of the Yokohama civilian police in order to house us. No changes had been made except putting the fence around it. Our food was cooked in the kitchen of the tea room, the tea room itself being divided into three rooms. We all slept on the hardwood floor, most with mattresses directly on the floor. There were good toilet facilities and an eight-person Japanese bath which could be heated. The showers had only cold water.

The building was only two or three years old but of course was never intended to house people for the winter. The only heat it had was the sun and Yokohama averages about forty degrees in the winter. At times we had as many as 32 male internees. From the 15th to the 24th of December we were kept segregated from the others in the smaller room which came to be known either as the "Tatsuta room" or the "missionary room." We were allowed a bit of exercise on the deck and after a few days got onto the grass inside the fence. Later the fence was moved back a little and we had a place twenty yards by thirty yards where we played softball. We were closely guarded both day and night. At least one policeman was stationed in our room all the time. He had a chair in the middle of the room and we slept around him. That was a bit galling and was to continue for three months. The guards were changed often, so that we never got well acquainted with any of them. Keeping the room clean was a problem and we immediately organized our own cleaning squads. The policemen used the same toilet and some were not accustomed to a foreign toilet and often missed it. It was our job to clean up the mess in the morning.

The day before Christmas we were allowed to talk to the

other internees. About half of them were Eurasians, and most had British citizenship. Some would prove to be good friends but others were from the riffraff of Yokohama. Our nine were no angels but they were saints compared with some in the next room. The partition was thin and we could hear almost everything. I have never in my life heard so much filth.

At first the police were stern with us. The first time Tsuru came he could not speak to me but I waved to him from a distance. The policeman on duty turned on me and yelled, "*Korah!*" I did not understand the word but there was no escaping understanding what he meant. Actually they were not prepared for this kind of duty. They were the ordinary civilian police of Yokohama and its suburbs and were under the permanent officers of that area of the city. They were used to dealing with criminals and did not dare treat us otherwise without getting different orders. The Yokohama internees had been arrested the morning of the 8th, Japan time, and had been put in the common jail. By that night and the next day most of them had been taken to two camps, ours and one at the racetrack which accommodated twice as many. The rest had been taken to prison as possible spies. One Englishman had been taken from our ship to prison for the same reason. Our police were afraid of our committing suicide and that was why our razors, ties, and belts were taken from us. One man did commit suicide with an overdose of medicine and we no longer could keep medicine in our personal possession. Some individual police no doubt hated us. One night two or three of the tough ones talked of throwing us into the sea.

However, the fact that they were civilian police probably worked in our favor. They were not military men and when the police orders on how to care for civilian internees under the Geneva Convention came down to them, most were prepared to obey the orders. One military man was attached to the main Yokohama office and he was sometimes the exception.

Christmas was a pretty gray day for all of us. Those of us on the *Tatsuta* had expected to spend the day with our families and here we were in custody and with no hope of getting out before the end of the war. We fully expected the Marines would eventually come marching up the Bund in Yokohama but were certain we would be incarcerated for at least two years and probably more. The police gave us a Christmas dinner in the evening and some officials came and ate with us. They brought along a Japanese Congregational minister from Yokohama. We were thankful for that much thoughtfulness. Ruth Hannaford, Gladys Walser, and Delphine Durgin, the wife of a YMCA man who had been with us on the *Tatsuta*, sent in special food wrapped in Christmas paper for all of us. Tsuru also brought small gifts for us.

The food in the camp was about the worst I have ever eaten. It was both bad and scanty. The cook of the Boat Club had been kept on but the police allowed us very little to eat. We had a slice and a half of toast with a little margarine and "naked" tea for breakfast. Some fish, usually the poorest, and two vegetables, carrots or turnips, were for lunch, and we had the same things over again for dinner. There were no fruits and no desserts of any kind. We ate on small wooden tables without tablecloths or napkins and with the scantiest of utensils. For example, we never had saucers for our cups and had only a knife for breakfast and never had spoons. Once in a while there was a little milk in the tea and once or twice a month there was a little sugar. We were always hungry. We could eat what we got in five minutes and never know we had it. Some could not eat at all at first but they got over that as hunger increased. We asked and asked for more bread. We were getting a total of five slices a day and asked for double that. We were scared to ask for rice, for more than half the men could not eat Japanese food. I lost 15 pounds in three weeks and others lost proportionately. With the lack of food and the cold we were up against it.

The Japanese were not entirely to blame. We were actually getting more fish and vegetables than their own people. They were living on rice. And they were treating us as they treated all prisoners. The system in Japanese prisons is to give the men only the bare minimum and allow their families to supply the rest. Our camp was run like that with three days a week when families could bring food. The men in our camp who had homes in Yokohama were in luck and were not hungry. Our *Tatsuta* nine had no resources in Yokohama. Only two of us had ever lived there and their homes were closed. Even if we had money we could not have bought things, for they were sold by ration cards and we had no cards. The Yokohama men in the next room ate at their tables and then went back to their lockers to eat what their families had brought in. We sat in the next room and watched through the glass windows of the partition as they ate meat and potatoes and sometimes pie. I know now how hungry men regard other men who have more than enough and do not share, and I would not be surprised at anything they might resort to.

Through Tsuru and then Hosoi San we were able to ask for some things. Howard Hannaford and Ted Walser were interned in Tokyo and were in much the same situation as we were. We learned that it was more difficult to visit but families could bring food. Gladys Walser and Ruth Hannaford were free to live at home and to go about within the limits of the city. They also had access to some money. They were not free to come and see us but they were free to send things with Hosoi San. At the beginning we were not permitted to speak with the two friends that came, but about the middle of January the atmosphere changed and we were free to make our needs known. That meant we had four women working for us outside: Gladys, Ruth, Hosoi San, and Lena (Dotty) Daugherty, a resourceful single woman of our Mission who was also in Tokyo. Before the end of January the food began to come in. The women realized that we would have to share and also that the others had few resources. So Gladys, Ruth, and Dotty began to send food in quantities with Hosoi San every five days for the balance of the six months we were there. We shared everything we got down to the last crumb. It was difficult to cut everything into nine pieces but we did it. We had no money to help pay for this, but at our request the people in Tokyo kept track of the money they spent for us and we reimbursed them when we later became able to do so.

It was at this time that we learned from Dr. Tsuru what had happened to Mrs. Hail. She had been taken to a hotel and then to a hospital and finally Tsuru had gotten her to Mrs. Hannaford's in Tokyo. There she died of cancer in February. Tsuru made all the arrangements for her and also for others who had no claim on him.

When the food began to come, we were able to get the kitchen to cook it for us at first. Then the man in the other room whom the police had appointed as our spokesman got into a scrap with the cook and we lost our access to the kitchen. It was a warm place, and we had been helping the cook to wash dishes in return for our use of his stove. But now we had to make other arrangements for cooking. At first Hosoi San brought bits of charcoal from her own scanty store. Then she found some briquettes made of coal. She also brought a small saw and we cut the briquettes in two pieces and each piece lasted us through breakfast and lunch.

Heinie was our cook and we began supplying some extras for breakfast, which was our worst meal. One morning we would have oatmeal and the next eggs, never both at the same meal. Tsuru got some extra bread from one of my seminary students whose father was a baker, and Ruth and Gladys got us some more. By this time we had a locker for each of us brought up from the basement and we had two extra lockers where we kept our food supply under lock and key. One man was in charge of apportioning the food. We always had something extra for lunch, usually some soup and occasionally a vegetable. Then we tried to get along with what the kitchen served for supper.

In addition, the day that Hosoi San came we usually had meat or a cake or even a pie. Those were gala days. Sometimes we got things from other people in Yokohama, but Tokyo remained our chief source right up to the end. Heinie and I never regretted our determination to share everything that we got. It cost us some money, although not that much, but it created a spirit which did much to keep up our morale and made internment livable. One evening after we had divided something we had gotten, one of the men remarked, "If anyone ever tells me again that a minister does not practice what he preaches, I'll knock him down."

Many friends came to see us and brought us gifts, but the core of them consisted of Tsuru, Ruth, Gladys, Dotty, and Hosoi San. Hosoi San was the one who kept this source open and transported most of the food. On that fifth day she came from Yokohama Station in a taxi with a big suitcase and some additional bundles. This was not all food, for she was still doing laundry for three of us. She was a Karuizawa woman who had worked for many missionaries, the last being the Smiths. When war came she returned to Meiji Gakuin knowing we would be back and might need her. Her name will always be remembered by the nine of us. We bought her a leather handbag before we left and all of us wrote our names in it as we gave it to her.

During this period of hunger and cold the greatest worry for some of us was the fact that we could not send any word to our families. There had been word to the Board that we were sailing so they knew about where we had been when the war started. We knew of no reports that the *Tatsuta* had returned, but there were no reports that the ship had been sunk, so they might have that satisfaction. On January 7 we were visited for the first time by a representative of the Swiss Minister. The Minister himself was in touch with the U.S. Government. We got his promise to send one cable for all of us to several addresses. It was, "Safe, well, busy, interned Yokohama." But of course we did not know if it went or not until he returned in February and said the American Ambassador had paid for its being sent.

Finally, through the Swiss, we got some of our luggage. We now had razors but not all immediately shaved off their beards. Lardner Moore had a vividly red one that got him the nickname of Wildcat or Tiger. Mine was black, sharply contrasting with my white hair, which I had had before the war. To many I was the black and white missionary. I had gotten some things from our home in Tokyo, including a Bible. Now I had my Moffatt's Bible and several of my Japanese books. I again began studying Japanese writing and reading. Later, with Lardner Moore's help, I began translating Kuwada's "Outline of Theology."

Heinie and I were close friends and were fortunate to be interned together. It was quite a blow when on the 3d of February he was suddenly taken away. We were all in bed when at 9:30 two police from Osaka came into the room and asked for Bovenkerk. They said he must pack what he had and go with them that night to Osaka. They assured him he would be all right and not to worry. We had learned by that time not to be taken in by assurances. I helped him pack and then, since neither of us had much money, I borrowed 100 yen from various other internees and then lent it to him. He was taken away in a car only twenty minutes after the police had come. We had arranged that someone in Osaka would send word to Hosoi San saying the weather was fine if he was all right. No word came until the end of February and then it was vague. In April word came that he had been released to the internment camp in Kobe, but I did not hear his story until June. He had been put in solitary confinement in an Osaka hotel and held there for two months. He had been questioned about his work, his ideas on Christianity, and the purposes of his study of rural sociology when the family lived for a year in a Japanese village. They were also trying to link him with the American consulate in Osaka through his work as Mission treasurer. They threatened him, tried to make him sign a confession, and slapped him in the face when he refused. The case finally fell through for lack of evidence against him as a spy and he was released to the camp in Kobe.

In our camp none of us were ever questioned individually except for routine questioning on family and where we had lived in Japan. Some businessmen were questioned about what they had been doing and who had worked with them. But occasionally a man was taken out by the police for questioning as a possible spy. Such men never came back to the camp, and there were well-founded rumors of torture or the threat of torture. One of these men was from our room and another was a close friend of some in our room. Here is a list I can vouch for. Three or four days after we were interned, a man in the larger room was marched off to prison. Heinie was next to go. A week later two men came in for the Rising Sun Oil man. Then in March, Jack Bellinger from our room was taken. In April another Englishman; and finally in May, after evacuation seemed certain, they came one day for Bond, our banker in the next room. They told him he was being taken to the other camp and gave him two hours to pack. We helped him with his luggage but when they came he was tied to a policeman, his baggage left with us, and he was marched off to jail. Each arrest threw a blight on the camp for several days. Our Irishman, Bobby Wright, expressed it when he said he knew now how chickens in a coop felt when they could any day expect a hand to grab them for a meal. Some of those arrested were later released after examination, but the proportion that were reported to have committed suicide was frightening. I can still shudder when I think about it. Any one of us could have been charged with breaking the finance control law or even the law against passing rumors.

Next to getting along with the police was the problem of getting along with the other men in the camp. We were crowded into so small a space so much of the time that we got on each other's nerves. Our room was 12 by 20 feet and in it we slept, ate, and spent most of our waking hours. The next room was just as crowded. I think that with one exception, however, we were more fortunate than they were in the men that we had. Here is a description of our group.

Heinie Bovenkerk has already been mentioned many times in

the foregoing account. He was the best friend any man could hope for.

The man who became my closest friend after Heinie left was *Lardner Moore*, a Southern Presbyterian. We had argued about theology and mission policy at the Kobe seminary. We could still argue, but in camp we stayed off that. He had a wife and three boys in Texas, a home that he talked about incessantly. He was born in Japan and knew the spoken language very well. He was then forty-four years old and full of pep. He was good at wisecracks and could imitate almost anyone, Japanese or American. He kept all of us in an uproar at times when we most needed it. Often after lights were out at 9 P.M., he would keep us going for another half hour. He could darn socks as well as anyone and after Heinie left he was our cook. He was a crack ball player also, and was admired by all.

The fourth missionary in the room was *Bobby Wright* from County Antrim in Northern Ireland. He was a Plymouth Brethren but fundamentally a dissenter. Lardner said he thought he himself was a dissenter but he could not hold a candle to Bobby. Bobby was against anything that anyone else thought about Christianity. He particularly hated Catholics and Episcopalians. Presbyterians were not that much better. I know that he thought I was not a Christian, but in the internment camp we buried our differences. His theology did not appeal to anyone but he was a good preacher. His Irish wit made him interesting if not logical. He was just thirty-three, with no family. He called himself a faith missionary, by trade a druggist, but he had little or no money. Sometimes his wit became tiresome. He would make a joke of anything one said. But underneath his joking he was not happy. More than once he said to me that he wished he were dead. He thought activity in this world was of no value and it was better to have it over with anyway. He was not good at games but made himself play them and sometimes talked his opponent into losing. He would share all he had and do anything for you—after all a pretty good fellow to have around.

The oldest of the other five was *Charles Horatio Nelson*, commonly called the Admiral and sometimes called the Archbishop of Hell. This last was to establish his right to be in the missionary room. He was an Englishman, born in Scotland, and had been a businessman in Kobe. He was a strong and vigorous fifty, with a wife and daughter in England. He was our treasurer and took charge of our store of grub. He had been a choirboy in England but now said he could not be a Christian and a businessman too. He was our Gloom King—never believed any report that was good and could always believe the worst. His gloom prepared us not to be too disappointed when a promising rumor was shattered by facts. He also could get more work out of the fellows who were inclined not to do their share than anyone else.

The sixth man was *John Wesley Palmer,* a native of Norwich, England, and an Episcopalian in spite of his name. He was the agent of the Norwich Union Insurance Company, and had been in Yokohama for sixteen years. His wife and child were in Canada. He was just a year younger than I, but raised the finest full beard in the camp. He had many of the qualities of a British businessman in the Orient. He was very blunt and sometimes profane, but at heart was an earnest Christian with insight that was sometimes startling. He had worked hard in the English Episcopal Church in Yokohama and had been treasurer and lay reader. He was largely self-educated and was a stimulating talker. I would like very much to have him on the session of any church in which I was the pastor.

The next man was *John Dalrymple Maple, Ph.D.* He will writhe if he reads this, for he does not like the "doctor" part. He was a California boy, just thirty, and an entomologist. He was in the employ of the U.S. Government and was studying various insects in Japan. He was not married and was very attractive to the ladies, tall and thin and witty. He was really the best man on puns that I have ever heard in my life. For us, puns were now either Mapleian or non-Mapleian, depending on their vividness. He had been in Yokohama for two or three years with the Yokohama consulate. His parents were Quakers from Whittier, California. He was a bit soured on religion, but he came to hear me preach sometimes and we had one or two serious discussions. And Johnny had a girl. She was a German girl whose grandmother had been English. She also had some Jewish blood through her mother, but her father was in the employ of the German news agency in Japan. She came to see Johnny. She could not get in but that did not matter. She still came and brought everything to eat that she could get her hands on. The police let Johnny see her sometimes and then the German Embassy sent word to the family and to the police that it was not to be permitted any longer. But she still came and the local police let her see Johnny. Johnny and the girl could not speak Japanese so I had to be their go-between with the police. Johnny was also sometimes sour, and we soon learned that anyone who spoke to Johnny before breakfast did so at his own risk. His friendship was one that will last.

Next in line was *Jasper Bellinger*, a young man of thirty from Oregon. Jack was the youngest of five children and his family spoiled him. He never played games and he was a sissy. He really had a good education as a journalist but not the ability or personality to put it over. He had been in Japan for some years and had taught at Aoyama Gakuin, a Methodist school. Later he got on the edges of the newspaper field. He was working on the Japanese-owned English-language paper in Tokyo before he sailed on the *Tatsuta*. He seemingly had never found himself. He made quite a fuss when we turned around on the *Tatsuta*, bewailing the fact that he had not gone earlier. Later he complained that he had not gotten a position that would put him with the foreign newspapermen and not in the internment camp. He thought, and we did too, that they would be treated better. In camp he was a pest. We tried to help him and he got somewhat better but the fellows outside our room detested him. Finally in March he was taken to prison. I packed his things and went down to see him after he was arrested and was still in the police office. I was able to lend him some money but not to talk with him. The cold sweat had broken out all over him and he was scared stiff. We worried a great deal about him. We were not supposed to know that he was in prison, but I went to the head of the police and told him what I knew of the boy and insisted that they try to understand him. Certainly he was harmless but his peculiar psychological quirks could get him into a lot of trouble. Later I made a chance to speak to the Swiss about him in front of the police. The Swiss Embassy was continuing to represent U.S. interests in Japan. Still later, when we thought he was being left behind, we tried to get the International Red Cross to get him out. It was certainly good news when the Swiss finally confidentially told me that he was surely going. I had some ten letters to write to the families of men who were not included on the first exchange ship. Thank the Lord I did not have to write to Jack's mother.

The last of the nine was a New Englander, a graduate of a New England college and a teacher in the schools of Japan for twenty years. I am not mentioning his name for I am going to say some pretty strong things about him and there may still be some members of his immediate family who are alive. I'll call him "The Professor." He would like that.

The Professor was forty-four in 1941. He had a wife in Japan who was a Japanese, and a daughter in college in the United States. He was leaving on the *Tatsuta* to see his daughter. At times he could be the nicest man you would meet; at other times he could be the most detested man that I have ever met. Internment made that evident to us. All the Americans mentioned here came back on the exchange ship. This time the Professor's wife was with him. Johnny Maple told me one day that when he saw the Professor he avoided him, for he did not want to think of the kind of skunk that was underneath that hide.

The Professor had a certain amount of culture and information but was the kind who tried to impress people with his intelligence, sat back and chewed his pipe and told you just how things were or ought to be. In argument he was more vituperative than logical. He thought himself to be an anthropologist and could talk at great length and in polysyllables about the origin of man and the development of the various races. His anthropological studies took the form of measuring heads. He had a slide rule and would gravely measure the length of a head and its breadth. He would then compare the two and tell you a great deal about your ancestors. He had no use for religion. Morals were merely a matter of taste. His personal habits were most disgusting. He was the squeamish member of the group but he used a personal teacup that he never washed and which was encrusted with grime. He was accustomed to leaving his clothing all over the place, cleaning his pipe at the table, sitting down and eating before we got there, and then leaving long before the rest. He never did any work if he could help it, and he had a vile temper. Heinie had the first scrap with him and it lasted three days. Palmer was next. He had asked us about Kagawa and we were discussing him when the Professor chimed in, saying that Kagawa was a half-baked peanut, and other things to the same effect. Palmer began reading the Professor the riot act for butting in and deriding a man with vile language who was being discussed seriously. The Professor then refused to accept the bread and other things at the table if they were passed to him by Palmer. Finally we all jumped on the Professor one morning and gave him a lesson he would never forget, Palmer leading the way in beautiful English. That silenced him in our room, although he did not speak to Palmer for three months. He tried to make friends in the other room but soon fell out with them. He was a good ballplayer if he was not mad, and he tried also to play bridge but it was no fun to play with him. He was a gambler and could be led on and set down too easily. In some ways we were sorry for him, for he did not realize the kind of person he was and I suppose he sometimes thought he was really the cultured gentleman he appeared to be.

The rest of the men in the camp were from Yokohama. Most of them were in some kind of business. There were five Eurasian boys who were students at the Catholic school in Yokohama. All of these were good ballplayers, and all had British citizenship. One was applying for Japanese citizenship and when he got it he was drafted into the Japanese army. The elite of the camp were a group of businessmen who were connected with good foreign firms. There were three Standard Oil engineers, all Englishmen. There was a man who was an accountant with Rising Sun Oil. We had three bankers, two British and one American. We had one Singer Sewing Machine man. Perhaps half of these were pretty straight fellows. The rest were so-so. In the business community most of the responsible men had left. Those who stayed were single and had Japanese concubines. Japanese law recognizes these relationships and they went about it openly.

I have left one man to the last. *Charles Moss* was part French, part English, and part Japanese with British citizenship. He had made a small fortune as a liquor dealer in Yokohama. His wife was French and was in France. He had had at least two Japanese concubines and was living with one of them when the war began. He spoke good Japanese and was well known in Yokohama, both among the Japanese and in the foreign community. The police put him in charge of the camp as far as internal affairs were concerned. He assigned duties to us and no one could officially approach the police except through him. He was very sensitive about his position and ran the camp's internal affairs as a dictator. The businessmen got his favors. The younger fellows and the "don't cares" would do nothing. Our room, of course, was hopping mad on more than one occasion. We had suggested to Moss that he ought to have a camp committee to help him. He ignored it. Finally when the fight with the kitchen started, Lardner and I volunteered to see Moss. Moss had one of his henchmen with him, a former prizefighter by the name of Westwood. We were as tactful as possible, saying that we knew he was trying to help us all but we thought he would get along easier with the whole crowd if he had some of the group to help him. He refused, saying that the police had put him in charge and we all had to listen to him. We still insisted that what he was doing was a dictatorship, benevolent and all that, but still not democratic, and we thought we ought to preserve as much democracy as possible. They laughed at that and when we persisted Moss left in a huff, saying that he would resign. At noon Westwood came and said that Moss had gone to the police chief and tried to resign. The chief said they had appointed him and he could not resign. The chief then wanted to know why he wanted to resign and Moss told him that one or two fellows were making trouble for him. The chief then said that he must give him our names and we would be put in prison. Moss had not given the chief our names and he thought he could patch it up if we would agree not to cause him any more trouble. We were almost certain his story was false but at the time there seemed no way of carrying it further and Lardner and I shut up. Moss had us over a barrel.

But it was not for long. The chief must have sensed that something was wrong, for in March he divided us into four groups of eight and asked each group to elect a leader. The *Tatsuta* room was a natural group and I was elected their leader. Moss was still nominally in charge but we learned how to work through and around him.

One of the Standard Oil men in the other room offered to let us have the grounds of his coffee pot for second-run coffee. (He had 200 pounds of Maxwell House when the war began.) It was spring and we were warmer, and eight or ten men would often congregate in the *Tatsuta* room after breakfast to sip second-run coffee and talk. The good fellowship we had then will always be remembered as one of the high spots of the six months. Moss himself had two or three scraps with his group and ended up eating by himself in a corner of the big room.

Conditions in the camp improved after the first of April. In March the police moved out of the building into a smaller one next to it. They kept an office in the room at our door but the day and night guard was removed. In April we had a sugar ration and the food improved somewhat. Many conjectured about this. Did rumors of exchange make them want to leave a good impression? The truth was probably that the various agencies in the government concerned with us had got together and sorted out what should be done. Now the police had guidelines instead of being unsure. These changes included a schedule of time for rising, roll call, and meals. We had a regular time for putting our mattresses in the corner for the day and for getting them on the floor in the evening, as well as airing them regularly in the daytime.

We had always had ample time and opportunity for exercise and on the whole were healthy. I had two slight upsets during the winter. Once it was because of food. Our fish was sometimes herring and if some were left we had it the next meal in "fish balls." It did not look appetizing; in fact Johnny Maple, our entomologist, said it looked like "owl regurgitation." Therefore we called it "owl meat." Sometimes it was slightly spoiled. One day after eating it eight or nine of us got sick, including one policeman. The doctor was called and he ordered medicine and brandy. We speedily recovered. Later in the winter I got a flu bug and ran a fever of 103. I thought the doctor would send me to the hospital but he didn't. I agreed with him when I discovered it would be the police hospital and that I would have a guard night and day. Lardner and Bobby took care of me. Bobby, the druggist, prescribed aspirin and gave me a good dose. In the night, after I had had a good sweat, Bobby took off the covers and my pajamas in the bitterly cold room and rubbed me down. Others, as well as myself, thought he was crazy. In the morning I was better. Bobby said the treatment would kill or cure. The folks outside sent me some powdered milk and soon I was built up again.

By the middle of the winter the police also gave us more freedom to talk with visitors. The word got around and visitors from Tokyo came. This process was slowed down for a bit when the police limited it to only two or three accredited visitors. I got Tsuru and Hosoi on my list but no more. Then the police allowed us to get around that by permitting us to thank people who brought us food, even if they were not on the list. I still scarcely believe that was true, but I have the record. Once in a while permission was not granted but much more often it was. Here is a reasonably complete list of my visitors as I remembered it and recorded it on my way home across the South Atlantic in August 1942. Because all had to register and talk in Japanese to me in front of a policeman, each one was a very brave person.

Kobayashi, a Meiji Gakuin professor and also a golfer at Karuizawa. He brought flowers and later came again.

Inouye, head of a language school in Tokyo and a Karuizawa friend. He called twice, once with Kobayashi.

Moderator Matsuo of Tokyo Presbytery called twice. He brought soup.

Professor Goshi of the Japan Seminary called twice.

President Yano of Meiji Gakuin came in Janaury.

Watanabe, head teacher of the Meiji Gakuin high school. He brought noodles and Japanese cakes.

Two students (Nisei), second generation from Tokyo Union Church, called twice.

Kiyama, a Tokyo pastor, brought gifts but was refused permission to see me.

Kikuta, Meiji Gakuin professor who helped others also, brought vegetables from the country.

Kashiwai, pastor of the Senzoku church, had been sick but came with a six-year-old boy in March on a Saturday. The boy gave me a crayon picture and church women sent me cupcakes. Kashiwai prayed with me and would tell the congregation to pray.

Sugano, a Wakayama and Tokyo student, came twice in March. He brought apples from his father, a lieutenant colonel in the Army. (I said "Thank you" for twenty minutes.) In May, Sugano came again with a permit to talk with me for one hour.

The Karuizawa carpenter who built our house came to see me and brought six oranges.

Three Meiji Gakuin teachers in the high school and five of my boys came June 1.

A Korean student from a Bible class who was a police suspect came several times as carrier of Hosoi's bundles to avoid registering with police. I could only thank him for coming.

Iwata from Shinmaruko did not come, only because he was called into the Army at the war's beginning. The work was continued by presbytery under a new young pastor.

All this was within the context of Dr. Senji Tsuru coming every week and Hosoi San coming every five days for six months.

The other Yokohama internees were quite surprised by the number of visitors I had, as were the police. Usually American businessmen did not have close Japanese friends. Christian fellowship had stood the test. My experience was unusual. Tokyo and Kobe internment regulations were interpreted more strictly by the police, as ours were from time to time. In Yokohama the pastor of the largest Presbyterian church visited Lardner just as Tsuru visited us.

The problem of money was a recurring one. Heinie as Mission treasurer had made arrangements for a Christian lawyer in Kobe to handle our funds in any emergency. The Mission still had some money both in a safe in Tokyo and in a bank. The funds in the safe offered no problem except that they were very limited. There was more in the bank but that was a problem. There were all kinds of permits to be gotten before these funds could be released. People who were free could push these requests along in the various offices of the bureaucracy, but those of us who were interned had to depend on the lawyer in Kobe and he had not enough time for all of us.

I appealed to the Swiss and the best they could do was borrow money from Mrs. Hannaford. The Swiss also got me $7 from the U.S. Government, which was all they would allow in a single month. Finally the lawyer made application for a permit to withdraw money from the Mission account so that I could prepare for evacuation on the exchange ship. That was delayed and I decided to sell our furniture in Tokyo. I had only the kitchen things, the dining room table and chairs, the living room furniture, and the beds. They had cost us under 1,000 yen and I thought I might get 500 for them. Miss Daugherty and Hosoi San called in a secondhand dealer and he brought me an application for the right to sell. When I came to sign it I found he was giving me 1,509 yen for the lot. I signed it, got the buyer to put the money in the bank for me, and then asked for a permit to draw some of it out. I could not draw it all and needed a lawyer to advise me as to what I ought to ask for. We settled on 1,300 yen, to pay my debts to Hosoi San and others, to loan some to internees who needed it, and to take some with me on the exchange ship. We could take up to 1,000 yen. (The yen at that time was worth about 30 cents.) I learned later that others of our Mission were getting money freely, but my request evidently had somewhere struck a snag.

The four or five of us in the *Tatsuta* group who were interested in a church service held one of our own in our room the first Sunday we were there. Then we had no Bibles and no hymnals, but shared what we remembered. We did this for two Sundays and then on the first Sunday in January, after Tsuru had gotten some Bibles and hymnals from Tokyo, we planned a service and then, without asking anyone's permission, invited others in the camp to meet with us. We had fifteen that first Sunday. The four of us missionaries took turns preaching. Palmer got some prayer books from the Episcopal church in Yokohama and we cut down the Episcopal service until it could be easily followed by all of us. Then he, as lay reader, and I, as preacher, took the Episcopal service every third Sunday. Palmer was also a good singer and could lead off. Most of the camp being English, the Episcopal service and Palmer's English accent were appreciated. On the other two Sundays Lardner and Bobby preached in turn after Heinie was taken. Neither of them would preach at the Episcopal service. Lardner would attend but Bobby would not. The services were well attended; even the Roman Catholic high school boys came sometimes.

In a way the services were difficult for the preacher, but challenging. We had the Bible but no other religious books. Living night and day with the men to whom we preached made shallow preaching impossible. Men wanted to hear what you really thought and practiced. Some had not taken time to think about religion for years. One said he had prayed as he had never prayed before. I would recommend to all preachers some form of our Sunday morning preparation. The man who preached would usually find that it was his turn to clean the toilets that morning. Getting down on your hands and knees to mop the floor and to wipe the urinals keeps one humble enough to preach the gospel an hour later.

In April, five or six of the men asked me to conduct a Bible class for them. They were mostly Englishmen and they wanted seriously to understand more of the Biblical background. They said they had not studied the Bible since they were children. We studied Mark twice a week for the rest of the time that we were there. The discussions were free and stimulating. It was by far the most interesting class that I ever taught. In the midst of this, one of the class members was taken off to prison, and the men who were left prayed for him regularly.

Our chief recreation in the camp was softball. The police furnished what equipment we had. The grounds were limited. There was no right field and left field was shallow. We could hit the ball over the fence easily but then the police had to run it down for us. They got tired of that and let one of us out the gate to get it. But that delayed the game so we called the men out who hit the ball, and if that did not work we called the side out. We played almost every day and sometimes twice a day.

For some of us bridge was our recreation on rainy days and in the evening.

I began to read five chapters of the Japanese Bible every day, and alongside it one book of the English Bible. I had never read a book at one sitting before. The last time I had read the whole Bible in a short time I was impressed by the Old Testament. This time it was the epistles. They stood out as never before. The Japanese Bible also was stimulating. The change in language throws a new light on some passages.

I had never expected to have such experiences as we had in the Boat Club at Yokohama. As I have reread what I have written, I have sometimes thought that it sounded like an adventure story. It was an adventure, but it was much more than that. We had more than two hundred days in the custody of the Japanese police, who were watching us as enemy aliens.

Every day we were faced with uncertainty. Often we were cold and hungry. Always there was the threat of going to prison and being tortured. Most of the time we had no hope of being released until the end of the war, some years away. We had no hard news; only propaganda and rumor. After hope was aroused there was endless delay. We were not even sure that our families knew we were alive. I did not agree with Bobby when he said that he wished he was dead, but I understood how he could say that.

We had the comfort of Christian friends, both inside and outside the camp. That was a great help. And we had our faith and the Scriptures. One day I found a verse which helped me understand the meaning of our experience. It was in Moffatt's translation of I Peter 5:9–11: "Learn to pay the same tax of suffering as the rest of your brotherhood throughout the world. Once you have suffered for a little, the God of all grace who has called you to his eternal glory in Christ Jesus, will repair, recruit, and strengthen you. The dominion is his for ever and ever: Amen."

I would not knowingly have chosen the experience of internment. But now that I was having it, I knew I was being prepared to identify with others in their hunger, isolation, and suffering around the world.

I'm sure we did not fully appreciate the visits from the Swiss Embassy. They and the International Red Cross were the only agencies authorized to report how Japan was complying with the Geneva Convention in the treatment not only of prisoners of war but also of civilian internees. They informed public opinion, but they could report infringements, which in turn would influence U.S. treatment of Japanese civilian internees. Japan still took some pride in keeping these laws intact.

The Embassy sent other representatives, but the only time the Swiss Minister himself came was on the 23d of February. Another man came at the end of March. That time I was able to send a telegram out to America and then paid for it the next month when he came back. They were getting better organized to do their work. Later the English changed from the Argentine Embassy to the Swiss.

We still read the English-language newspaper the Japanese printed and we read between the lines, interpreting the reports often differently than the Japanese intended. That was true with the naval battles of the Coral Sea and of Midway. There was no getting around the results in Hong Kong and Singapore and in the sinking of the British battleships by Japanese planes. These were especially dark and bitter days for our British friends in the camp. We had no other sources of information; no letters at all except old ones that had strayed and now arrived. Floy's letter of October 1 came to me at the end of January. In February I received a letter from my father, written in October, in which he had put his personal scorecard of a World Series game.

On February 18 we were allowed out of the camp for the first time. A couple of days before, the police came saying that in celebration of the fall of Singapore we would be allowed to walk in the parade. We talked it over among ourselves and reported to the police chief that we would not go out under these conditions. So the next day it was reported that we would not have to march in the parade but that we would go for a walk and would carry Japanese flags. We reported back that we would not do this either. I remember that I talked on the phone to the police chief, explaining to him that we were not prisoners of war but civilians. If he were caught in America, would he want to be made to walk down the street on a day which celebrated an American victory and be asked to carry an American flag?

That night the flags were brought down and kept in the police office. Some of our men played sick the next morning and one excused himself because he did not have proper shoes. But 27 of us lined up waiting for what could have been a confrontation. At the last moment an order cancelling the flag-carrying came down. The other Yokohama internment camp had accepted the flags and were ready to march. Both camps walked about a mile to a park in front of the New Grand Hotel where the Japanese military man attached to the police office addressed us through an interpreter. His theme was that Japan had nothing against Americans. They were not to blame; Roosevelt was. Every morning when his own children started off to school with inadequate clothing and poor shoes he wept and blamed Roosevelt for the embargo that had deprived Japan of supplies. We Americans agreed he must be a Republican.

On the way back to the camp we stopped at the American consulate and met the men who were under house arrest there, and then over to the British consulate, there the consul made a brief speech. Then we walked back home, 21 policemen guarding the 27 of us. We were tired from the unusual exercise and surprised when the cook gave us a special meal that evening.

Up to that time the only way to get out was to go to the doctor or the dentist. I got to the latter three times while he repaired one filling. He could have done it with one visit. He was a German Jew and his wife was his assistant. We all enjoyed talking freely for a change. For those who wished it, he served drinks.

The first of April we were taken out to see the cherry blossoms in the park. We had a picnic lunch and then a ball game between the two camps, which we lost, and then a speech by the military man. His theme was that the lives of Japanese soldiers were like the beautiful cherry blossoms, living for the moment and then fluttering to the ground.

On April 12 we got out, those who wanted to, for a Communion service at the Yokohama Episcopal church. The

British chaplain from the Embassy came down from Tokyo to conduct it.

The last of April the men who had relatives in Yokohama were allowed to go home from 9 to 2 one day a week without a police guard. Concubines counted as relatives. A Scotsman who had neither wife nor concubine and had to stay in camp remarked that this was "the reward of virtue." However, two weeks later we got our reward along with the Scotsman. The original group had their time extended from 9 to 4 and the rest of us were allowed to go to the Yokohama Country and Athletic Club, a beautiful place with clubhouse and grounds on the edge of Yokohama. We played tennis, took a Japanese bath, had lunch, visited the bar, and played at lawn bowls, a game that Englishmen play with a ball in one hand and a glass in the other. There were 15 of us who went every Wednesday from then until we sailed the middle of June. We had three policemen along with us and after the first week I was in charge of the behavior of the group. Our Scottish friend had had too much to drink and the police chief said if this happened again we could not go, so the men themselves selected me as their policeman. I hesitated for I had had no experience whatsoever, but I was told I would have a core of experienced advisers when the time came. No one got drunk after that.

My most thrilling trip came in May. In the back of my mind I was determined to get that pearl necklace back. Our money, neckties, pens, and pencils had all been given back, but no necklace. It had been taken at the same time and I insisted they look for it, but no luck. When we suddenly learned we might play tennis, I asked permission to go to the customs police and get my summer things and my racquet out of my baggage. I got permission but others who asked were refused. I volunteered then to also get things for the rest. I found all the luggage from the *Tatsuta* nine kept in one room. I got my things and then the things others had asked for. I was pleased that we had found all the luggage intact for the nine people. There remained a cardboard carton in the corner of the room. The customs officer asked me if I knew to whom that belonged, for it had no name on it. I went over and opened the box. On top was a small parcel tied up in a man's handkerchief. I took it and saw the name Robert Wright on the handkerchief. I opened it and there was the Mikimoto Scotch-plaid case and in it were my pearls. I explained what I had found and commented that this carton must have contained the unmarked private property taken on December 15 and not identifiable. The police had attached it to the other property in the room which they knew belonged to the same people. I then asked the policeman and the customs officer what I should do with the pearls now. They both replied, "Put them in your pocket." I did so and brought them home three months later to Floy in the United States. (I took the police guard to lunch at the New Grand Hotel on our way back to the camp.)

We were all in camp during the Doolittle raid on April 18 but we saw little of it. It was our interview day so I remember the date. Just at noon the guns began to bark and then we caught sight of a plane over Kawasaki. Later a plane was over the bluff in Yokohama, flying very low with shells bursting around it. Whether it was the same plane we did not know. As far as we could see, no damage was done. Our police were scared. They got their pistols out and we were careful not to give them any reason for starting on us. Later I learned from people who saw the raid in Tokyo that it was a small affair. Heinie in Kobe saw only one plane and no damage. Nagoya was reported to have large fires but we could not check that. Of course it triggered a tremendous amount of discussion in the camp, with many theories about it. One was that the Japanese staged it to awaken their own people to the danger. I'm sure this was not true but that was part of the result. By its very nature the raid was a kind of stunt. Land planes flying off carriers and then landing behind the lines in China could not have been expected to produce much damage. But the psychological impact on the Japanese people was important. They now could anticipate that it would happen again and in increasing numbers. And there was a probable U.S. military gain. Japan had launched the war with a minimum of planes and other equipment. Expansion at that point was impossible and even replacements were very difficult. Japanese planes were striking into the South Pacific. If Japan had to divert some of those planes to protect the main islands there was a clear military gain in the raid. All in all it was a gamble that may have had important results. Toland emphasizes that America did not beat Japan by better equipment and better-trained soldiers. We won because of our capacity to increase material and to replace losses of ships and planes. It was to be a war of attrition.

It seems strange from this point in time that our only interest in being moved from the Boat Club was in anticipation that a better place could be found somewhere in Yokohama that would provide accommodations better suited to our needs. We all wanted to be moved to a better place but we never expected to be exchanged. Originally we thought the war might be over in two years at the earliest. After the fall of Singapore we extended our estimate to three or four years before the Marines would march up the Bund in front of the New Grand Hotel. We knew there might be an exchange of diplomats, but an exchange of ordinary civilians never entered our minds.

But on February 23 the Swiss Minister himself said that we would definitely be exchanged. The diplomats would go within a month and we would go on a second boat within two months. The British received the same assurance. No definite date was set. I cabled Floy in March that there was some hope of evacuation "this year." The last of March the British were assured they were going the end of April and it appeared that we probably would go with them. A slightly drunk police sergeant told us on April 15 that we were slated to sail on the *Kamakura Maru* on May 6. (By that time we did not know what to believe.) A few days later there was news of a delay to May 15, then to the end of May, and then to the end of June. On May 27, upon our return from the Athletic Club, the police asked all the Americans to assemble and then told us that we would be going soon and that on the next morning we were to meet at the Yokohama United Club for instructions. There were about twenty who met the next morning from the two camps and from the prison. We were told that all but two or three of us would surely go. The date set for sailing was June 10. It was then delayed to the 12th, to the 15th, to the 16th. We actually got on the boat on the 17th. With such delays we were skeptical about going, until on the morning of the 13th the *Asama Maru*, a sister ship of the *Tatsuta* and the *Kamakura*, came into the harbor with white crosses painted on her side against a gray background. The British by this time knew they were not going with us but there would be a later boat.

We were told we could not take any printed matter, rugs, blankets, sheets, or silverware. Yokohama men went home for two days to pack. We asked for special consideration of our baggage in the customs office and it was refused. Yokohama men all had red stickers on their luggage and we still had nothing. Finally on the 14th we were told that a man would take us to the pier the next morning to repack our luggage. In the morning it was raining and the man called suggesting we did not need to go. We insisted and we got him a taxi and we all went. Our baggage was all on the pier. The others got through in a hurry but the police balked at my big box of books. I had insisted that our baggage had been all placed in bond when the *Tatsuta* came back, and after consultation with his chief, the customs officer agreed. I was missing one file of papers that the customs officer said they had taken to examine and I would get it on the *Asama*. I never did and I never protested that loss. I already had more than I expected to get.

It was hard to leave the British on the morning of the 17th but far harder on them to see us go. We had many fast friendships. We got our cabin assignment at the Yokohama United Club, had our money counted, and said good-by to some of our friends who had come to see us off. At the pier we had five different examinations before we got on the boat. There were people from Sendai, Kobe, and Tokyo joining us, and we Presbyterians had a grand reunion. There were ten of us sailing. Heinie and I were quartered in the same cabin. Ted and Gladys Walser, Howard and Ruth Hannaford, and Dotty Daugherty came from Tokyo; Alice Grube came from Osaka and the Bill Kerrs from Korea, where they had been working with Japanese. The U.S. Government ruled that people in prison and in internment camps, together with their families and those who were ill, should come first. Alice had been in jail and Dotty got in on health grounds. We left three behind. Helen Palmer and Martha Ann Wilson had been interned in their own home and would come on the next boat. Lillian Wells would choose to stay through the war with her Japanese friends in Tokyo.

The Presbyterian contingent was to be increased at every stop, but we doubled our number immediately when the Korea people came aboard at Yokohama. They had a hard time in that Japanese colony. Some of the men and all of the women had been free, but other men had been interned and three were imprisoned from one to six months. All three had had the "water cure," being tied upon their backs and having water poured down their noses until they passed out. One had it done to him five or six times. The purpose of the Japanese was to get a confession and they got none.

We had plenty of time to hear these stories, for at 6 P.M. we steamed out of the breakwater and turned up toward Tokyo and anchored. The next day we went farther up the bay. Speculation was rife as to why we did not go. The most common story was that the Lanes and a Mr. McKinnon were in jail in Hokkaido and that the United States was insisting they be put on the ship. The Lanes were friends of ours, and their twins, just six months younger than John, Jr., were already on the ship. In any case we did not sail for more than a week. On the 22d we came back to the breakwater and took on water, then went back up the bay. We were still in sight of our internment camp and I suppose the British had a hard time figuring out what we were doing. At 1:30 A.M. on the 25th the engines turned over and we started. I stayed up until we were out of the harbor, following a destroyer as we had done six months before. It was a fine feeling to be on our way.

On the night before we left the camp the police gave us a dinner and the military man gave us another speech, telling us what we might say when we got back to the United States, assuring us that they had always tried to protect us. I do not think he expected a reply, but we had Lardner primed to give it in perfect Japanese. He was very polite and had all the police listening to him. He thanked them all and then said that we hoped we would never be interned again, but if it happened we hoped they would be the ones to care for us. Then he said, "As a boy I was proud to have lived in Tosa." Later he had lived in Gifu and he used to take his own boys to the park in Gifu and show them a statue of a Tosa man. This was of Viscount Itagaki, who was a noted liberal hero and had been assassinated in Gifu. On the statue were inscribed the words that he had uttered as he died at the hands of the assassin: "I die but freedom lives forever." Then Lardner added that that was the spirit in which we had lived in the camp. We were prisoners and sometimes conditions were bad, "but in our hearts freedom lived forever." The police knew exactly what he meant but there was no reply.

On the *Asama* we were in third class, twelve men to a room. Women and older men were in second class, but most of the diplomats ate with us. At first the food seemed good by comparison with the camp, but we soon got tired of fish and the speed with which we were served. We ate in three shifts, thirty minutes from the time we sat down until another shift was taking our places. We had water in our cabin only a half hour in the morning and a half hour in the evening. The *Asama* was usually a combination of passengers and freight. One of the holds had been made into a dormitory. We had about 430 passengers on board. Later we pulled into Hong Kong just off Hong Kong Island and took aboard 370 more Americans, leaving 2,000 British behind. We talked into the night with some of our missionaries from Hong Kong. Eight thousand British, including volunteers, had resisted fifty thousand Japanese before surrender came. Soldiers who surrendered early were bayoneted; the last who surrendered were saved. Later we stopped just below Saigon in the river and took aboard 125 refugees from Thailand, 26 from our Mission, the rest having escaped early in the war through Burma and India. We talked again into the night. Fifty miles off the harbor of Singapore we met the Italian ship *Conte Verde*, which was under Japanese control and which had 600 refugees from China. The two ships then proceeded through the strait between Java and Sumatra, across the Indian Ocean, around Madagascar, and into the Portuguese port of Lourenço Marques in Mozambique. During all this time, five weeks in all, we were under Japanese control but turned to Ambassador Grew and the Tokyo Embassy people for guidance in American community affairs.

The Embassy turned to me, as the last acting pastor of the Tokyo Union Church, for the church services on the *Asama*. I got the pastors of other port city union churches together and we organized the services. The first Sunday while still in the harbor at Yokohama was a memorable one. I preached and felt at home with the Ambassador as my Episcopalian lay reader. We sang Old Hundredth and "Faith of Our Fathers." There was not a dry eye in the audience. I used the words in Moffatt's translation of the Lord's Prayer, "Thy Reign Begin," and emphasized that the experience of the last six months had given us all personally an opportunity to reflect and begin again. As one of our men in camp had prayed, "I ask God to set me free, but most of all I pray that God will make me fit to be free." God's reign begins in us and then extends into all our relationships.

The harbor at Lourenço Marques is up a river and the dock is alongside the river's edge. The *Gripsholm*, a Swedish ship under the American flag, had already arrived and was tied up at the dock.

In the river itself were anchored a score or more freighters, most of them British but two American. In fact, the first one we sighted was an American tanker, the *Malaya*, flying the American flag, with antiaircraft guns forward and a big gun behind. We steamed slowly past, less than a hundred yards away, and its crew let out a yell of greeting. There were tears in our eyes as we replied. Then its whistle began to toot out a message which some could spell as "Welcome Refugees." The next boat was British and its crew also greeted us and its whistle spelled over and over again the Morse for V and then V-I-C-T-O-R-Y. Other British boats joined in. It was the first real outburst we had had, anticipating the freedom we were about to enjoy. The *Conte Verde* with the 600 or more refugees from Shanghai was immediately behind us and got the same greeting.

The dock was more than a mile long and there was room for us to come in ahead of the *Gripsholm*, and for the *Conte Verde* to come in behind it. All three of the ships were about the same size, but the *Gripsholm* was a passenger ship and at the time held 1,500 Japanese refugees from the United States, for whom we would be exchanged. We docked about 10:30 A.M. The Swedish crew on the *Gripsholm* began throwing cigarettes to our fellows and then fruit to the children. Oranges were most in demand. Heinie and I got pieces of two oranges. We had forgotten that they could taste so good. Newspaper reporters were also down at the ship and gave us some garbled news and asked what we knew. We had heard that Alexandria had fallen and were glad to know it was not true. The Russian news, however, seemed bad.

We went down to lunch, and for a time when we came up we watched the children catch oranges. Then someone said there was mail. We had expected that we would get mail but never expected it the first day. We ran to get in line. Heinie and I were disappointed as there was none for us. The Merrill Adys from Hong Kong had mail from her sister in Muncie, Indiana, and she mentioned in her letter that she had been at my sister's and their saying that we would be on the same boat. We heard there was another box of unsorted mail and we stood in line for that. Heinie got a letter from Hester but there was none for me. Later I went into the line for the third time and there was still no mail. I gave up and went to sit on the hatch beside Heinie. He read me scraps from his letter. About twenty minutes later we heard there was more mail and on this fourth time I got two letters, one from Floy and one from my mother. As I read them my heart was very, very full. It was the first word that I had had since October. Nine months and a half without knowing how they all were. I never want to go through that again.

Reading and rereading the letters filled the afternoon. The Japanese passengers on the *Gripsholm* were ashore and the *Conte Verde* passengers got ashore in the evening. We were kept in.

We were up early the next morning, July 23, Louise's birthday. We had everything packed before breakfast and then stood in line an hour and a half. I had one suitcase, a golf bag with five clubs, and my typewriter. Then the lines began to move. One line each from the *Asama Maru* and the *Conte Verde* made small circles and entered each end of the *Gripsholm*. Two from the center of the *Gripsholm* separated and circled wide to enter each of the other ships. After we got started, it was all completed in less than two hours. Now 1,500 passengers from each side were at last under their own flags. Heinie and I did not stop to join the line that was getting Portuguese money. We had a few U.S. coins in our pockets and we went ashore without a police guard for the first time since December 2. At last we were free!

We had traveled halfway home without any fear of danger. We did not know then what Ambassador Grew learned later from a young U.S. submarine commander. In the misty dawn one day in the China Sea he saw in his periscope what he thought was a fat Japanese transport. He was about to fire his torpedoes when the fog cleared and he saw on the side of the ship the Swiss cross. He told Grew, "You were within seconds of receiving two torpedoes right in the middle."

Chapter 5

Missionary to the United States
(1942–1948)

THE FIVE WEEKS that we spent on the *Gripsholm* before we met our families in New York were quite different from the five weeks we had spent on the Japanese ship, the *Asama*, in getting to Lourenço Marques.

The first thing was freedom. Heinie and I, since the war began, had been literally prisoners under the Japanese flag for 228 days. All of those days had been filled with uncertainty. Seldom, if ever, were we out of sight of a Japanese policeman. We had hoped and dreamed of being free. Now we were. That explains the emotional thrust that struck us when we were greeted that first morning by the cheers of the men on the American tanker.

After our walk that first morning without the shadowing of a policeman we returned to the ship to enjoy the next difference. It was food. Lunch for the 1,500 of us was served on the deck, picnic style. It included almost everything that we had missed for months—ham and turkey, cheese and fruit, and ice cream will always be remembered. For the next five weeks we were to eat at a more leisurely pace in the dining room and actually have tablecloths and napkins.

Before the day was over we also knew that we still had human problems. The cabins had been cleaned during the day and after dinner we lined up to get our cabin assignments. I was in line for an hour and a half and I got through quickly. Some were in line for four hours and some never did get a cabin and slept all night in the lounge. At the same time some cabins were empty. We all put up with it the first day, but the next evening they asked us all to line up again to be reassigned. Then the fun began, for they started assigning people to cabins that continued to be occupied by people who did not yet have new assignments. In some cases children were already asleep and were put out into the corridor with no place to go. I did not join the line that night but went to sleep in the cabin I was first assigned. I was not put out until after breakfast the next morning. Then I went off the boat for sightseeing and when I got back in the evening they were looking for me to give me my new assignment.

Of course the assignment of cabins was a difficult task. It had been easy on the *Asama*. We were still enemy aliens on a Japanese boat and we took the assignments we got without question. But now we were under our own government and all the claims for better assignments could be voiced. The *Gripsholm* was a Swedish boat but it had been leased by the American Export Line for this particular trip. Each of us was paying the same price, $575, for the whole ten weeks. Therefore we had no choice as to what class we were to be in; in fact, some had to stay in cabins built for the crew because there were more than the ordinary number of passengers aboard.

The American Export Line had no office in Lourenço Marques but flew down some of their men from Lisbon to make cabin assignments. Either they underestimated the task or had had too big a party the night before; in any case they were not prepared the first night and then not prepared for the demands that a great many made for better assignments. Some of them came from as far away as the New York offices of the firms employing the men. Few, if any, of the missionaries got the better cabins. Heinie, Lardner, and I were all in separate cabins. There were four men in mine, all named Smith.

The task that Ambassador Grew had given to me on the *Asama* as chairman of the committee to plan the religious services was expanded on the *Gripsholm*. We had several new people on the committee from China, including a Roman Catholic bishop. There were now just under 600 missionaries and their families among the 1,500 on the *Gripsholm*. One hundred seventy-one were Northern Presbyterians, including twenty-five children.

We were pressed for worship space on Sundays, but after conferring with all groups and with the purser we planned nine services: two Protestant services, as well as junior church, an Episcopal Communion, and two Catholic Masses. Provision was also made for a Sunday school, a prayer service, and a song service. Ambassador Grew took a great interest in the worship provisions and participated as a lay reader in the Episcopal service.

Because of overcrowding there was some friction between the missionary group and the more secularly oriented passengers. Both sides were crowded and at times irritable. At Lourenço Marques the wife of an American naval attaché had heard a Japanese internee from the *Asama* ask at the gangplank for Russell Durgin, our YMCA Secretary. She turned on him, cussed him out, and would have beaten him if she could have gotten to him. On the other hand, a missionary was irritated by the drinking and smoking that went on in the next cabin. When the door was open he went in and threw the liquor and the tobacco out the porthole. Most of the irritation found expression in remarks that were meant to be overheard.

We shared among ourselves the letters and magazines we got hold of. We learned that the Board of Foreign Missions was planning to keep us in New York for a few days of debriefing and for some orientation to wartime America. Spouses of internees were to be brought to New York to share in this. We were to be at the Prince George Hotel, $2.50 per day single and $4.00 double.

The magazines caught us up on the news, although sometimes it was like starting a long story in the middle without knowing the beginning or the end. In the internment camp we had discussed and discussed the outbreak of the war. What we learned on the *Gripsholm* did not change our thinking much. We now knew the substance of the last communication from Washington to Tokyo before Pearl Harbor. It was that the embargo on trade with Japan could not be lifted without Japan withdrawing from Indochina and South China and recognizing fully the Chiang Kai-shek government's claim. Anyone following the negotiations carefully must have known that Japan would find this difficult and would almost immediately, while it still had resources, decide between withdrawal and war. That led to the following question: Why, knowing this, were we not prepared for the attack on Pearl Harbor? In the camp I leaned toward the possibility that the Roosevelt government was willing to risk a Pearl Harbor if it then precipitated our entry into the war with full commitment. I changed my mind on the *Gripsholm* when I read the news that Clark Field in Manila under MacArthur was attacked a few hours after word had come of the Pearl Harbor attack and *all the American planes were destroyed on the ground*. The attack on Pearl Harbor had certainly warned Manila to be prepared, but the result was the same. I therefore was obliged to believe, and still do, that we Americans had simply grossly underrated the Japanese. We believed they could not harm us until they had done it twice. All this in spite of the fact that Japan had started its war with Russia at the beginning of the century with a surprise attack.

Food on board the *Gripsholm* was the same for every class, and decks and lounges were the same. We had a steam bath and a saltwater swimming pool. All four dining rooms had two servings and we took our time. American breakfasts were most attractive. All of us turned thumbs down on fish. Meat, catsup, and potatoes got a great run.

The only stop we made in the five weeks was at Rio de Janeiro. We came into the harbor in the early morning. The sunrise was beautiful and the harbor the finest I have seen. We were amazed at the skyscrapers and the size of the city. We were allowed ashore just before noon. We did some shopping and got lunch, and then eight of us chartered two taxis and went to see the town. Later we went up the inclined railway on the mountain where the figure of Christ towers above the city. As we watched, the *Queen Elizabeth*, with upwards of 10,000 Allied troops aboard, left the harbor below us and started out for India or Australia. The *Gripsholm* is a large ship, but the *Queen* was almost five times larger and fast enough to outrun submarines and had no need of a destroyer escort.

Lardner had a surprise when we docked at Rio. We were standing on the boat deck watching the dock when Lardner yelled: "Hey, you rascal! What are you doing here?" I thought he was fooling, but a man on the dock looked up and there was his brother, Wallace. Wallace said he was in Rio on business and would ride back with us to New York. It turned out, as we later learned, that he was with Navy Intelligence, which had a group riding with us and seeking information.

The last lap was now just ahead of us. It was rumored that we would arrive in New York on August 25, just 269 days after Heinie and I had left Yokohama on the *Tatsuta* expecting to get home for Christmas. Quite a voyage! It was not one we would have chosen, but now that we had had it we were sort of glad for it. I had learned a lot about people and about myself, and in some respects would never be the same again. As friction occurred between missionaries and others I was glad I be-longed to the missionary group and had heard no griping among missionaries over cabin assignments. All in all we had done a good job in maintaining fellowship in spite of war. In a small way we in Japan were doing the same thing that those Christians in Geneva were doing: trying in wartime to build the bridges that would establish the reality of the world Christian fellowship and would hasten the forming of the World Council of Churches.

We entered New York Harbor early on the last Monday morning in August, stood at attention on deck to greet the Statue of Liberty, and docked on the New Jersey side. Diplo-mats got off first. I had a message that Floy was waiting at the end of the pier, but now we were confronted with our last hurdle. The rest of the passengers had to be screened. We were all given numbers; mine was twelve hundred and something; so we waited. I got onto the dock on the second day to assemble my baggage but I could not see or talk with Floy.

My turn at the screening came on the afternoon of the third day. The Government had to be assured that we were the persons we claimed to be and that our loyalty to the United States had not changed. Visits had been made to our families and inquiry about physical characteristics had been made. Neighbors had been asked about the loyalty of the families and dossiers had been prepared. Three intelligence officers—FBI, Army, and Navy—examined each passenger.

My intelligence officers seated me at a small card table with my dossier before us. I was asked additional questions. Identi-fication was easy as I have a broken finger on my left hand, among other things. My being a pacifist and a member of the Fellowship of Reconciliation was no problem. They knew the organization and accepted that. But they questioned me care-fully about my attitude concerning this war. Finally two of the officers stepped away from the table to talk. Then one of them came back to stay with me while the third went to talk. When they all sat down again, they asked me one more question. Producing a letter from the file, they asked me if I knew a certain newspaperwoman on the *Gripsholm*. I said I did. Then they asked me if I knew of any reason why this Canadian woman should have sent them a letter warning them to question me as a possible spy. I said I did. I had met her once. I was on the committee that had prepared a letter for the Swiss representative to present to his government thanking them for arranging the exchange of internees. I was getting the signature to the letter of a Colonel Rush, who was well known in the Tokyo American community. I found him at a table with several of his friends, including this Canadian newspaperwoman. When she overheard what I was doing she said: "That's just like you missionaries, always wanting to do something nice for people. You should have been gone from Japan long ago. Your government warned you to go long before the war. If you had gone, there would have been more room for us." I presumed that she had been drinking but I could not let the statement stand. I replied: "Our government's warning was that all those who did not have essential business should leave Japan. And my business was as essential as yours." That was the way we had parted and could explain the letter. They accepted this explanation; at least they approved my entering the United States.

The customs officers were ready with my baggage and even had a man who could read Japanese who approved the Japanese books that I had. The Board of Foreign Missions was arranging the transfer of baggage and I proceeded down the pier to meet Floy. What a reunion after nineteen months! She remembers I was carrying my Bible in a Japanese *furoshiki* and I remember the striking dark-brown hat that she wore. We went immediately to the Prince George Hotel by taxi, got settled in our room, and went down to dinner with a dozen or more friends from Japan. By that time we knew that Walser, Hannaford, and Bovenkerk had been taken from the ship to Ellis Island on the ground that their examination would take more time. All three joined us a day or so later. I'll never know why that letter did not send me to Ellis Island. The best explanation would seem to be that Lardner Moore's brother, the intelligence officer, had been convinced by Lardner's report that I was all right.

Our old friend Winburn Thomas was one of those at the dinner that night, and his questions drew out of me the answers that those waiting were anxious to hear about Japanese friends in churches and schools now on their own in Japan.

The next morning we checked in at the Board office at 156 Fifth Avenue and got our instructions for the days that we were to spend in New York. I found that Dr. Leber wanted me to speak the next day about my experience in Japan at a luncheon that the Board was holding for some representative Presbyterians on the East Coast. Korea, China, Thailand, and Japan were to have fifteen minutes each. We also stopped that day at Wanamaker's store. I had the internment psychology and wanted to buy everything in sight for fear there would be no more.

That night in the hotel room I wrote what I had to say very carefully, ending with the verses of Scripture that had come to mean so much in the internment camp. "Learn to pay the same tax of suffering as the rest of your brotherhood throughout the world. Once you have suffered for a little, the God of all grace who has called you to his eternal glory in Christ Jesus, will repair, recruit, and strengthen you. The dominion is his for ever and ever: Amen." I made many friends at that luncheon and was to use the substance of that speech on many, many occasions in the future.

The same evening I wrote the speech we phoned Harrisville, Pennsylvania, and talked with my parents and with John and Louise, who were staying there while Floy was with me in New York. We assured them we would see them all in a few days. (Even writing these things thirty-eight years later brings tears to the eyes.)

Our first church service in the United States was at First Presbyterian in New York. Elmer Homrighausen was the guest preacher. He was one of the first to introduce the theology of Karl Barth to the American churches. I had thought that I might not understand American preaching but I soon found that reading Kuwada in the internment camp had prepared me to understand Homrighausen.

The conference with the Board lasted most of two days. It was welcome home, a sharing of the American scene, and a description of how we could be used in the days ahead.

It began with reports from the field. This time Howard spoke for Japan and used a letter given to him that last day in Tokyo on the way to board the *Asama*. He was to read it and destroy it. As best he could remember it went like this: "Even now, in spite of war, we approve your Board's policy in maintaining a maximum force consistent with the situation. Now you must go to America in sadness and with loss of personal possessions. But you do not go defeated. By staying until now you have given us courage and strength. You have done something lasting for us."

All of us were to have three months of vacation and rest. Then first termers would go on furlough study. The rest could go on Furlough Fellowship of Service, being assigned to a presbytery for interpretation or being given a general assignment. Those from Japan might also go for service in the Relocation Centers for Japanese Americans set up by the Government for those evacuated from the West Coast. For the moment we were too busy getting reacquainted with our families and a wartime America to pay much attention. We would face this matter later.

The last day of the conference, Floy and I took the night train from New York to Pittsburgh, where my brother Walter and his wife Van met us with a car and drove us to Harrisville. All of my family were there. That night Floy and I with the children went on to Ellwood City and the little house on the back of the lot which had been home for Floy and the children for more than a year and which now would be home for all of us for almost another year.

Floy had made that little house a home to come back to. It was furnished principally with borrowed furniture, but it also had our dishes, rugs, pictures, and curios from Japan. It would soon have my books. She also had bought a secondhand washing machine and a refrigerator. With my brother's help I now bought a secondhand Dodge for $300 and passed my test for a driver's license. Later in the fall we bought some furniture and stored it pending our decision as to where we would go. Its cost was met by the money we had gotten for our Karuizawa house. The early purchase was not due to internment camp fever; it was based on the fact that good furniture was really becoming hard to get. We still are using most of what we bought then.

We all had to review and relive time and time again the events of December 1941. The family had anticipated my being with them for Christmas. On December 7 in the afternoon they were attending a piano recital in their music teacher's home when the news came of Pearl Harbor. It took several weeks before any definite word came that I was alive and interned in Yokohama. Through it all Floy's special hymn was "Be still, my soul, the Lord is on thy side." Louise, six years of age, also had a verse, "Let not your heart be troubled."

Both John and Louise had had some difficulty in adjusting to school in America in the middle of the winter of 1941. Most of that was over now and they knew about Boston and Washington as well as about Kobe and Tokyo. I was overjoyed to have a family and they were glad to have a father again.

After I had relaxed I found I needed that three months' rest. Before completing the rest period I tried to preach in the Presbyterian Church in Ellwood City and just managed to get through after shedding some tears at the end. For some six months more I could be ill when I was under tension. That was all over by spring and I was myself again.

Several Japanese missionaries were employed under interdenominational auspices as counselors in the Relocation Centers. A Presbyterian, Gordon Chapman of Kobe, was in charge. We all did some of this: the Bovenkerks, the Hannafords, Betty Evans, and Alice Grube were among those who served in the camps. I made two trips to the camps and was used in preparing churches in communities where resettlement was taking place.

Floy and I decided that in the long run we wanted an experience in the American church if we could get it. In the meantime I took a general assignment for the Board to speak in churches, especially in Pennsylvania. Herrick Young of the Personnel Department of the Board was alerted to find a possible opening of service in a church.

I was still a pacifist and tried to register as one. The draft board in Ellwood City registered me as a minister and therefore exempt. I had by this time modified my pacifist position and no longer advocated this as a possible present position for a nation as a whole to take. An individual could take it and prepare himself for the results which might advance the cause of peace. But a nation was not prepared to accept the results and could not make a strong witness. Muriel Lester, a British pacifist, had said in Kyoto after visiting China during its resistance to Japan, "In such cases the choice is not between Christian pacifism and war but between courage and cowardice." After Pearl Harbor I no longer thought that America could or should have stayed out of the war.

My speaking was aimed at reporting what happened to me personally and how Japanese Christians had stood the test of war and would prove to be loyal to their faith. I found many American Christians thinking that all was lost in Japan. Repeatedly they said, "Too bad those twelve years you spent in Japan were wasted." I tried to answer and to lead people to pray for Japan and its people that peace would come soon and we could resume our work. Many people were surprised to hear my story and some of them were glad. I later was to meet opposition when I suggested concrete action, but theoretically people went along with me. I had one experience with the superintendent of schools in Pittsburgh. He had me address all the principals of schools on the subject, "How Japan Got Into the War." I stated the case and answered questions. The superintendent then said to all of us, "If I am ever tried for murder, I hope I will have Mr. Smith to defend me." He said it with a smile but I never knew just how he meant it.

Floy and I often drove to my speaking assignments in Pennsylvania. One of them was at Harrisburg in the late fall. The leaves were at their height in the mountains and gas rationing had not yet entirely closed in. In January I was in Philadelphia for more than two weeks, speaking at least once and sometimes twice a day in churches. I was also at First Church in Pittsburgh one Wednesday evening, and after the service went with Dr. Clarence Macartney to a reception at the Shadyside Church for Dr. Robert E. Speer.

In the spring the Board also assigned me to do some preaching in Japanese at the Rowher Relocation Center in Arkansas. At that time there were 106,000 Japanese Americans in ten of these centers. They had been taken abruptly from the West Coast when war came, regardless of their citizenship or past records. Most lost their possessions or had to sacrifice them at ridiculous prices. In the camps they were guarded by soldiers within barbed-wire fences. They lived in hastily built barracks. Food was also furnished and they were given a small wage if they served within the camp as teachers, office workers, doctors, dentists, ministers, or small farmers. In no case did this wage reach $20 a month.

The reason for all this was the unreasoning fear in the first days of the war, especially in California. There was never any proof that the fear was justified. Many Americans who knew the facts were aghast and some in the Government were working hard to change the situation. Dr. Milton Eisenhower, the brother of the general, was the head of the program for relocation in other parts of America for all those who had been cleared by the FBI. In the spring of 1943, 6,500 had been relocated, 700 of these as students in colleges. There were at least 20,000 to 25,000 more employable people waiting for relocation. More than 1,000 were already combat soldiers in the U.S. Army and others were awaiting call. Later a regiment of these soldiers in Italy became the regiment with the highest level of casualties and the most decorations in the U.S. Army.

My week in Rowher was a stimulating one and was followed by a week in Cincinnati preparing the churches to welcome those who were seeking relocation there. This program was all done under government auspices, but with civilian committees helping. Cleveland, Toledo, St. Louis, and other such cities were responding. As yet, Pittsburgh had turned down the government program.

Also in the spring the Board had a conference in New York about the future in Japan and asked some of us to write papers for it. Reischauer, Hannaford, Thomas, and Bovenkerk were all there. My paper is still in the files and is, at points, embarrassing. I prophesied that when we had won the war by landing troops in Japan and the Japanese had fought to the last ditch as they had done already on some of the islands in the Pacific, it would be years before the feeling in Japan would allow Americans to serve them in any numbers. I was glad to be proved wrong, probably because Japan surrendered before invasion was necessary and MacArthur emphasized peace and not vengeance.

The conference gave us all a chance to be together and compare notes. We were interested in how Fuji Thomas was getting along and were glad to hear that in most areas she had been well received. Heinie, Tommy and I talked long into the night about the American church that we were discovering. One thing we agreed on. We found many ministers who had done little or no studying beyond preparing their sermons since they had been graduated from seminary, or so it seemed from their conversations and from the books on their shelves. At least Japan had lifted us missionaries out of that rut.

In May I was at the General Assembly as an advisory delegate from the Japan Mission with voice but no vote. My main interest was in the report of a special committee on the church's relationship to the war, which had been appointed at the previous Assembly. Hugh Thompson Kerr was the chairman of the committee and was reported to be bringing a strong supportive recommendation. Henry Sloane Coffin was the

Moderator. The report was not available until the morning it was presented. (This was before the day of the Blue Book.) We got the report at our desks when we came in. It was to be presented and voted on between 11 and 12 that morning. It was a strong report. I consulted George Buttrick, who was a commissioner. He advised that little if anything could be done. He encouraged me to speak if I wished.

When the hour came for the report Dr. Kerr was introduced and proceeded to read the whole report, which was already in our hands. When he finished it was almost 12 and time to vote and recess for lunch. Someone suggested that we recess, take time after lunch to discuss it, and then vote. That was ruled out, but it was permitted that we take an extension of fifteen minutes for discussion and then vote before lunch. Advisory delegates were seated in the back of the Assembly and I was the first to be recognized by the Moderator.

I told the Assembly my name and where I came from. Then I said I thought the report too closely identified the Christian faith with the purposes of the nation, good as they might be. I told them the story from Wakayama at the time when Japan was at war with China and Christians discussed whether they should pray for victory. Our Japanese pastor said he prayed that God's will should be done, adding that that was not the same as praying for victory, for God's will might be done even if Japan was destroyed. I added that the spirit of that prayer might be a part of the Assembly's action. God is still the judge of *all nations*.

There were two or three other speeches but no amendments and the vote adopting the report was almost unanimous, with only a scattering of five or six in opposition. Upon reflection I wondered if the timing of the presentation and vote was not deliberate, so that no significant debate could be prepared, and that the refusal to postpone the vote until after lunch was also for the same reason. In the long run it would not have made any difference. But after supper that night I was literally sick because of my very first speech in a General Assembly.

Earlier in the spring Floy and I had been at Third Presbyterian Church in Pittsburgh for an evening meeting. Dr. Louis Evans, Sr., had been the pastor before he went to Hollywood and he had been followed by Dr. Stillman Foster, who had graduated ahead of me in seminary and was some years older than I. He and his committee proposed that I become their

Assistant Pastor for Christian Education. I said I was not qualified for the Christian education task but might fill in for a year if they wanted me with the understanding that I might be leaving at the end of the year if a call came to me. They accepted this condition and Herrick Young of the Board agreed with us that it could be a good preparation for something more in the Presbyterian Church. I moved my presbytery membership from Zanesville to Pittsburgh and we moved into a rented house in the East End early in June of 1943.

There were no strict presbytery rules in those days about assistant pastors. I served under a Christian education committee of the session, but I was not invited to session meetings. "Stilly" was my boss. I called on the sick and sought new members. Floy and I took charge of the high school department on Sunday morning and evening. I participated in the morning service, including Communion, and preached at most of the evening services. I continued to have invitations to speak outside Third Church and took a good portion of them. One of these was on a weeknight at the Mt. Lebanon United Presbyterian Church, which was vacant. I attended a conference on peace, under the auspices of the American Friends Service Committee, where Eleanor Roosevelt was the principal speaker and I was invited to have lunch with her.

In the fall I picked up my interest in resettling Japanese Americans and talked with the chairman of the Allegheny Council of Churches, who was an old friend. He said the original initiative had failed because of the opposition of a retired colonel who was connected with the American Legion. He said we could take it up again through the related Council committee which was chaired by a Mrs. Samson, the wife of one of the leading funeral directors. She invited me to lunch with her committee at the William Penn Hotel. I told my story and then proposed that the Council indicate to the office of the War Relocation Authority in Cleveland that we were now ready to cooperate with the Government in forming a committee to work with them in Pittsburgh.

Mrs. Samson's first reply to me and to her committee was to say that she had a sister in California and her sister and her friends all said that no Japanese American could be trusted. I had the facts from the FBI and from the Army to disprove this, but I had no opportunity to present the facts during the meeting.

Early in January of 1944 "Stilly" called me on the phone one night to tell me that he was making a change in his own schedule and that I would not have to preach so much at night. Then he asked me if I would promise to stay another year beyond our original agreement. I told him I could not promise to do so since I wanted to be free to accept a call to be pastor of a church if it came. He then said that he was free to go ahead with plans to secure my successor. I agreed, and in fact helped interview the two men who eventually came from Princeton.

But that put us in a hole. We could go back on the support of the Board, if necessary, but in the meantime I would have no job and be placed in a bad position to seek a church.

We started then to look in earnest. Don Campbell, the assistant pastor at Shadyside, helped me, along with Herrick Young, but few church committees initially considered missionaries and fewer were interested in one from Japan.

In April Don arranged for me to preach at Cranbury, New Jersey, so that pulpit committees in the East could hear me. The one from the West End Church in New York City which we expected to come did not show up, but one from Easton, Pennsylvania, which we did not know about, came. We had dinner together and I went back to Easton with them to see the church. They said they would be in touch with me. This was the only nibble we had had, and we were getting anxious. But then West End invited me to preach at the Fort Washington Church in New York for the whole committee on Mother's Day. We went to dinner afterward with the committee and I was asked to come back to have breakfast with the chairman the next morning. He was a professor at Columbia University and we met at the Faculty Club. He told me that the committee had been impressed and believed I would be a good preacher and pastor. But Negroes were moving into the area of their church and the committee thought my sympathy for Japanese indicated I would be sympathetic with blacks. I said they were right. Then he told me they had a rule that no black people could join the church.

That same week the Mt. Lebanon pulpit committee sent two of their members to our home to invite me to be their candidate and preach for the congregation on the last Sunday in May. We had not as yet met the committee. They doubtless had heard me preach one or more times in the evening at Third Church but had never made themselves known. The only intimation we had was the telephone call asking if they could come and see us. But we had had time to think about it and I agreed to preach for them.

Still that same week, I had a telephone call from the West End Church. Two of their committee were on the way to Pittsburgh and wanted me to have dinner with them at the William Penn Hotel. They told me that they had solved their problem. They would get the congregation to make irrevocable the rule that no black person could be a member of the church. That would remove the onus from me, for I could do nothing about it when I became their pastor. I was glad to turn them down with enthusiasm!

I preached the end of May at Mt. Lebanon. The vote of the congregation was a good one and we moved from the East End to the South Hills on July 1. I transferred from Pittsburgh Presbytery of the Presbyterian Church U.S.A. to the Mononga-hela Presbytery of the United Presbyterian Church of North America, and my father preached the sermon at my installa-tion.

Earlier in 1944 I had been back to the Rowher Relocation Center on a preaching mission with Dr. E. Stanley Jones. It reminded me that Pittsburgh still lagged behind with regard to the relocation program. Then one day at Presbytery meeting Dr. William Orr of Pittsburgh Seminary, whom I had known at Hartford, asked me if I had something I could say to a group of young pastors who met for lunch on Mondays at the First Presbyterian Church. I said yes, and then told them of the experience I had at Rowher and my failure to get a response in Pittsburgh. Bill himself headed a committee of three that went from the meeting directly to the office of the Council of Churches and demanded that they do something about it. And at long last they formed a committee, got a Government man from Cleveland to come and help, and opened an office in Pittsburgh. The committee of some fifty people was chaired by Dr. Kinsolving of the Episcopal Church. I was on the commit-tee but kept a low profile because an old Japan hand might be the center of attack if we had trouble.

Floy and I will always be thankful for what the members of the Mt. Lebanon church did for us. It was not just that they took us at a time when we needed a job. Their taking us meant a declaration of faith in us of very sizable dimensions. They were the largest congregation in the United Presbyterian

Church of North America. We were going back to our previous denomination and to what many regarded as its top church. We knew it was a challenge at the time but we had no way of knowing how great that challenge was to be. We were summoned to do our very best. The Mt. Lebanon people believed in us and they helped us to do it. The church was almost 150 years old.

It was in 1904 that Edwin McCown graduated from seminary and became Mt. Lebanon's pastor. Soon afterward, Pittsburgh put twin vehicle tunnels through the hills along the Monongahela River and opened up the South Hills suburbs. Mt. Lebanon was ideally placed right in the middle of this development. The church grew and Edwin McCown grew with it, or maybe it was the other way around. From 178 members in 1904, the church in thirty-nine years grew to 2,700 members. In 1929 they had dedicated a new Twin Tower Tudor Gothic church that would seat almost 1,500 people and whose doors behind the pulpit could be opened up so that more than 2,000 people could be accommodated. Dr. McCown had retired because of illness in 1943 and a year later they were ready to call a pastor.

By the time we got there in 1944 there were many other sizable churches in the area, including a Methodist church on one side of us and a Roman Catholic on the other.

We had known the church since seminary days. Jim Leitch, my classmate in college and roommate in seminary, came from the church. I had seen the new building under construction and I knew the high regard in which the people and their minister were held.

I found the session of twenty-four men well organized to function in leading the church and committed to making this ministry a success. McCown had had an aptitude for organization.

I was fortunate also in another factor. Mrs. Clara Mercer stayed on as church secretary. She was absolutely loyal to me, as she had been to Dr. McCown.

Getting a staff was a major question. Harry Rankin, a senior at Pittsburgh Seminary, was our student assistant. The session and the young people liked him. We increased his responsibility and he became assistant pastor in May. We also secured Margaret Dawson, an experienced educator, to assist the excellent lay staff in Christian education.

The church year for the first time around was both interesting and amazing. The Christmas services were new and unusual. On Palm Sunday we received almost 150 new members, half of them young people. We had been warned that we would be amazed at Easter and we were. The doors behind the pulpit were rolled back and I preached from a side pulpit to more than 2,200 people.

The summer of 1945 was to be a testing period. Early in the fall of 1944, at the request of members of the congregation, I had repeated the sermon I had preached about my own internment experience. Later I spoke on the Japanese American situation and the resettlement program in Pittsburgh. If I remember correctly, this was at an evening service in our church to which the Methodists also came.

Early in 1945 Kinsolving called me to say that he was being selected the bishop of another area and that at a meeting I had not attended I had been elected the chairman of the committee. I protested that I would be vulnerable in case of trouble but he assured me that they thought there would not now be trouble. The office was functioning well and several families had found work and housing. I agreed to accept.

At about the same time the Government office suggested that resettlement could be speeded up if we had a hostel. Housing was more difficult to secure than jobs, and in other cities having a temporary hostel had solved the problem. The men got jobs, the families stayed in the hostel, and landlords who saw the families were more willing to rent to them.

We had a good committee and we found a possible hostel. The Gusky Orphanage on the North Side was vacant because the Jewish community was turning to foster homes as an alternative. Late in May I went to see the Orphanage committee, explained our need, and got permission to use the Orphanage with its beds, furniture, linen, and dishes. Our only expense was for space heaters when it turned cold.

We arranged a press conference so we could make the announcement and not surprise people. In a few days I had a phone call from a doctor's wife who had been a member of my father's church. She informed me that a small protest meeting was being held that night on the North Side and that I could come.

I went and discovered about twenty people led by a man named Hendershaw who, with his lawyer, was planning a larger meeting in the American Legion Hall in order to stir up support for an injunction against our use of the Gusky buildings. I spoke at some length but the leadership was not in a mood to listen. I then insisted we should be represented at the protest meeting and that the Gusky people should be informed.

Bright yellow posters announcing the meeting appeared on telephone poles on the North Side. I was one of the three speakers and Floy insisted on going with me. The biggest and burliest of our elders went with us as Floy's protector.

There were some 200 people at the meeting, most of them noisy. We had police protection and a few soldiers on furlough were present but did not speak. Hendershaw presented the case for the injunction and then called on the U.S. Government man from Cleveland. He was telling how resettlement was working in that city and how the new people were proving to be good citizens, when at that point he was booed and shouted down. I was next. I explained our plans, said we had not tried to pack this meeting with supporters but I had a list in my pocket of people in this community who had volunteered to take turns in the Orphanage so that no unseemly incidents would occur. At that point a woman charged up, demanded the list, and said they would take care of such people. I was then shouted down.

The meeting proceeded to raise money to support injunction proceedings in the courts. About $200 was raised. Five or six ministers were in the meeting. Two of them spoke in our support. The others sat on their hands.

The next morning the story made the front page of the newspapers in Pittsburgh. There were pictures, one of me with the headline, "Mt. Lebanon Pastor Shouted Down." For the next few days we had obscene phone calls and anonymous letters. Our Presbyterian neighbors suffered because the callers sometimes got the wrong church.

We soon found out that the injunction would not be sought unless we occupied the buildings with some Japanese Americans. This we did in early July. An able lawyer, who was an elder in Shadyside Church, volunteered to take our case at no cost. He defeated the request for a temporary injunction and later for a permanent injunction without our appearing in court. The case was based on the claim that Gusky had lost its exemption from the zoning ordinance because it had not used the buildings for more than a year as a service institution. Hendershaw was a furniture dealer and real estate man who wished to buy the property on which to build apartments. If Gusky had lost the exemption, the buildings could not be used for institutional purposes and thus would fall in price. Hendershaw, incidentally, was a Sunday school teacher in a nearby Presbyterian church. The woman who had shouted me down was the president of the Women's Missionary Society in a Methodist church.

I do not remember that we ever had any vocal criticism that reached us from the congregation about the things we said and did in the summer of 1945. We had one anonymous letter that might have come from a member. It accused me of tearing down all that Dr. McCown had done in all the years of his ministry.

But we had many friends also. The city government and the newspapers were on our side. The *Post-Gazette* had a thin edition it sent to servicemen and it ran the story there. Several Army men in Italy sent in reply a letter which was printed. It charged that the North Side meeting made it hard for the parents of the Japanese Americans who were fighting at their side in Italy. In a fall meeting of the Pittsburgh Council of Churches called to review the program, the canon of the Episcopal diocese said our action was the best thing the Council had done for many years. One of our trustees was there and relayed the canon's statement to our annual congregational meeting in January. It also led to my becoming a vice-chairman of the Council and chairman of the Committee on Race Relations.

That summer the war ended with the dropping of the atomic bombs on Japan and the surrender of the Japanese to MacArthur. In September I preached two sermons on the atomic bomb, one on the enormous responsibility we now had for the basic power generated by the atomic process, and one on the ethical significance of the bomb's use. They were hard sermons to write and preach, especially the second one. I took my stand against the horrible nature of war itself, now illustrated by the use of the new weapon. It only highlighted war's awfulness. One of my friends who sang in the choir and looked at me from that angle told me years later he remembered how my knuckles were white while I preached that day.

The church building had been dedicated in 1929 with most of

its debt covered by pledges. The Depression changed all that and it came through the 1930s with a debt of $200,000. When we arrived fifteen years after dedication it was $80,000. The psychology of the debt had been so long with the congregation that the first priority budgetwise had to be to get rid of the debt. We started a program to do that in four years.

The denomination had a postwar campaign for worldwide Christian Advance. The trustees wanted to postpone this until the debt was paid, but the session refused and we raised most of our share and finished it after we burned the mortgage in April 1948.

There was a wealth of skills and energy at our disposal if we spent some time in organizing it. In general the congregation was young, much younger than at Third. The session always had some new people coming up as members.

I now had old friends in two Pittsburgh Presbyteries—the Presbyterian U.S.A. and the United Presbyterian. In addition I had new friends in Mt. Lebanon. My best friend among the ministers was the Methodist, Lloyd Wicke, who was next door. We both remember the day we met. It was in the middle of Scott Road, which separates the two churches, and each was going to greet the other.

Both Tokyo Union Church and Third Church in Pittsburgh had prepared me for my preaching tasks. I think I would be classified as an evangelistic preacher, not one who asks people to come forward, but one who seeks in every sermon to challenge people in some way to follow Jesus Christ. The challenge could be to accept Christ as Savior or it might well be to participate as a Christian in making a more just society. In Japan I had been accustomed to preaching to people who were not Christians. At Mt. Lebanon in a morning congregation of 1,000 people or more I would be sure to have some who needed the challenge. If I did not give it, who would?

There was still another intangible aspect by which a young minister grew at Mt. Lebanon. I know now that when I came to the church I had not made the most of some of the opportunities that had confronted me. Now I began to realize the potential for service which such a position held for the pastor. I could not use it to enhance my own prestige. I dared not abuse it so that its usefulness would cease, but I must dare to use it in the service of people and of God's Kingdom. I learned to understand that I was in a position not just to protect the institution but to use it as God would lead us in the accomplishment of the task he had entrusted to us.

These experiences in Pittsburgh confirmed experiences we had had in Japan. Often when the way was not clear and we began to worry, we found that by taking one step at a time in the direction we believed to be right, other steps opened up and we were surprised by the rewarding results. Our plans were inadequate but Someone had a plan for us that was beyond our own. We came to believe that the Holy Spirit does not lead us while we sit on our hands. He can lead us when we begin to move, even if it may be in the wrong direction. In such things our family saying was reaffirmed, "When the time comes, we'll know."

During the war our congregation had literally hundreds of young men in military service. My experience as a missionary in Japan was possibly a handicap in some situations. At the same time, my experience in the internment camp and my separation from my family gave me a sensitivity to the soldiers' needs. We spent considerable time preparing memorial services and planning the sermons that dealt with the questions of war and peace. The war was coming to an end in the early months of this ministry and the note of hope was appreciated.

Largely by accident and not by planning we had a few guest preachers who were unusual. Dr. Irons, a black pastor of national prominence, brought a needed message and was the first black minister who had ever preached in our church. Later Dr. Tolliver, a black Presbyterian minister, spoke of the particular situation in Pittsburgh. Dr. Marc Boegner of the French Reformed Church kept us abreast of the developments in the ecumenical movement. He very soon was the first Reformed churchman to be one of the presidents of the World Council of Churches. In 1946 Rev. Tamaki Uemura, the first Japanese pastor to visit America after the war, preached for us at a union evening service. We had 900 people present to welcome her. In 1947, on Reformation Sunday, we had President John Mackay of Princeton Seminary. These people were remembered with appreciation by the congregation.

At the congregational meeting in January 1948 we were able to announce that the balance of the debt was pledged and would be paid within the next few months. The congregation appointed a planning committee to study the needs of the congregation and to bring recommendations about future budgets now that the debt was about to be paid.

Meanwhile, in the fall of 1945 the two denominations, the United Presbyterian Church of North America and the Reformed Church in America, were talking union and the joint committee met in our Mt. Lebanon church. The committee included Dr. Luman Shafer, who had been a missionary in Japan and a good friend. Luman was now the Secretary of the RCA Board of Foreign Missions and as such was one of four American churchmen who were going to Japan to make the first contacts with Japanese Christians. This was regarded as the return visit in response to the visit of Japanese Christians just before the war.

Luman was flying to Japan in October. I talked with him about sending letters with him to our friends. He took 26 letters with him which would be addressed in Japan and sent to our friends. We got 23 replies and three letters were returned because of inadequate addresses.

We then got recommendations as to what was most needed by families in Japan and asked the Joseph Horne Store in Pittsburgh to prepare to send packages as soon as the Post Office would receive them for delivery. Two packages went to each address. They contained the following: blanket, underwear for men and women, knitting needles and 4 skeins of yarn, 16 spools of thread, needles, pins, sugar, 2 shirts, 4 towels, dress goods, scissors, Band-Aids, gauze, cotton, soup, can opener, toothbrush, razor blades, adhesive tape, shoe laces, buttons, writing paper, envelopes, notebooks, pen points, soap, powdered milk, and a fly swatter.

We still have the letters we received from Japan. Five hundred churches had been burned in the fire bombing, mostly in the last days of the war. Professor Yamazaki in Wakayama wrote, "You can't identify the exact location where the church used to stand in the wide wilderness of ashes and mud." Wakayama had not yet been visited by the committee from America and our letter was the first communication from outside. Yamazaki wrote, "We hunger and thirst for a warm word of comfort. We know now that at least one friend speaks kindly to us and to the Japanese churches." Dr. Hail's house had also been burned. Christians met in homes that had survived, until a quonset hut was secured a year or so later.

Goshi's church in Tokyo had been burned, along with the houses of twenty of the families of his congregation. They also got a quonset hut through the American church organizations. Iijima in Osaka had lost his church, the manse, and his library. Okada was homeless in Wakayama.

The school buildings and residence were gone at Joshi in Tokyo, but Meiji Gakuin had survived, along with the seminary. We had letters from Yano, Tsuru, Matsuo, Murata, Watanabe, Kiyama, Iwata, Kashiwai, Kuwada, Sugimoto, and others, including Hosoi San, who was now in Karuizawa. Shinmaruko was gone but Senzoku survived. Most Christian friends had lost one or more members of their family in the war.

We had kept in touch with Hannaford, Bovenkerk, and Reischauer. The latter was acting secretary for Japan while the Secretary, Dr. Leon Hooper, was making trips to the Philippines and Thailand after the war. Luman Shafer's committee had come home, but a select group of six missionaries was chosen to go back to Japan to begin relationships with the United Church and help plan the future. Heinie was the Presbyterian among the six. When the plans began to take shape and the first missionaries on a permanent basis went back, Hannaford was among them and was the Presbyterian contact person. By the time our packages got through both Heinie and Howard were there or had been there.

Mrs. Uemura had a special message for us when she came in 1946. It was from the new Union Theological Seminary and from its president, our friend Kuwada, and was an invitation to come to teach Greek. We were honored and knew that Greek was the first step. However, we told Mrs. Uemura that we did not believe that we could go immediately. Mt. Lebanon had been good to us and we ought to see the congregation through another year or two until the debt was paid. When the official invitation came to us from Reischauer, we told him the same thing and added that we thought by the spring of 1948 we might be ready. When Dr. Mackay preached at Mt. Lebanon on Reformation Day in 1947, he had dinner with us and we talked Japan.

On the last Saturday in January 1948, I was at the church in the morning and had a call from Charlie Leber. He was preaching in Washington the next day and would like me to meet him at the William Penn Hotel in Pittsburgh at 5 P.M. for dinner. I agreed but informed him I'd have to be back for a 7:30 evening service. I knew that sometime along the road Hooper would retire, but I had never discussed this with anyone and had no indication that he was now retiring or that my name was being considered.

At dinner that night Charlie spoke to me about Hooper's early retirement as Secretary for the Far East and the committee's wish that I would consider taking his place. I would need to meet the committee in New York in February. Floy and I had already agreed that if this was what Charlie had come to discuss, we would consider it. I told Charlie I would meet with the committee.

It turned out I did not meet with the committee but met each of several members separately. I talked with Henry Pitney Van Dusen while riding back with him in a taxi to Union Seminary. I saw Mackay in the hall at 156 Fifth Avenue and he told me he had dreamed of this since October when he was in our home. The first man I went to see, however, was Heinie. He had been secretary of the Presbyterian deputation to Japan after the war and I wanted his opinion. He said he was becoming the Secretary for the committee of all denominations working with the Kyodan (United Church in Japan) and that we would be working together if I came. The Board nominated me, subject to the final approval of the General Assembly.

I had talked to Wicke before leaving Pittsburgh. He said, "It is a natural," and added, "Our paths will cross again," which indeed they did when he became Bishop of New York. My father wrote me the last letter he was ever to write to me. He knew we would probably go and he added, "Remember you are a preacher." For a time I thought he was disappointed. Later my sister told me I was mistaken; he wanted me to go but to remember to continue preaching. I knew that already, but it was good to have him write it.

Father died in April at the same age and year that Robert E. Speer died. He had retired at seventy and he and mother went to live in Harrisville to care for grandmother. He preached occasionally but finally was not permitted to drive his car. He would get it out of the garage and up to the sidewalk as he waited for someone to drive him. We were glad to be near enough to see him during those last years. All of the family was at Harrisville when he died and stood around the bed as he passed away. He and mother are buried with her parents in Grove City.

The first person I told in the church about my possible

mission assignment was Charlie Campbell. He was most likely to understand me. He was in business but had also been, almost full-time, a volunteer in the church, usually in the Sunday school. He did understand why I would have to accept. We had both been bowling in the church league that night and talked afterward.

After the Board had taken its action we shared this with the session and then with the congregation one Sunday morning after the sermon was over. Some tears were shed.

The congregation selected a pulpit committee. I had hoped they would get at it quickly and they did. Their chairman was James B. Graham, an executive of United States Steel who, believe it or not, had been an elder and my Sunday school teacher in my father's church in Elyria thirty years before.

I began my new job on July 1st, we took our vacation and moved in August, and by the end of September I was on my way to the Orient. My first letter on that trip was to my successor at Mt. Lebanon, who had been called within three months after I had left. He was Dr. Cary Weisiger from the Presbyterian U.S. church in Augusta, Georgia.

Chapter 6

An Institution Begins to Change

ON JULY 1, 1948, I began as Secretary of the Presbyterian (U.S.A.) Board of Foreign Missions for Japan, Korea, Thailand, and the Philippines. It was very much like entering a new profession. I had been a pastor, a preacher, and a missionary. In each case I had had time to prepare and I had had models to follow. This time I knew no models well enough to follow them, and I had a bare two months to become familiar with my title and my duties before I had to begin to act like a Board Secretary. In September I was to leave for a three-month trip to the Orient in order to perform specific duties as well as to become acquainted with the new situation.

The month of July was spent in New York. Dr. Leon Hooper, my predecessor, introduced me to the offices at 156 Fifth Avenue and to his able secretary, who now was my secretary. She taught me what I had to do in the office. Dr. Hooper also sent me to my first committee meeting on my very first day in the office. It was a committee on the founding of the International Christian University in Japan. Several old friends were there and when, that day, we organized the board of the Japan International Christian University Foundation, we all became charter members.

The vacation month of August was spent in selling our Mt. Lebanon house and moving into our new home in Leonia, New Jersey. Dr. Wicke had once been pastor there. We bought our house from one of his friends and got the mortgage from still another of his friends.

On September 1, I began commuting to New York by bus. The family joined the Leonia Presbyterian Church and John and Louise entered the Leonia school system. John was a senior in high school and Louise was in her third year in junior high. Floy was no longer the pastor's wife. As a parishoner she began teaching in the Sunday school. Later she also became program secretary of the Women's Association.

Staff meetings picked up in September and I learned their real importance. This was where actions were introduced but it was also where we learned what others were doing and thinking and where each of us had a chance to discuss actions and to vote. No wonder my friend Herrick Young told me, "Where two or three are gathered together you'd better be there."

The plans for the trip to the Orient were already worked out. The reason I was sent so soon was the problem of the final designation of money from the Restoration Fund. The fund was being raised in the churches and a large portion of the more than $20,000,000 was slated to go to the Far East. But there was delay in getting designations from both Japan and Korea. The fund raisers needed them and I was briefed on this before I left.

I was also briefed fully on a new change that was being tried out in Thailand and the Philippines concerning Mission Secretaries. In prewar times the *Manual* provided that every Mission should elect its own Secretary. In Japan this was done annually. Usually we got good ones, as we did with Willis Lamott and Howard Hannaford, but twice we had done less well. The Secretary at the time we arrived in 1929 was so anxious to be reelected that he cut short his furlough in order to be back for Mission Meeting. When he later became ill we elected a person who lived far down at the southern end of Honshu, the main island, who rarely saw any other missionaries and who was far removed from the church headquarters in Tokyo. Information to the Board and from the Board depended on the Secretary, and this location was less than satisfactory.

The Board had instigated the new change and was trying it out. After consultation with the Mission, the Board had appointed Horace Ryburn as field representative in Thailand. He had served one term there as a missionary and had served as a mission interpreter in Pittsburgh Presbytery during the war. In the same way Henry Little, an experienced interpreter in the Chicago office, had been appointed to the Philippines. Their terms were for three years and each served as Mission Secretary, with a Mission executive committee to advise him. I was to report back as to how this was working out in practice from the standpoint of the mission community. Incidentally, these two were also the administrators of the Restoration Fund in their countries.

There had been deputations from the Board which had visited each of the four countries sometime after the war and which had established relationships. On these and other matters I was simply to get acquainted. While I was away, Dr. Ruland, Secretary for China and vice-chairman of the Administrative Council, was my contact person in New York. I was ultimately responsible to Charlie Leber, the chairman of the Administrative Council.

Korea, 1948

We made one change in my itinerary. One influential missionary in Korea had written to Dr. Leber and protested my selection as Secretary for Korea on the ground that I was a former missionary in Japan. Did the Board not know that Korea was no longer a colony of Japan? Charlie gave me the letter to answer! I wrote a brief answer and promised to talk about it when I visited Korea. My normal first stop would have been Japan but I went first to Korea, lest after visiting Japan I should be caught talking about how things were done in Japan as I talked with others in Korea. In 1948 the trip by air was swift compared with the lengthy boat ride we had taken in 1929, but it was also slow compared with jet travel today. I was two nights and most of three days on the plane, stopping at Minneapolis, Edmonton, Anchorage, Shemya, and Tokyo before finally arriving in Seoul. The trip was tedious, except for the tremendous view of the mountains in Alaska.

I really had no personal difficulty in Korea. I knew some of the younger missionaries, for they had studied Japanese in Japan. Some of the others had been on the *Gripsholm*. I soon became acquainted with all of them. I also knew some of the younger pastors whom I had met in the Kobe Seminary or had taught in Tokyo. I could speak Japanese to them in private conversations. They had been required to learn it when Korea was a Japanese colony. But I preached in English with a missionary or pastor to translate for me. It would have been embarrassing to preach in the former colonial language. I preached almost every day of the three weeks I was in Korea. In at least six different places there were audiences of 1,000 or more.

This was South Korea. Before the war there had been larger numbers of Christians in North Korea. When after Potsdam a boundary was drawn at the 38th parallel, separating the Communists to the North from the democracy to the South, Christians voted with their feet and went south. There were tens of thousands of them. In many instances they formed their own churches, even in Seoul. The largest of these was Yung Nak, with a beautiful stone building and a thousand or more at each of three services on Sunday morning. Most of the northerners, however, were still in refugee camps in South Korea, but even there they set up churches and filled them. Grammar schools were not adequate, and the church established Bible clubs, which taught the three R's as well as the Bible. There were literally thousands of students in such clubs. A special service in Seoul at an athletic field attracted many thousands. The demands on the pastors and missionaries for leadership in these activities were tremendous. At that time it was estimated that there were more than a million Christians in South Korea. There were several denominations, but the Presbyterian Church was the largest. Here, as in Japan, Presbyterians from abroad participated in one Presbyterian Church. In this case it was Southern Presbyterians and Canadians with whom we were associated in the Korean Presbyterian Church.

I soon understood why the Restoration Fund designations had been delayed. There were some few buildings that needed to be rebuilt or repaired in South Korea, but the buildings the refugees needed in South Korea were still in North Korea. They needed churches and institutions now in their new location in South Korea. This was complicated by the fact that almost every presbytery and every school from the North wanted to be transferred literally intact to the South. A missionary who got to Korea after the war told me that at one time there were at least six presbyteries with headquarters in Seoul—the original Seoul Presbytery and five others that had transferred themselves from the North. Refugees were often in desperate need, but they were not docile, especially if they were committed to preserve something that was precious from their past.

Fortunately it was not my task to decide what should be built and what should be merged with existing organizations. Leaders in the church, with assistance from the older missionaries, could do this and I could interpret their needs to the Restoration Fund people in the United States.

In 1948 in Korea I wrote, "One is always conscious of the potential size of the Korean Church." It was a million then. Now in 1980 it is estimated at six million, if one million Moonies and such are included. There are 2,700,000 Presbyterians in one form or another.

I also wrote in 1948 that in Korea one is always conscious of Communism being close by. We must recognize that Korea in Asia is as important to the Free World as Berlin is in Europe.

At the same time we were alerted to friction in the church, some of it generated from within Korea but a small part encouraged from outside. Already there were two Presbyterian seminaries and two Presbyterian denominations. I knew I would have to return soon if I was to keep up with Korea.

Japan

I had visited every mission station and every Presbyterian institution in Korea. I would do the same in Japan, but this was different now, for Presbyterians worked within the larger context of a United Church. This had survived the war, although when the pressure was off, the Baptists, Lutherans, and some others left the "Kyodan." In Kobe the Central Seminary was also the core of a small dissident group that called themselves "The Reformed Church in Japan," but were our old Southern Presbyterian friends. There was also some unrest in Hokkaido but it remained quiet for the present. There were numerous openings for evangelism in Japan.

At the same time all manner of new missionaries arrived in Japan, attracted by the invitation that MacArthur was giving and by the popularity of work in a former enemy country. Our relationships to the institutions largely followed former denominational lines, except in the seminaries and in the new Japan International Christian University. I visited the Tokyo Union Seminary and also the site that was about to be bought for ICU with funds that were raised in Japan.

I was immersed immediately in the familiar atmosphere of Japan and faced with the enormous damage that had been done by the war. Korea, on the other hand, was a country that had been freed from foreign control. In spite of their enormous problems, the people now had the spirit of a new country where they could plan their own future. In Japan we faced at least as much destruction but it was in a defeated country and the people had been worn thin by the long years of war. There was hope, but it was still at the end of the tunnel. The binding up of wounds was the order of the day.

The reunion with old friends was overwhelming. Many had lost everything in the fire bombing. I was surprised to learn that in one night in Tokyo more people had perished in the fire bombing than had perished at Hiroshima. Families that still retained their homes were living an "onion skin existence." They had a residue of cherished family possessions but week by week it dwindled as they peeled it off layer by layer and got closer to the core. They were still a proud people and hated to ask for help, but they also were a humble people, often speaking of the mistakes that Japan had made and the destruction that it had brought upon others and itself.

Howard Hannaford was the Presbyterian correspondent and we traveled together. I was twenty days in Japan, spending eight nights on trains, only one of them sitting up. I brought greetings from the American churches and also personal family greetings to Sapporo, Tokyo, and Wakayama. Wakayama was the hardest for me. We met in the quonset hut that was now the church. We spent most of the day together. The night their church had burned, twenty-six members had lost their lives. They needed many things, but at the moment they wanted a missionary friend. Howard and I had stopped in Kyoto and had brought Louis Grier with us. He was a Pittsburgh boy and I had participated in his ordination. Later he had volunteered for Japan. Now he and his wife were in language school in Kyoto. Before that day was over the seeds were sown for an invitation to the Griers to come to Wakayama. They accepted and have been there to the present. Their assignment is an interesting one, assisting the Japanese church in its program for a suppressed minority within the culture of Japan.

Allocation of Restoration Fund monies in Japan was simpler than in Korea. We were spending the money to help restore the buildings that had been destroyed and were still needed. The problem was that we could not do it immediately because materials were very scarce and were being allocated by the Allied occupation for the most-needed things first. This was why it was easier to import a quonset hut or a prefab temporary building than to get permission to use scarce Japanese materials. No contractor could give us an estimate because he did not know what the costs would be when the building could be built. We had to resort to allocating lump sums for each project, subject to adjustment when the time came to do the work.

I was made aware in Japan that administering funds for Japan from several different denominations in the United States, to be used by the one United Church (the Kyodan), would be difficult and challenging. Even the missionaries found it hard to think of themselves as sent to the United Church and no longer in Japan belonging to their particular denomination.

The Kyodan in Japan was related in America to the Congregational, Disciples of Christ, Evangelical United Brethren, Evangelical and Reformed, and Methodist Churches, the Reformed Church in America, the United Church of Canada, and the Presbyterian Church U.S.A. I was fortunate to be present at the General Assembly of the Kyodan and to bring greetings. Our old friend, Kashiwai of Senzoku, was the Vice-Moderator. The highlight of the Assembly was the adoption, at long last, of a creed, the Apostles' Creed plus the addition of some evangelical statements on the Bible, the church, and the Holy Spirit.

I had one last satisfying experience on one of the last nights in Tokyo. Our American friends had found it hard to believe us when we asserted that the Japanese are essentially honest. In fact, just after the war there had been some dishonesty and robbery in the cities where there was desperate need. I had been visiting the Sam Franklins at the seminary and came back late in the evening on an electric line to Shibuya Station. I took a taxi and the driver got confused and started in the wrong direction. He had gone some distance before I could correct him. It was a meter cab and when I turned to pay him he subtracted a significant amount because he had made the mistake. I paid the metered amount and went home happy— the old honesty was still there. I've tried this story on cab drivers in New York and they do not believe me.

I planned to stay three weeks in each country with one week in the middle in Shanghai, where I could rest and visit with the Winburn Thomases. Tommy was the Secretary of the World Student Christian Federation in the Far East. Trips like these are exhausting. The guest is like a baton in a relay race. At every stop he must be taken to see everything. That is tiring on both host and guest, but the host can rest after he has passed the baton on to another host. The guest, as baton, cannot rest but has to run with every host. Thus I looked forward to being with Tommy and Fuji.

But the schedule had been nibbled at both ends of the week and the plane from Tokyo was late. I had the possibility of only part of one day in Shanghai. I was first off the plane and on the bus at the airport. I went to the Pan American office to check my plane that evening for Bangkok. The man at the desk looked at my ticket and then said, "We have been looking for you. Your plane left last night." I leaned back against the wall and laughed and laughed, and at that moment Tommy came in. We booked the next plane three days later, cabled Bangkok, and took a pedicab to Tommy's home. There was a curfew on in Shanghai because of the fear of Communist infiltration and everyone was off the street by 5 P.M. That was the reason my plane had left early.

Thailand

I relaxed and rested some during those three days, but the National Council of Churches of China was in session and I attended one or two meetings. I also talked with Presbyterians in our Shanghai office and Tommy and I talked with another of Tommy's guests, Dr. Charles West, a promising Presbyterian missionary. Our principal subject was the future of China. Then came the question, what should missionaries do, leave now, or risk the possibility of being caught by the Communists? It was like Tokyo in 1940. Some got away from Shanghai, some stayed and suffered imprisonment. No Presbyterian missionary lost his life. Tommy's assignment was to the Far East, and by the time I was leaving Thailand, Tommy's wife Fuji had established their home in Bangkok.

Most people I talked with agreed that the Chinese government was totally rotten, but Communism in China was not agrarian reform. One man from the north said all of China would go except Hong Kong and Taiwan! The United States could help, but not without a core of Chinese people who would stand firm. One felt he was watching a whole era gradually sinking into a caldron of massive uncertainty. In a country the size of China this was startling and ominous.

In the early nineteenth century, Thailand (then called Siam) had been one of the first countries to which the American Board of Commissioners for Foreign Missions sent missionaries. Many of these missionaries were Presbyterians, and the Presbyterian Foreign Board inherited the responsibility there when it was formed in 1837. Growth was exceedingly slow. The Disciples also associated with us in the Church of Christ in Thailand. The Christian and Missionary Alliance, the Seventh-day Adventists, and a few others completed the Christian forces.

The prevailing religion was Buddhism in its Hinayana or early orthodox form. Priests in colorful yellow robes were often on the streets and Buddhist temples were sightseeing attractions. The social and cultural control of Buddhism was all but complete. Ordinary Thai could not imagine being other than a Buddhist and still being a Thai. I was later to visit Pakistan and Egypt where the Muslim controls are similar. Being a witness to Jesus Christ in Pakistan is like hitting your head against a stone wall. In Thailand it is similar except that the stone wall is a feather bed. That hurts less but the ultimate results are the same.

These featherbed characteristics make the Thai very charming indeed. They are courteous, their tonal language is musical, and their leisurely life is a refreshing change from the bustle of Korea, Japan, and Shanghai.

The center of church life in Thailand is not in Bangkok but in Chiang Mai, which is twenty hours by train to the north. I spent a week there, a week in Bangkok, and a week in four other, smaller places. A combined meeting of Church and Mission was held in Chiang Mai over Thanksgiving and I got to meet everyone of importance in the church. The greatest Christian impression as yet has been made by medical work, and the second by education. The former was largely initiated by one man, Stuart Cort, a graduate of Johns Hopkins and an excellent doctor and leader. He and his wife had no children and they chose promising young Thai and supported them through Johns Hopkins. These have come back to serve the church in its hospitals. The highest-ranking medical man in the government service was one of these doctors. Education has also thrived in the church, though not to the same extent. Most mission stations have both a hospital and a school, and those in the two large cities have national prestige.

Led by Horace and Mary Ryburn, the Mission and Church leaders now realized they had to put equal emphasis on training leadership for the church. The center of this would be in Chiang Mai, and an able group was being assembled there, both Thai and missionary. During the last two years the church had grown from 9,000 to 14,000, most of the gain being among young people. I found my study of Hinayana Buddhism at Hartford was a help in understanding the Thai. I was continually charmed by the people I met. I use the word "charm" advisedly; there is no other word to use. They are a free people, never subdued by a foreign nation except under the Japanese during World War II. They are sometimes proud and easily hurt, but they are also able and free to move out in a vigorous program when challenged by their own leadership.

The Philippines

My last three weeks were spent in the Philippines, visiting in Manila, Legaspi, Tacloban, Cebu, and Dumaguete. My hosts were Henry and Agatha Little.

The Philippines were difficult for me to analyze. The people were of varied racial backgrounds—succeeding waves had overrun the islands from Asia, Europe, and America. On top of many local dialects, Spanish, Tagalog, and English were national languages. Most people spoke the local dialect at home, but English was the language of the schools. To the foreigner this made conversation easy, but it was deceiving if the American then assumed he could readily understand the thoughts and feelings of the people. There is more to communication than the use of a common learned language.

The influence of Spain was marked. The family names were Spanish and the religion of the vast majority was Roman Catholic, but in the cities the immediately apparent influence was American—seen in the names of streets, motor cars, the movies, the radio, even the form of government. The war had also left its mark on the Philippines. Manila may not have been the most destroyed city in the world, but in 1948 it still showed the ravages of war as few others did. Some of its downtown sections were still massive ruins, with windowless, roofless buildings standing above the rubble. Place names such as

Corregidor, Leyte, and Bataan were constant reminders, and everywhere I went I heard stories of courage and guerrilla warfare against the Japanese and of joy in the freedom that was now theirs. Like Korea, that other newly freed country, the Philippines were demonstrating that there was character there and that the nation would be developed and realized.

The Filipino people were among the most hospitable in the world. The farm mother, standing beside her nipa hut in the mountains, had just as warm a smile for us as the Protestant woman who was a member of the President's cabinet and attended its meetings in an evening gown.

The Roman Catholic Church in the Philippines was like that in many other countries where Catholicism came in with colonialism and was the majority religion. It became a vast landowning establishment and some of its people simply added a new superstition to those they already had.

Protestantism also came in with American colonialism and was welcomed by many. By 1948 there were almost half a million Protestants in the islands. The stronger denominations were the Methodist, Episcopal, and Baptist Churches and the Philippine United Church. This last had been formed in early 1948 by the Presbyterian, Congregational, United Brethren, and Philippine Methodist Churches. With 130,000 members it was the largest Protestant group.

There was also the Aglipayan Church, which was a split off the Roman Catholic Church in the Philippines, and there was a sizable minority of Muslims in the southern part of the islands.

I met many of the leaders of the United Church at an Executive Committee meeting in Manila. I had to get used to bishops, four of them—one for each of the uniting churches. They were working out relationships and preparing leadership for the rapid growth—12,000 in the last two years.

Silliman University at Dumaguete is one of the great Christian schools in the Orient. It has high standards of education in the arts, law, science, and theology. At the time I was there the enrollment had doubled since the war.

The Sunday before Christmas I preached to the largest congregation of the United Church. The next day I heard Handel's *Messiah* sung by sixty voices in Manila. The following morning I left by plane, and at noon I was in Shanghai seeing a plane leave with evacuating missionaries for Canada. That same night I stayed in Tokyo, and then I took off for New York.

This time I did get home for Christmas.

Postwar Changes

January 1949 continued my learning process concerning staff and Board procedures and action. In my report to the Board, the first I had ever made, I stressed the importance of the field representatives. In Thailand and the Philippines the knowledge and experience of Ryburn and Little made an impression on me. They had become accustomed to keeping track of Board policy as well as the Church and Mission opinion in their own area. In both ways they filled the gap in communication. Japan and Korea had good people also, but they did not have the responsibility to be sure that both Board and Mission were well informed. As long as we did not make the field representative a tool to impose Board policy, this would be acceptable. We must try to ensure a meeting of minds so that all decisions could have the benefit of all the wisdom we could get.

We continued to expand the appointment of field representatives (FRs). They had the status of Board staff in New York. They came back together once every two years and the Foreign Secretary from New York visited them once in the interval. Among them were former Mission Secretaries, New York staff members, and one former Board member. I have never been in more creative meetings than when the FRs came to meet with us.

As far as policy matters were concerned, the most important observation after World War II was something we seldom articulated, but it was the immediate assumption behind most of our planning. The so-called younger churches had stood on their own during the war, many of them without any help. This fact was an amazing achievement to some and now must be recognized by all.

I remembered how frustrated I was when I came home in 1942 and some church members who heard me would remark, " Too bad those twelve years you spent in Japan were wasted." I was at a loss to answer that. The remark really meant that those church members did not recognize the first thing about what we were doing. It implied that after decades of work the only thing that sustained the churches and their institutions were the American missionaries; that when the missionaries were gone the Christian community ceased to exist and the gospel was never preached! This is silly, of course, but the remark came often enough to indicate that many American Christians did not think it to be silly. (Some of them still don't.)

For four or five years American missionaries had not been present and at work in Japan, Korea, Thailand, and the Philippines. That ought to be long enough for everything to come apart if it was dependent on the missionary. But the churches and their institutions had survived under their own leadership, as we had been confident they would. In Japan, catastrophe had struck in many areas, and 500 churches were destroyed, but the Christian community was still there. The people worshiped in homes when churches were burned, and there was no mistaking the fact that courage and hope were present. The Holy Spirit was at work. This ought to make us humble and teach us that we were working with a Force that is beyond our planning and our own strength.

There was still another fact we recognized. This period of separation offered us a God-given opportunity to change our relationships and start over again. During the period of growing up it is often difficult for missionaries to give up authority and let the church go ahead on its own. But now we need not start over in the old rut. We could change; at least we could structure our relationship so that change could occur.

The deputations that went to these four countries after the war realized this and made some provisions for it, but this was a continuous thing and the postwar years were to be filled with various plans for carrying on together. We were to speak of this in various ways. It was "Partnership in Mission," it was "A New Day in Mission," it was "Ecumenical Mission." In these latter days a missiologist has called it "The Decolonization of Mission," and a perceptive psychologist has said, "It was meeting each other at eye level." All this points to the fact that the modern foreign mission movement had come to the end of an era. But it was not the end of mission, and we had, under God, to find a way together by which we could move into the new era of mission, the whole Christian community working together for eveyone in the whole world.

In the meantime we had to deal with the everyday things that would lead us onward, never losing sight of the ultimate objective.

Charlie Leber was the stimulus for much of what the rest of

us were doing. He had never been a missionary, but he grasped the context of a problem as though he had been there. He was always ready to move ahead. He had a clear vision of where we ought to be going and was flexible enough to change tactics on the way. If in the evening he seemed to be deciding to do something one way, it was always wise to check with him the next morning before doing it, for he might have changed his mind. Once he had confidence in a staff person, he trusted that person. There was a sense of movement together, and this included all of the staff. Part of this was our collegiate system, but it was enhanced by Charlie. The spirit extended to the Board members as well. We were one family. Before coming to the Board, as a pastor in Scranton, Pennsylvania, and a member of a General Assembly committee, he had helped initiate World Wide Communion Sunday. With a leader like this, often supported first by the women of the church led by Margaret Shannon, and then by the Board members with John Mackay, Peter Emmons, Inez Moser, and Pitt Van Dusen advising, the Presbyterian Board of Foreign Missions was one of the major forces in progressive mission policy and action. We were fortunate also in the personnel that we had on the field, both the mature missionaries that had returned after the war and the new people that had been recruited. We were in many ways prepared for this transition period.

As we proceeded into the '50s the problems we were facing in East Asia were soon seen as throwing light on the problems of churches and boards of missions all over the world. If, after the war, churches in East Asia needed new relationships that would recognize their independence, then this must apply to other younger churches. This was soon clear in Africa, where colonialism was to be supplanted by freedom. We were being compelled to face change in the whole world more quickly than we had anticipated. In the new United Nations these new countries were being accepted on a par with our own country and with the same vote in the General Assembly. In the World Council of Churches, which was formed in 1948, the younger churches were admitted on a par with the older churches. There no Board of Foreign Missions stood between us.

After the first centuries of the Christian church, the mission had been carried on both by the state and by missionaries. Roman legions had been accompanied by missionaries in Europe and Great Britain. Later when the New World was opening up, the Vatican authorized the kings of Portugal and Spain to divide that world between them and to colonize and evangelize. Sometimes the governor of a colony was also the archbishop of the church.

It was in this colonial era that the modern Protestant foreign mission movement was born, beginning before 1800 in Europe and then in America. In fact, initially missionaries were most likely to be sent to countries that were colonies. Churches in Britain, France, Spain, Portugal, Germany, and the Netherlands initially sent missionaries to their own colonies. The United States had no colonies but after the Spanish-American War, President William McKinley encouraged missionaries by saying the church now had a God-given opportunity in the Philippines and Cuba.

I do not mean to say that the missionary was a part of the colonizing movement, but I do mean to say that church and state were partially motivated by the same desire to explore and change, and each influenced the other. Even the United States, when it had no colonies, still had to get its missionaries validated by colonial governments rather than directly by the colonies. The freedom from colonialism that came after World War II was bound to affect the churches and their desires to be free.

We Presbyterians, including both the Presbyterian Church U.S.A. and the United Presbyterian Church of North America, very largely had our missionaries under colonial governments. Those colonies were Egypt, the Sudan, Pakistan, the Cameroon, Spanish Guinea, Cuba, the Philippines, Korea, India, Syria, and Lebanon.

We had missionaries also in Iran, Japan, Thailand, and Ethiopia, which were not under colonialism.

We also had missionaries in Latin America, in Mexico, Guatemala, Venezuela, Colombia, Ecuador, Chile, Argentina, and Brazil. But Latin America had been among the first to be colonized, and its nations still spoke European languages and followed many of the customs of the colonial period, including the relationship to the Roman Catholic Church.

To sum it up, a sizable majority of our related churches abroad were in countries that were facing as many changes in the postwar period as the new United States had faced after the Revolutionary War. Needless to say, it would be a time of troubles and change for all of us, and we in the United States were part of the problem. Four hundred years of colonialism had deepened Western superiority complexes, mixed them with racial feelings and often left us unable to understand our fellow Christians. In a small way this also was happening in the United States between white churches and minority churches, and for many of the same reasons. We have begun to dig out the roots of centuries of colonial and racial prejudices, but it will take decades longer before we make substantial progress. Some Christians do not yet know that these roots exist.

Korea, 1950: Evacuation

We had not forgotten that Korea had priority for a second visit. We decided that I should attend the Korean Mission Meeting at the end of June 1950. I followed the same route I had taken in 1948, but at the Minneapolis Airport I saw a man I had known in Osaka before the war. He was in the State Department and was escorting Mr. and Mrs. John Foster Dulles on a trip to Korea and Japan which was primarily concerned with negotiating the peace treaty with Japan. He introduced me to Dulles, who was a Presbyterian elder. The plane was not full and we had plenty of opportunity to talk. We got to Tokyo about 5 o'clock in the morning and the Dulleses got off to meet the American Ambassador. When they came back to the plane he came up to where I was sitting and told me that he had received a letter from Korea at the airport informing him that they were invited to attend a reception for me that evening in Seoul. He said that they had consented to go. Ned Adams, our field representative, had been on the alert, but the only time he could invite them was the time of the reception already scheduled for me. Of course after we got there it became the Dulleses' reception. After the reception Mr. and Mrs. Dulles went to an evening service in the Yung Nak church. They went back to Japan after two or three days.

Ned Adams and I visited churches and projects in Seoul that had been built or repaired with money from the Restoration Fund. We also went over plans for Mission Meeting, which was to be held the last of the week at Taejon Beach, 100 miles south of Seoul on the Yellow Sea. Taejon was being developed as a summer vacation place, but this was its first season and the buildings were still in process with no running water and no electricity. We drove down on the 22d of June, 1950. Everyone from the Mission was there except one family in Seoul where the husband was ill.

We were well into the agenda during Friday and Saturday. On Sunday morning, the 25th, we had a worship service and I reported on other churches in East Asia. In the afternoon we had a vesper service and bade farewell to Mission young people who had graduated from high school in Seoul and would soon be going to the United States to enter college. We completed the day with a surprise visit with a honeymoon couple who had come to the beach.

About 11 P.M. a jeep came into the camp carrying the husband of one of the families that was staying there for the summer. He brought the news that the North Koreans had invaded the South that morning and were on their way to Seoul. We rigged up a hand-operated generator-radio and got the news at midnight that all of us should be evacuated as soon as possible.

There was not much sleep that night. A guard was set up armed with baseball bats, and at daybreak we hurriedly packed and ate breakfast. We were talking together about plans when another jeep came in with two men from the American Embassy. They were instructed to lead us out to Pusan, where there would be a ship to Japan. There were 76 of us, more than 20 children. We had two station wagons and seven jeeps and lots of baggage. The plan was to drive across to Taejon, where we could get a train south. We hired three trucks to carry the baggage. A new station wagon would not start and we abandoned it. We had food with us and stopped for lunch on the way. The road was gravel, but rough. It took us the rest of the day to go 80 miles.

Taejon was also a base for a unit of KMAG, i.e., of an American Korea Military Advisory Group. They had been ordered out of Korea, and all had gone except a captain and a sergeant who were waiting for us. We made reservations on the first train in the morning, ate our supper in the KMAG barracks, and went to bed. A little after midnight we were awakened with the news that the train might not go in the morning and that Seoul advised us to get underway immediately.

Two of the trucks had returned to the Beach and the third man refused to go farther. But there was a new Mission one-

and-a-half ton truck at Taejon which we took with us. We had to abandon all but the most minimum baggage. The truck was our best vehicle and we put that at the end of the line, piled the baggage on the floor, put some mattresses on top of that, and then put the children on top of the mattresses. I rode on the tailgate of the truck. The Embassy jeep led us and we started a little after 1 A.M. for Taegu, some 130 miles south of us along the back roads, the main road being reserved for the military. It took us all night and until 3 P.M. the next day. After dawn we had a series of flat tires and finally had to abandon our one remaining station wagon, but we made it.

Taegu was on the railroad line and we Presbyterians had a compound there. While the Embassy people hired a three-car train to take us to Pusan, a hot meal was prepared and we ate it on the lawn of one of the residences.

Safely on the train, we held an Executive Committee meeting. I was able to advise them, based on my Japan experience, on what I thought would be Board policy. We decided that all women and children should go to Japan and stop, if possible. Fathers with small children should go with them, but six men should stay. The Executive Committee had to decide who these would be, since all wanted to stay.

We boarded a freighter in Pusan about midnight. There were prayers and tearful farewells for the six men, but good news on the radio. Truman was ordering KMAG back into Korea and there would be military resistance to the invasion, and this under United Nations supervision.

We were landed the next day at Fukuoka in Japan and were able to send a cable through the Red Cross to the Board, who would notify families. We then went to Beppu to sit for a week while MacArthur's troops were using the railroads to get to Korea. Beppu was a hot springs resort fixed up for recreation for the occupation troops. We rested a bit, got some money from Tokyo, and made preparations for the future. I used an occupation telephone after hours to Bill Kerr, a former missionary to Korea who was in Tokyo. He transmitted our needs to Darley Downs, who was secretary of the Interboard Committee. We had some Methodists with us, but the main body of Methodists had been evacuated by plane from Seoul to Kobe. The missionary community in Japan made all the provisions to entertain the refugees.

We Presbyterians were lucky. There was a Korean Presbyterian denomination in Japan and they wanted assistance. They had not counted on it coming this way but were glad to have help. When we finally got to Tokyo we set up an office in the Kyodan headquarters and I operated from there with two secretaries, one Methodist and one Presbyterian. I had a good ad hoc advisory committee from among the refugees, and we arranged housing and assignments for work in schools and with the Korean Church. We also organized a Korean language school in Karuizawa for the winter for our first-termers, as well as a school for their children. We lost two couples, both of them first-termers. Three or four men soon got back to Korea; others were gradually returned as the United Nations army drove the Communists back. For a time MacArthur occupied our compound at Taegu as his headquarters. We later discovered that the old Presbyterian compound in Pyongyang in North Korea was being used at the same time by Kim Il Sung, the Communist leader.

I stayed on with Bill and Grace Kerr in their apartment, visited some points in Japan, and went home in early August. By this time John was a student at the College of Wooster but was working in Leonia for the summer, so both our children had been with Floy when their father got into his second war.

The intent of the trip to Korea was to have conversations about future Church-Mission relations. That did not happen. But the respect and the love that we had for one another was deepened by the experience and it was in that context that we could move ahead. It also was the only time I know of when a Board Secretary was actually on the spot in a major crisis. I did some things that were not provided for in the *Manual*. For example, I authorized buying three Japanese houses in Japan without consulting the Treasurer. We used them for a year or more and then sold them as people went back to Korea.

One more comment on that experience. The first lodging assignments were made from Beppu, filtered through Tokyo. Newt Thurber in Kyoto was informed to prepare for six guests who would arrive as we came through on the train. I will always remember the look on his face when he met us and I informed him that there would be at least three times that many. But he was game and handled it well. On that train to Tokyo there were some Americans on tour in Japan. When they learned who these refugees were, I got the old time-worn response, "Too bad all those years they spent in Korea were wasted." Fiddlesticks!

Beyond Colonialism

I had been surprised when I learned that Dr. Robert E. Speer had never had a title that labeled him the head of the Foreign Board. He was a Senior Secretary of the Board, but there were two of them. However, it was immediately added: "Wherever Dr. Speer sat was the head of the table."

When Dr. Speer and Dr. McAfee retired, no new Senior Secretaries were elected. Instead, a chairman of the Administrative Council was elected every year by the Board on nomination of the Staff Council. After two or three years, Dr. Charles Leber was always reelected. The other major agencies of the church had General Secretaries.

In a staff of some twenty-five to thirty executives there were several councils: Foreign Council, Home Base Council, Functional Council, etc. All these councils also elected their chairman each year. The chairman's duties were limited to presiding at council meetings and attending to whatever other duties his council assigned. All chairmen were ex officio members of the Administrative Council. Since a council chairman held his job for only one year at a time, he still retained his original title and tasks.

Every executive belonged to the Staff Council and had one vote. Actions began at the lowest level and moved up through the Administrative Council and Staff Council to the Board. Thus every executive had an opportunity to discuss and vote on all the recommendations. This was democratic and was called collegiate, I suppose because of its similarity to a college faculty. We thus welcomed a new executive to the whole task of the Board and assigned him a part of it.

Toward the end of 1950 I was elected the Foreign Council chairman, about the same time that L. K. Anderson, our former chairman, returned to the Cameroon as field representative. Two years later, when Gus Ruland was assigned a new task in anticipation of retirement, I was elected also as vice-chairman of the Administrative Council and soon after was given additional help when a Philippine layman was made Foreign Secretary for Thailand, the Philippines, and Indonesia.

He also became our Secretary for Evangelism. Mateo Occena brought new insights to our discussions.

These changes reinforced our commitment to slow but significant change as we faced the future. As early as 1948 there had been a "sleeper" in the annual report of the Board to the General Assembly. Charles Leber was listed as before in the role of chairman of the Administrative Council and Home Base Secretary. Now he was listed also as a Foreign Secretary. That seems puzzling until one looks at a new listing under the Foreign Department. It was Benjamin J. Bush as "Field-Executive for Work in Europe," and Bush was responsible to Leber. That was because the General Assembly had committed to its Foreign Board the task of helping rebuild Christian communities and their churches in Europe after the war. This was entirely new, for we were now working in an area where the churches were older than ours. I'm sure no one understood at that time that this would lead to a new kind of relationship which would become worldwide. But it did.

Ben Bush often told the story of how he went to the headquarters of the French Reformed Church in Paris and presented his card as a Secretary of the Board of Foreign Missions of the Presbyterian Church U.S.A. They thought he had come to the wrong place and referred him to the Paris Mission Society, which was down the hall from the office of the Church.

This one item set us to thinking in our Board and staff. If it is not proper for our Foreign Board to be related directly to the Reformed Church in France, at what point does another church, in Brazil or India, for example, achieve the status of an equal in the World Christian community? And how do we relate ourselves to other churches in mission when we are all equal? Charles Arbuthnot and Paul Frelick, who were among our first people in Europe after the war, were the first to articulate these questions when the field representatives met with staff. It did not change anything then but eventually we had to deal with it. The forming of the World Council of Churches in 1948 and the admission of the so-called younger churches as full members made this an increasingly urgent question. It was another indication that we must hurry to find the pattern of mission which would follow the end of the present era. We still lived in the old era but we were getting glimpses of the future.

These problems were not peculiar to Presbyterians. Other denominations might face them in different ways but they were the same problems. At times this meant close consultations and new plans between denominations. These occurred in the Foreign Missions Conference of North America, which became a part of the new National Council of Churches in 1950. Dr. Leber was the first chairman of the Division of Foreign Missions of the NCC. At the world level, mission consultations were in the International Missionary Council, of which Dr. Mackay was chairman. We were thus involved at every level.

I'm sure that none of us had a blueprint worked out for the future. Rather, it was a step-by-step process. This was God's mission through all the churches and his Spirit was leading us one step at a time. We must be careful but we must also be able to move. Before the decade was over, the "new day" had dawned.

Perhaps the best way to report on how the changes came about is to look at some of them step by step. Each one of them may seem routine, but added up they make a whole.

This approach to an end of the colonial era in history continued to stimulate us to expand our new church-to-church relationship, which we discovered in Europe, into other parts of the world. This relationship would take the place of one which was confined to the Foreign Board. Some were already beginning to think of the Board of Foreign Missions as the "Colonial Office" of the church. These changes had to be made carefully and with time and patience to work out details.

The most difficult areas with us U.S.A. Presbyterians were in the Cameroon and Cuba. With the United Presbyterians it was Egypt and Pakistan. In these countries we had established presbyteries and then synods and made them integral parts of our church in the United States. Their membership and all other statistics were listed in the *Minutes* of our General Assembly. Even judicial cases were ultimately referred to our higher courts and the rules in these churches were translations of the rules in ours. This pattern had become embarrassing.

In 1956 we jointly celebrated the freedom of the Presbyterian Church of the Cameroon. A year later the UPNA did the same in Egypt. Two or three years later we did it in Pakistan. Cuba, which was related to the Board of National Missions, remained a part of the Synod of New Jersey until 1966.

Most of the younger churches with which we were related

were members of the World Presbyterian Alliance and some were members of the World Council. We encouraged them to join such organizations, although there was never any pressure to do so. They were free and could make their own decisions. Those who did attend such meetings, however, appreciated the opportunity to meet other churches as equals. We profited, also, in such a setting, for we were no longer simply donors and they were not primarily recipients of our gifts. Our relationships in these world organizations were carried by the General Assembly's Committee on Interchurch Relations and not by the Board of Foreign Missions.

At the General Assembly in 1953, where Dr. John Mackay was Moderator, we added a significant detail which we had not planned. At the Assembly the Committee on Interchurch Relations always introduced fraternal delegates from sister churches to the Assembly. These introductions were an annual event. Fraternal delegates from the younger churches were also introduced at the same time by the Board of Foreign Missions. I was responsible at this Assembly for introducing the Stated Clerk of the Presbyterian Church in Brazil. A half hour before the time I suddenly decided not to do it but to ask Ralph Lloyd, the chairman of the Committee on Interchurch Relations, to do it at the same time he was introducing such people as the delegate from the Church of Scotland. He consented and did it, and John Mackay and the man from Brazil, who were old friends, embraced each other before the Assembly. I had not asked Charlie but I knew he would agree. Thereafter that was the way we always did it.

We already had Matty Occena from the Philippines on the staff. We added Sybil Bailey from India as a Women's Secretary and Kyoji Buma from Japan as a Secretary for Youth. In a sense they were missionaries to the United States. We added to this by bringing a young German pastor to fill a position in an industrial community in New Jersey and a Frenchman to be a student worker in a Westminster Foundation in the Midwest. These were good people, carefully selected to do a necessary task, but they also demonstrated that mission was a two-way street in a pagan world. Later, in 1957, when I visited Ghana, I was authorized to invite the Presbyterian Church there to send a man to work with a project in Detroit Presbytery. I gave the invitation to the leaders of the church in Accra, the capital, and then talked about it when I preached in a church eighty miles in the interior. Some understood English and some did not, so I preached with an interpreter and got two laughs with the same story, once when I spoke in English and once when it was translated. They were amazed and pleased that we should think they had something to contribute to the American churches.

We became aware that we could not depend upon recruiting candidates and then sending them to the field with only a few interviews, a week or so of orientation and a commissioning service. In this day of change we needed more than that. We started with one semester at Hartford, with part of it under our own curriculum. Then we moved to some New Jersey summer hotels in the winter and operated our own studies. With this experience behind us, we built the first buildings at Stony Point, New York, on some land that had been given to us through a bequest. This we called the Ecumenical Training Center. No candidate was finally appointed without having successfully completed a semester there. We had many illustrations of our need for this. One young man who had been carefully screened and sent to Stony Point listened to one of my lectures and then came to me in much distress and said, "Why, Dr. Smith, if what you say is true, it is like demoting me from a colonel to a buck private." I answered, "Who ever told you you were going to be a colonel?"

A major concern was finding another name for "foreign missions." Once, after speaking in a church in Illinois, I was taken to dinner by a university professor who asked me if I did not realize that the name was misleading and inadequate. I replied that we all did and were working on it. We first dropped the "s" from "missions." There is only one mission of the church, unless we describe each separate group or project as a "mission." But "foreign" was also outdated. It depends on where you are, who are foreigners. And there ought not to be any "foreigners" in a community of believers. We struggled with this over and over again. One day when our Administrative Council got away from the telephones at "156" and was meeting in the Auburn Library of Union Seminary, I asked Charlie what the World Council would call its Division of Mission if it had one. Charlie replied, "Ecumenical Mission." That seemed probable. Any world organization is nowhere foreign. We considered this from time to time and began to use it informally. A women's meeting at Purdue University highlighted it. My sister Margaret attended and my mother, who at first disliked the term, wrote me that after she heard Margaret use it freely, she liked it. "After all, sometimes it is good for us to learn something new."

We began to use it as an explanatory phrase on a letterhead. "In Ecumenical Mission and Interchurch Service." When I got my first copy of the letterhead, I was in Argentina. Dr. John Baillie of Scotland was lecturing there at the time and I showed it to him. He was a president of the World Council. At first he was puzzled and said: "You are using 'ecumenical' in a new way. We use it only for those things we all do together." I replied, "We have not abandoned that meaning." He thought again and then said: "I see. You mean you are engaged in the Presbyterian share of the worldwide mission of the worldwide church." He was exactly right.

We were not so fortunate in getting a substitute for the word "missionary." We tried "fraternal worker" but it was not widely accepted. We used it in Europe successfully and also for non-Americans who served in the United States. We used both words in commissioning new people. "We commission you as missionaries of the Presbyterian Church in the U.S.A., who are to serve as fraternal workers with the church in Japan" (or wherever it might be). Otherwise the two terms were often used interchangeably.

Usually Charlie and I shared in speaking for the Board to the annual meeting of the General Assembly. I would speak to the Board's report and he would present the challenge of mission to the church. In 1954 at Detroit I held up a copy of the report at the close of my speech and said, "This may be the last report of the Board of Foreign Missions. Next year we may come with a recommendation for a new name."

Thus the institution began to change in our move from colonialism to world community.

Chapter 7

An Idea Whose Time Had Come

ONE OF THE MOST exciting things about the Board of Foreign Missions under the administration of Charles Leber was the holding of informal meetings of Staff Council and Administrative Council. These meetings were often held. They were in addition to the regular monthly meetings and not for the purpose of taking actions or adopting policies. They met away from "156," sometimes at Buck Hill Falls but more often at Stony Point, which was as convenient for most of us as New York City. Staff Council for all of us did this once or twice a year and Administrative Council three or four times a year. Field representatives from abroad always were invited when they were in town, and we sometimes invited guests from overseas churches.

The agenda of the meetings was adjustable and anyone could introduce an idea or comment on ideas introduced by others. No minutes were kept, but the secretary kept track of the ideas which we might want to consider later for action. These ideas then became agenda of the next Administrative Council meeting and, if they survived that, came to the Staff Council's formal meeting for discussion and action.

In a period of change these meetings were both exciting and essential. They kept us all thinking together as participants in the change. Later, after reading Catharine Drinker Bowen's *Miracle at Philadelphia*, about the Convention that wrote the U.S. Constitution, we gave the name "committee of the whole" to these informal meetings.

In all this we did not forget to consider the statement that I had made at the General Assembly in 1954, that this might be the last report of the Board of Foreign Missions. But bringing about the changes we had in mind proved even harder than we had anticipated. Part of it was the difficulty in finding another adequate name. In any case the deciding factor against haste was the growing possibility, even probability, that this time union with the United Presbyterian Church of North America (UPNA) could become a reality. To rename and restructure in the midst of union negotiations would be impractical.

One of the ideas we developed was a study fellowship on the Christian approach to Communism. Events in China had highlighted the need for this. Dr. Charles Forman, one of our missionaries in India, was selected as leader of this study, and several able missionaries on furlough were added to the group. They had access to people and libraries and made significant recommendations. Besides training people to meet and understand Communist ideology, one recommendation was to train people who were Christians in how best to prepare to live in a Communist country. This project was under the direction of Hal Leiper, a young missionary from China and the son of my old friend Henry Smith Leiper. His paper was greatly appreciated and widely read. I remember especially his recommendations for the preparation of national Christians who might have to live under Communism. They must be carefully trained in the Bible, especially the laity, both men and women. They almost surely will not be permitted to have professional ministers and must themselves find guidance for Christian living. Secondly, they must love one another. Any outside threat will tend to divide the Christian community. This threat of division may be stimulated intentionally and must be guarded against. Whether we had anything to do with it or not, I do not know, but events in China proved the importance of this advice. The church has survived in substantial numbers, and what has been learned in the process will make the new church oriented in the direction of the laity.

Toward Ecumenical Mission

Sometime in the fall or winter of 1953–54 we had a staff conference at Buck Hill Falls. Several field representatives were present as well as three or four leaders of younger churches. In our discussion of ecumenical mission as we talked about how all Christians should join together in making Jesus Christ known to the whole world, one of our visitors from Asia asked how his church could join in ecumenical mission. We did not discuss it much then but it was jotted down as an idea we would discuss further. Later I was asked to consult with the International Missionary Council office about how a discussion on this could be launched. I talked with William Decker, the IMC Associate General Secretary, about it and he said that IMC could not initiate such discussions, but if two or three of its members initiated it and asked for help, IMC could give it. Bill's answer was correct. As one of its English members once said to me when I suggested an executive committee for IMC to act on projects, "We are not that kind of organization." There had been an Asia Conference in 1949. Subsequently an Asia Secretary for IMC and WCC had been appointed, Rajah Manikam, a Lutheran from India. He complained that he had no authority or budget and that his Asian Advisory Committee could not function. I reported this to our Administrative Council and we placed the idea among those we would try to do something about.

Hong Kong, 1954

On that day in Detroit in 1954, after we had told the General Assembly we might recommend a new name for the Board of Foreign Missions, Charlie and I went out for coffee. This was the middle of May and I was leaving for Asia in June. As we talked, Charlie wondered if I could get together representatives of related churches in East Asia to look at the idea of joining together in mission. I thought I might and we began working on it.

Hong Kong was chosen as the site and the date was early July. There would be a Board meeting in early June and Charlie would get an action officially calling the meeting. I would follow up in Korea and Japan and the field representatives would handle it in the Philippines and Thailand.

Since most of the sister churches were united churches, we shared this with other boards in New York. By this time Alford Carleton of the Congregationalists, Eugene Smith of the Methodists, and I were very close friends. We often talked and planned together. We trusted one another and shared responsibility for the same things in many parts of the world. Along with Virgil Sly of the Disciples, we were often charged by others with running the Division of Foreign Missions of the NCC. That was not true, but it was true that nothing was done without us. Gene appointed a Methodist missionary to attend our meeting in Hong Kong as an observer. Al did the same with a Chinese pastor in Hong Kong.

We had five churches in East Asia represented: the United Churches in the Philippines, Thailand, Hong Kong, and Japan, and the Presbyterian Church in Korea. I had personal satisfaction in the appointment of my old friend Kashiwai as the Japanese representative. We met for four days in the Peninsula Hotel. It was hot—very hot. We had one air-conditioned room where Bishop and Mrs. Navarro of the Philippines slept at night and where we had our meetings in the daytime.

I knew all the representatives from the East Asia churches and they knew me, *but they did not know one another.* We wanted an Asian chairman but they were not ready to nominate one. I consented to be chairman for the first day, and then one by one the others took turns. The theme of the meeting was the question of how we could help one another in mission in East Asia. It was soon evident we were all in agreement that we ought to do this. By this time we were becoming acquainted and asking questions about each of the churches. We therefore centered on three questions: (1) What are the needs for help in each country? (2) What help can we get from each other? (3) How can this be arranged?

Each church had had experience in listing needs for help from the United States. They now listed the things they might hope for from fellow Christians in Asia. This was followed by listing possible sources of help. Then we faced the last question of how we could do this now and in the future. The process was exciting. I had rarely seen people so enthusiastic.

Some definite needs were met by promises to furnish support. One was met while we were together. Thailand needed a nurse and could furnish support. The Philippines had a nurse who would go if her fare could be paid. And a Chinese in Hong Kong bought the ticket. That was a simple thing to do but it opened up possibilities that went deeper than money and people. We adjourned with the promise that all would go home and see if their churches wanted to engage in this further.

Hong Kong, 1955

In 1955 the Asian churches themselves met in Hong Kong. No one went from the United States, but Horace Ryburn and Rodney Sundberg, Henry Little's successor in the Philippines, were there as field representatives. All voted to form a committee to pursue the purposes we had discussed the year before. They called it the "Asia Council on Ecumenical Mission" and elected Bishop Enrique Sobrepeña as chairman and Rodney Sundberg as secretary. The name was a bit all-inclusive, but they authorized the officers to invite other churches to join them.

Bishop Sobrepeña was from the United Church in the Philippines and at the time was one of five Asian churchmen who were members of the Central Committee of the World Council. The Central Committee met in Europe that summer and Bishop Sobrepeña informally told some of them of the newly organized church group for ecumenical mission. He did it enthusiastically and two of his hearers were appalled. They were Charles Ranson, General Secretary of the International Missionary Council, and Dr. W. A. Visser 't Hooft, the General Secretary of the World Council. Ranson, in the name of IMC, sent a letter to all national Christian councils in Asia warning them about the new organization.

No one at the meeting really had adequate information, so that the opposition to it was all that came to our ears from the meeting. Adequate information did arrive in our offices, however, and as a result the Congregationalists, the Evangelical United Brethren, and the Reformed Church in America people, as well as ourselves, joined in supporting the Asia Council on Ecumenical Mission. There were often discussions among us in New York as to what the results might be. I remember one discussion in Gene Smith's office that centered on substance and that may have led to an ultimate solution.

Gene had called ten or twelve of us together on the occasion of the visit to this country of Canon Max Warren of the Church Mission Society. He was an Anglican and a staunch member of the IMC. Charles Ranson and Bill Decker of the IMC staff were both there, and Searle Bates, professor of missions at Union Seminary in New York, was also present. At first the discussion was general, but it soon centered on Max Warren and myself. Warren attacked the idea of missionaries going from one country to another in Asia. The Asian churches were too weak to spare any of their leadership and this would result in only switching people back and forth between countries and would destroy the missionary movement. My reply was that we thought the missionary movement was for all Christians and should be presented to all. If the challenge was accepted, this in itself would produce its own leadership both at home and abroad. That was what had happened in our own countries and it would happen in Asia.

Bangkok, 1956: Regionalism Begins in WCC

Perhaps it was that day that produced the recommendation that since IMC was holding a Conference on Theological Education at Bangkok in the early spring of 1956, representatives of the Asian churches should be asked to stay on for an extra day to discuss the new organization. The invitation was sent to all councils of churches in Asia and we exerted ourselves to be sure that all of the Asia Council churches would be represented. We also had enthusiasm on our side.

It was agreed that I should represent the Board of Foreign Missions at the Bangkok meeting. Charlie told me before I left that if I thought it would give me more status in the meeting he would resign as General Secretary and have the Board elect me instead. I was touched by the offer but assured him that if that was the way he felt, that was sufficient. I would act as though I were the General Secretary.

Invitations had now gone out from the officers of the Asia Council inviting other churches to join them. The IMC, which had sent the letter condemning it, now sent a letter to all councils of churches to send representatives to Bangkok. We were assured of a good crowd at any rate.

I was not a delegate to the Theological Education Conference and did not arrive until its last day. I was greeted by an American National Council of Churches executive who told me that I should not have come; only Charlie Leber would be adequate for this occasion. The Horace Ryburns had Dean Liston Pope of Yale Divinity School and myself to dinner that night. Dr. Pope, along with others, had just come from the

World Council's Executive Committee meeting in Australia and told me this matter had been discussed there and that the WCC's General Secretary, Visser 't Hooft, had come prepared. We had a brief meeting of the Asia Council that evening and then prepared for the morrow. Bishop Sobrepeña had all his files and got up at 5 A.M. the next morning to go over them once more.

The chairman was Rajah Manikam, the Secretary for Asia of both IMC and WCC. This pleased us for, if anything, he was on our side. Ranson, whom I knew, and Visser 't Hooft, whom I was meeting for the first time, sat on a bench beside him and carried the attack on the Asia Council. Sobrepeña was in front on the left of the rest of us, thirty-five or forty in all, who were the audience throughout the morning.

The facts were presented by both sides and then questions were asked of Sobrepeña. The thrust of the attack was that the Asia Council was an idea from abroad and that the Asia churches had not had a chance to accept it for themselves. Sobrepeña read the record and insisted that it was Asians who had formed the Council. The exchange at times was very heated and on a hot day.

I had not spoken in the morning but I was increasingly irritated by the roughness of the questions they had used on Bishop Sobrepeña and by the implications that some non-Asians (Presbyterians?) had imposed this from the outside.

When we broke for lunch I walked back to the dining room with Ranson and Visser 't Hooft. As we walked, one of them spoke sharply in criticism of the administrative ability of the officers of the Asia Council. That triggered an equally sharp reply from me. The tension continued as we entered the dining room.

I could not eat lunch. One friend jokingly wanted to know how it felt to be questioned by a prosecutor. Another said, "The IMC is the dog in the manger and you are vulnerable."

The Asia Council people met briefly after lunch and then I was glad that in Asia a group rests after lunch and meets again only at tea time.

When the meeting reconvened later in the day, none of us had spoken yet, but now I asked Manikam if I could speak first. He nodded. I said only this:

The genesis of this organization begins with a question asked of us more than two years ago by Asian Christians: How could they participate in the world mission of the church? We asked an IMC officer how to go about this and he said IMC could not initiate this. He added, however, that if some Council members started this and asked for help, they could furnish it. We have proceeded on this course. I have not come across the Pacific to this meeting to be discredited. I have come to discuss an idea, and I move that we get on with it.

There was silence for a bit and then the reply began. The Secretary of the Council of Churches in Burma said he had known nothing of this except that the IMC had attacked it, but he thought it was a good idea. Probowinoto of Indonesia supported the concept along with several others. Alan Brash of New Zealand said this was something that would be difficult, but it was what we ought to do. There were no Asians or any others who supported the attack on the Asia Council. Finally the pastor of a Presbyterian church in Hong Kong, a small Chinese man, said: "We belong to the Hong Kong Council of the Kwantung Synod of the Church of Christ in China and we are separated from our brothers. When the World Council met in Evanston in 1954, we thought we would find fellowship. But the World Council is too far away, it is high up in the sky. Then the Asia Council came and we found a home."

There was another silence, finally broken by Dr. Visser 't Hooft, who observed, "As in so many ecumenical conferences, the sinners bench has moved to the other side of the room and Charles Ranson and I are sitting on it."

That evening we all worked on an action that would call a meeting of the Asian churches for the spring of 1957 at Prapat in Indonesia. Visser 't Hooft asked me to draft the purpose of the meeting. By the time the day was over he and I were close friends. The vote was unanimous. The meeting was called so that all the churches in Asia related to the World Council could participate in forming an Asia Christian Conference, where we could face together the unfinished task of evangelism in that part of the world.

We had had sharp words but they had not led us to a lack of respect for one another nor to an inability to work together in Christian mission. On our side we had made some mistakes. We should have had someone at the meeting in Hong Kong in

1955 to advise about the name, and at some stage we should have gone back to the IMC to confer about what was happening. But the idea was right and had prevailed. We all had shown how deeply we felt about it and we now could go ahead.

I was not privy to the thinking among IMC and WCC staff. I suspect they were afraid of a regional council more than anything else. The Bandung Conference had been held recently for representatives of Asian nations, and the spirit for the most part was anti-Western. They did not want that to happen in the church. In his memoirs Visser 't Hooft reports that there was some idea that the Asia Council would become the agency for all the work done by some American boards in Asia. I had never heard of that idea. I personally am of the opinion that the Asia Council was somehow regarded initially as a threat, a movement among Asian churches to take control of their own relationships and to rebel against possible control from Geneva.

On our part we were undergirded by faith in the need for all churches to be in mission in the world. And John Mackay had convinced me in 1949 that regionalism had a valid place in the structure of society, including the church. I also had talked with a management counselor in our hometown who had some experience in international business. He said that they would never begin with people from all over the world in one meeting. The smaller groups would be crowded out. They would begin with smaller regional meetings before they were ready to participate fully in a greater conference.

Thus regionalism began in the World Council. In a few years there was a council in Africa, in the Middle East, in the Caribbean, in the islands of the Pacific, and in Europe.

Prapat, 1957

At the meeting of Asian churches at Prapat, Indonesia, in 1957, Gene Smith, Alford Carleton, and I were all present. I roomed with D. T. Niles and Alan Brash. Niles became General Secretary of the Asia Conference and Brash, from New Zealand, was his Associate for Inter-Church Aid for Mission and Service. Later Brash was Associate General Secretary of the World Council and D. T. and I were elected together as two of the six presidents of the World Council in 1968. M. M. Thomas of India was also at Prapat. He later was chairman of the WCC Central Committee.

Niles was a Ceylonese British Methodist. Franklin Fry, another chairman of the WCC Central Committee, called him the most brilliant mind in the World Council over a period of fifteen years. He had been the preacher at Amsterdam in 1948 and was the preacher again twenty years later at Uppsala after Martin Luther King was killed. He often visited our staff in New York, was in our home, and once was the preacher at our United Presbyterian Church's General Assembly.

Bangkok in '56 and Prapat in '57 were learning experiences for all of us. The tactics of the IMC and the WCC at Bangkok would have defeated them even if their cause had been right. To a meeting in Asia among Asians they allowed a considerable number of Westerners to attend who were on their way home from Australia. As one Thai remarked, "They brought in the elephants to stamp out the grasshoppers." Then in that meeting in Asia they attacked an Asian publicly. That was bound to rally the rest to his defense. But "Wim" Visser 't Hooft showed his greatness when he confessed his mistake.

At Prapat he made two remarks that indicated he was still learning. The Asians at Prapat insisted that the new Asia Christian Conference should not be an integral part of the WCC. It should be related but not subject to it. Visser 't Hooft remarked, "This is the first ecumenical conference I have ever attended where I could go swimming while the Executive Committee met." Later he said, "I hope this does not mean that you will cease to knock on the door at Geneva." Someone replied, "We will knock harder than ever before." That turned out to be the truth. At a later meeting of the Central Committee of WCC, Visser 't Hooft referred to the emergence of regionalism as an advance for the ecumenical movement.

Later, when what happened at Prapat was reported to a Methodist group in Singapore, a Chinese pastor said to me in the presence of his American bishop: "Do you mean that I could be a missionary? I thought that was an American monopoly."

Lake Mohonk, 1956

The climax in the first phase of our movement into the new era of mission came in the conference that was held at Lake

Mohonk in 1956. The Board of Foreign Missions had had decennial conferences before World War II. At first they had been for representatives of the mission organizations. Later a few national leaders had been added. No conference had been held in the '40s. Now we determined to hold a new kind of conference. It would be for Board and staff but would include the heads of all sixteen churches overseas with which we were closely related, plus some other selected national leaders and missionaries.

The first purpose of the conference was to share information about our thinking and action in the first decade after World War II. We had moved slowly at the beginning but gradually with a greater sense of purpose. As we realized we were in the beginning of a new era and as we sensed its direction, the pace of change had increased. Now we must take a good look at it together, Board and staff and related churches, and make sure that we understood one another.

The second purpose of the conference followed after the first. We must share our plans together, churches and Board, so that we could move together into the future of the "new day" in mission.

Some of these things were shared with our guests before they left home so that they could prepare in anticipation. This included the staff of field representatives and the heads of the churches. In addition, we had representatives of the Southern Presbyterians and the United Presbyterians with us as well as NCC leaders in mission.

Lake Mohonk was the ideal place. It was near New York but far enough away to escape interruptions. It was to last for most of two weeks and we would have the hotel almost to ourselves. The first week the staff and the overseas guests got acquainted with one another, each church having a chance to report on its own life and work. At the beginning of the second week, Board members and American guests joined us. An experienced author on mission subjects also was present to record our findings and possibly to write a book afterward.

Many of the new things that we had done together since World War II were explained and discussed so that we had a chance to understand the general sense of direction. These included the following:

1. The churches in Japan, Korea, Thailand, and the Philippines, which had survived the war without missionaries, had shared with the Board in establishing new relationships that recognized their strength and maturity.

2. Gradually all other related churches shared in this new relationship of mutuality.

3. The relationship with older churches in Europe was informing us about what it would take to establish similar relationships.

4. Field representatives were now in almost every country and made possible more adequate information and understanding as we worked together.

5. "Ecumenical mission" was a familiar term in all our conversations.

6. The term "fraternal worker" was being used in Europe and the United States, and its meaning was applicable everywhere.

7. In addition to fraternal workers in the United States we had now three Christians from overseas on the staff of the Board, one from India, one from the Philippines, and one from Japan.

8. The Asia Council on Ecumenical Mission had been established and would soon be enlarging its purpose in the East Asia Christian Conference.

9. In Latin America the Presbyterian churches had established a similar organization in which to share their life and work.

10. A study course training center for new missionary candidates had been started which was to become the Stony Point Ecumenical Training Center.

These were in no sense completed projects but they were on their way.

It was the leaders of the overseas churches that made the conference significant. Almost without exception they were able and articulate and soon felt at home. The factual material they presented was important but it was the spirit generated by our fellowship that was more significant. It is hard to say which of them made the most important contributions.

There was Ah Jan Leck, the Stated Clerk from Thailand. He

was a former Buddhist and now a sober-minded Christian, concerned about details and anxious to get on with the job. Underneath was a man of staunch loyalty, sometimes easily hurt, but committed to working things out together.

There was Ibrahim Dager from Beirut, a solid churchman with a glint of humor in his eyes, who could discuss the problems of the Middle East seriously and then tell you a story that would make you laugh the next moment.

There was the Japanese Moderator, Dr. Muto, a Methodist pastor before the union of churches, skilled in the problems of church union and glad for the welcome the Presbyterians gave him as though he had always been a member of the family.

There was Kyung Chik Han, the pastor of the fabulous Yung Nak church in Seoul, who told the story of how Christians had escaped from North Korea and come to find a home and build churches in South Korea. One could readily see how he had built a congregation of several thousand members in a few short years.

There was Bishop Sobrepeña of the Philippines, who had been an Evangelical United Brethren before the union and was now the chairman of the Asia Council on Ecumenical Mission, articulate in English and a dynamic leader.

There was Dr. Moreno of Mexico, a medical doctor and a pastor and Moderator, who had a clinic in his church through the week and a sermon on Sunday morning.

There was the Stated Clerk of the Cameroon church, a big man, gentle and full of fun, but quite evidently an African leader to be reckoned with.

There was a young pastor from Colombia, beginning to find his way and later to be a pastor and Bible Society Secretary in Mexico City.

And there was Dr. José Borges dos Santos of Brazil. In some ways Borges and Han were the stars, both intelligent and committed and with what we would call charisma today.

Such variety and spirit was bound to make a lasting impression upon all of us—staff, Board members, and visitors. It was not like attending a large ecumenical gathering. It was like a reunion of an extended family, members getting acquainted and reacquainted with one another and enjoying it. Charlie Leber was in his element as the leader of such a group.

Later we would point to many things that were accomplished at Lake Mohonk. Perhaps the outstanding one for all of us was the writing of the purpose of our Christian mission. The Board of Foreign Missions had a purpose of its own but quoting it in such a setting emphasized its inadequacy. It had been all right for us U.S.A. Presbyterians, but it could not include other churches which were now so obviously partners with us. We needed to do more than change its name. And so we set about to compose a common purpose for Christian mission that we all could use. It took time. I can point today as I read it to phrases that a particular person contributed to the whole. Here it is as we adopted it:

> The supreme and controlling aim of the Christian mission to the world is to make the Lord Jesus Christ known to all men as their Divine and only Saviour, and to persuade them to become His disciples and responsible members of His church in which Christians of all lands share in evangelizing the world and permeating all of life with the spirit and the truth of Christ.

The Lake Mohonk conference was not only the celebration of "The more we get together the happier we will be." It was that, but it was much more. It was, "The more we get together the better God can use us in advancing His Kingdom."

At the end we were no longer separate entities with our own personal worries. We were a family. New York was no longer the center with outposts around the world. We each were centers in our own right and part of the whole body of Christ. We still had problems but we had shared them. Dr. Moreno did not understand how Andrew Thakur Das could be a pastor in a united church, yet he respected and loved him. On the last day Borges said it this way:

> What is ecumenical? I've often been asked and have found no adequate definition. But now I know. It is like sugar. You can't know it by describing or analyzing it. No one will understand you. But taste it and you know it is sugar. What is ecumenical? I cannot tell you even now, but I have tasted it. I know now. It means that when I pray I will see you all. Han and Thakur Das and all the rest. That is ecumenical.

After Lake Mohonk the pace of our participation in change accelerated. Practical ideas had been shared and would be implemented in a variety of ways. All of us, Board and staff as well as colleagues from overseas, had been exposed to a truly ecumenical experience and would carry it with us for the rest of our lives. This would also rub off on others in the churches, even in the United States. We were sure that God was leading us to work together in mission in this way.

Now as I write this a quarter century after Mohonk, I am increasingly of the opinion that Lake Mohonk might have been the decisive factor in the restructuring of foreign missions in our denomination.

In 1956 the Presbyterian Church in the U.S.A. (PCUSA) was on the verge of union with the United Presbyterian Church of North America (UPNA). The final votes were in 1956 and 1957. Committees were setting to work to propose how the agencies of the two churches should be united. As far as we were concerned in the Boards of Foreign Missions, our experience at Lake Mohonk increased our conviction that *relations* with sister churches and *joint mission* with them belonged together.

The leaders of the two churches who could prepare such a proposal were very largely with us at Mohonk. They also may very well have become convinced that what they had experienced there could not be expressed fully by simply uniting two Foreign Boards into one larger Foreign Board.

The Methodist missions professor who was at the Mohonk conference and who wrote a book about it, *New Day Dawning*, was impressed and cited a World Council statement on unity and mission made at Rolle, Switzerland, in 1951:

> The word ecumenical is properly used to describe every thing that relates to the whole task of the whole church to bring the Gospel to the whole world. It therefore covers equally the missionary movement and the movement toward unity, and must not be used to describe the latter in contradistinction to the former. We believe that a real service will be rendered to true thinking on these subjects in the churches if we so use this word that it covers both Unity and Mission in the context of the whole world.

That sounds like John Mackay; at least it is the way he taught us.

I was not a part of any committee that planned the union, but I knew a good many of the participants quite well. In both churches they were relatively young leaders. Don Black, Sam Weir, Sam Shane, and Theo Taylor in the UPNA; Ralph Lloyd, Charlie Leber, John Mackay, Gene Blake, and Glenn Moore in the PCUSA. The last two had been elected Stated Clerk and Secretary of the General Council respectively in 1951 and were strong leaders with vision. There were doubtless differences among this group of leaders, but I never heard of any. They were unanimous in recommending that in the new church, The United Presbyterian Church in the U.S.A., the two foreign boards and the three denominational committees on inter- church relations should all be merged to form "The Commis- sion on Ecumenical Mission and Relations." Union of the churches took place at the General Assembly in Pittsburgh in 1958, and the Commission was also approved. There was little or no opposition. One ministerial commissioner rose to ask why we had to use the very difficult word "ecumenical." An Indonesian woman, who was a fraternal delegate seated on the platform, leaned forward and said in a loud whisper, "Doesn't he read his Greek New Testament?"

We had had to make two concessions. One was on name. We would have agreed to the name "Commission on Ecumenical Mission," believing that "Ecumenical" also included relation- ship. But that meant the committees on Relations would not be represented in the name. So we became the Commission on Ecumenical Mission and Relations of The United Presbyterian Church in the United States of America. That was a mouthful. Charlie at first would not permit the use of the initials by any of us but it soon became known as COEMAR. That was inevitable and probably right.

The second concession came about for the same reason. We had to begin with two divisions in COEMAR, a Division of Ecumenical Mission and a Division of Ecumenical Relations. Each side could then see its interests visibly continued in the new agency and its administration. We put up with this administration by ecclesiastical carpentry for some five years.

Theophilus Taylor, a seminary professor and longtime mem- ber of the UPNA Ecumenical Relations Committee, became the first Moderator of the new church, and then the first chairman of COEMAR. Charles Leber was General Secretary, Donald Black of the UPNA Board became Associate General Secretary for Administration, Margaret Shannon became Associate Gen- eral Secretary for Ecumenical Relations, I became Associate General Secretary for Ecumenical Mission, and Dan Pattison became Treasurer. Eugene Carson Blake as Stated Clerk was an ex-officio member of both Commission and staff.

The use of the word "Commission" in place of the word "Board" proved to have some advantage. Commission in

Presbyterian circles implied representation of the whole church's participation and not just the action of an agency. And the acronym "COEMAR" in many places came to stand for the new and fresh approach to mission that we had hoped for.

From the beginning the new church (UPCUSA) was free from division. The work had been carefully done and no surviving UPNA existed. Less than a half dozen congregations protested the union and not all of these left the united church. In COEMAR both constituencies remained loyal.

For both Floy and myself the union was a time of rejoicing. It put two halves of our lives together. Our education and pastoral services had been with the UPNA. Our missionary service overseas and with the Board had been with the PCUSA. Now our experiences in all these places could be used in the future service of the new church. Our families and friends in both former churches rejoiced with us.

Chapter 8

COEMAR

IT WAS NOT an accident that the union of the two Presbyterian churches and the formation of COEMAR began with so much promise. In the first place the larger Presbyterian Church in the U.S.A. had been willing to take an important part of the name of the smaller United Presbyterian Church in North America. We were now The United Presbyterian Church in the U.S.A. Dr. Mackay had been on the committee and argued for this, saying we could reserve the old name (Presbyterian Church in the U.S.A.) for the reunion with the Presbyterian Church in the U.S. (the Southern church) at a future date. After all, that was the name both had before the Civil War.

And we had prepared very carefully for the Commission on Ecumenical Mission and Relations (COEMAR). After all, we were not only combining the two Foreign Boards of two churches, we were also combining with them three standing committees of the same two churches, each of which had a loyal constituency. It was thus a major reorganization.

After union had been voted but before it occurred one year later, we held all our meetings together. The chairmen of each Board and committee presided during the time when their business was on the agenda, but all the rest of us were present without vote. Thus all of us learned about the details of the business which would be considered by the new body after union. And of course we got to know each other in more than a social way.

We then arranged that the new Commission, which would now manage the business, would be enlarged temporarily to include all the former members of the Boards and committees whose terms had not expired. The numbers were gradually reduced as terms did expire.

All of this took time but it was worth it. Don Black once said to me during that year that he had spent more time in my New York office than he had spent in his own office in Philadelphia.

This experience meant that we could begin to handle with considerable confidence the problems which were normal for the Division of Ecumenical Mission. The staff were all accustomed to that. The Division of Ecumenical Relations was a different thing. We had never in our Foreign Board experience handled these relationships. We were helped immeasurably by four people: Theo Taylor, who was now our Commission chairman; Ralph Lloyd, who had been our Interchurch Relations chairman and was now a member of COEMAR; Gene Blake, who as Stated Clerk had responsibilities in this area and was experienced; and, most of all, by Margaret Shannon. She was an imaginative leader and ready to explore new ways by which COEMAR might function as the mandate of Mission *and* Relations began to be carried out. In all these we were very fortunate. I can illustrate the spirit by a story. Later, when I was General Secretary, we began making charts of how we operated. In our organization structure the Stated Clerk had a box on a level with that of the General Secretary with a dotted line between them. When Gene Blake saw it he remarked that the dotted line meant that I was not his boss. I replied that it also meant he was not my boss. We both laughed and that was the way it was. There was never any trouble between us, nor between Bill Thompson and myself when he succeeded Gene.

For both the uniting churches there were new geographical areas to become familiar with. For us U.S.A. Presbyterians, the Middle East now meant more than just Iran and Syria-Lebanon. Pakistan, Egypt, and the Upper Sudan had been added, thus making us directly concerned with a larger portion of the Muslim world. In like manner our conception of Africa was enlarged. The U.S.A. church had had missionaries only in the Cameroon and Spanish Guinea, which did not begin to acquaint us with the whole continent. Now Ethiopia and the Southern Sudan had been added in Mission; and in Relations, we were now becoming acquainted with Christians all over the continent, many of whom were Presbyterians whose churches were founded by missionaries from Europe and Great Britain. All this was a mind-expanding experience for the new church.

Twenty years later this still continues to influence our vision of the future.

One of the features that both Boards carried into the union was the practice of holding a staff meeting for prayer at the beginning of each working day. It was only for fifteen minutes, but we started the day together. These meetings were led by all levels of the staff and often by missionaries on furlough. In the course of a year we absorbed a comprehension of the magnitude of the task we participated in and of the quality of the people with whom we were at work.

Our faith was reinforced by the strong emphasis on evangelism that came out of our experience at Lake Mohonk. As one younger churchman put it, "Without evangelism we will disappear in one generation." Some of us Americans later began to realize that this was true in the United States also.

Some of the new things in which COEMAR was involved were expansions of the experience we had had in the two Foreign Boards. Both churches had been charter members of the National Council of Churches in 1950 and the two Boards were charter members of the NCC's Division of Foreign Missions (DFM). Here we took counsel together about mission policy and action.

The DFM had area committees in which we participated. After World War II these committees were expanded. For example, in many areas new committees had to be added because in those countries significant church union had occurred and denominations that were still separated in the United States had to meet together and learn how to be related in support of their friends abroad. We were learning much from such ecumenical experiences. I personally had had experience in such committees for the churches in Japan, Korea, and the Philippines. I suppose that as a Foreign Secretary I spent as much time in such interdenominational committees as I did in our own Foreign Board committees. The work done was very similar but the people present changed.

The International Christian University

One of the most important new ecumenical tasks the American churches supported after the war was the Japan International Christian University. Late in the nineteenth century the

Japanese became determined to make education available to everyone. Universal compulsory education was enforced and by the 1920s the level of literacy began to surpass that of the United States. Christians had been part of this, especially at the kindergarten and high school levels. Most denominations also had a small college but there was no high-level Christian university. The dream of a Christian university began in 1918, but when it began to take shape in the 1930s the denominations were involved in their own colleges and these found themselves unable to merge their interests in one more important venture.

In the last year of World War II Japanese Christian leaders began to dream again. Meanwhile in the United States, after the dropping of the bombs at Hiroshima and Nagasaki, a Southern Presbyterian pastor in Richmond, Virginia, told his congregation one Sunday morning that the American churches should plan to give a gift to the people of Japan as an assurance of their friendship.

At a meeting of the NCC in Cincinnati which heard a report from the first Christians who had gone to Japan after the war to meet Christians there, the NCC was impressed by the desire for a Christian university, the idea of which had been brought back from Japan, and also by the Richmond pastor's plea that a gift be sent to the Japanese people. The NCC united these two ideas and set up a committee to join with the committee in Japan and plan for the university.

With this encouragement, the Japanese committee authorized a financial campaign in Japan for money to buy a site for the university, while we in the United States set out to raise $10,000,000 to supply the budget with which to start the university and to provide endowment for the future.

Our leader in the United States was Dr. Ralph Diffendorfer of the Methodist Board, while in Japan the governor of the Bank of Japan was chairman of the fund-raising committee.

In Japan where people were recovering from a crippling war, a sum of approximately $400,000 was raised and the site was bought. In 1949 a board of directors was formed and Dr. Hachiro Yuasa was elected president of the university. We launched our campaign in the United States in early 1950. Funds were solicited primarily from the general public.

Late in the summer of 1950 it was known that the campaign was failing and suddenly the professional fund raiser for the committee had a heart attack and died. Dr. Diffendorfer had retired from his Board and was now running the campaign. We had a new chairman of the board, Dr. Kenneth Scott Latourette of Yale, who accepted election only on condition that I be the chairman of the Executive Committee.

With the help of Dr. Yuasa, Harold Hackett, the treasurer from Japan, and Dr. Maurice Troyer, the organizing dean of the university, we sought to save the campaign. We were in the midst of failing when, at the end of January, Dr. Diffendorfer died of a heart attack on his way back to his office with Dr. Yuasa.

Early in the spring we called a meeting in New York of the heads of mission boards in order to face the crisis. Ambassador Joseph Clark Grew, who was our honorary chairman, came from Washington to preside. Dr. Yuasa explained the possible effect in Japan of our failing to support the International Christian University after a national committee there had raised all the money to buy the site. Hackett and Troyer presented a plan and budget that would enable us to take the first step in Japan. We called it a "bread and butter budget" and challenged the denominations to pick up their share, which we had spelled out. Dr. Leber led in pledging our support, and the three from Japan could go back now with assurance that we would begin.

The Executive Committee met every week at noon for several months. It was the kind of problem one woke up at night to think about. Gradually support increased. A Women's Committee for the university raised significant amounts. The denominations kept their pledges. As we got going and needed money for buildings, we received larger amounts—a half million dollars from a friend of Dr. Diffendorfer who had promised him he would help, and a quarter million from John D. Rockefeller III after his son Jay had spent two years as a student at ICU. It took us about ten years to match the amount we had hoped for in the original goal. But we made it.

From the beginning, able professors and top students were attracted to ICU. Some leading Christian professors left top positions in government universities in order to help. Emil Brunner, a leading theologian from Switzerland, volunteered. We have always had far more applicants than we could take. The school intentionally has been kept small, with some 2,000 in the College of Liberal Arts and the balance in three graduate schools and several institutes. Ambassador Edwin O. Reischauer has called it the only international university in Japan. Dr. Yuasa is fond of telling the entering students that "there are no foreigners at ICU." Its graduates are now literally all over the world, serving international institutions.

After the war ICU furnished an outlet for many of us on the international scene. It was something two nations could do together. It has remained Christian; every professor with tenure and vote belongs to an evangelical church. By the term "evangelical" we mean any church that proclaims the Good News in Jesus Christ. This is true also with members of the board of directors. But the university is also open to all students and to all streams of thought, although a church building with a cross occupies the center of the campus.

Recently our financial problems were reduced to a minimum. Land in the area had increased in price enormously, and the university had more land than it needed. The board's Finance Committee in Japan handled the sale of unneeded land carefully and the university now has more than $100,000,000 in endowment. We are glad that this means the university is now supported primarily from Japanese financial sources. We still help in the support of American professors and assist in other international activities. After all, we do belong together.

More than incidentally, this project has given wives of former missionaries in Japan an important task in which to participate. Men like myself were very busy, but often at tasks that did not directly involve our wives. After serving in a local church on program committees and becoming officers in larger area women's organizations, the wives still needed something to challenge them. They were still "Japanese missionaries." They were needed desperately, and the success of ICU is due to their efforts as much as to any of the rest of us. I was chairman of the Executive Committee for twenty-one years, but during all that time Floy was on the Women's Committee, whose Executive was Miss Ruth Miller, who has been from the beginning an irreplaceable leader of the Foundation. When we retired, Floy became an honorary vice-chairman of the Women's Committee and I became honorary president of the ICU Foundation.

WCC and IMC: Toward Integration

Through the Division of Foreign Missions of the National Council of Churches, we were members of the International Missionary Council, as well as related to the Division of Inter-Church Aid and Service to Refugees of the World Council of Churches. After that mouthful, we need to pause for a lengthy explanation.

As yet I had never been directly involved in either the IMC or the WCC. However, I had attended some meetings and had talked with some people. In Leonia we had a car pool to New York and the driver of the car was Henry Smith Leiper, one of the founders of the WCC and at that time its Secretary in the United States. Almost every workday morning I had a short course in WCC history. Then our daughter Louise decided she would shift her schedule at the College of Wooster from music to history so she could enter Princeton Seminary, and she chose for her independent study the history of the ecumenical movement. I had to recommend books and I had to read them.

There are two forerunners of the modern ecumenical movement: the World Student Christian movement and the missionary movement. The two overlap at some points. Men like John R. Mott were in both of them. Which should have the preeminence is debatable. Let us look at it from the standpoint of the missionary movement.

Until 1921 there was no world missionary organization of any kind. There was the Foreign Missions Conference of North America, and similar organizations existed in other countries, notably in Europe. In the nineteenth century there had begun to be a series of conferences, every ten years, usually in Europe, of such missionary organizations, but there was no continuing organization of any kind, not even a committee. The largest of these conferences was held in 1900 in New York and was called "The Ecumenical Missionary Conference." The chairman of its program committee was Dr. Arthur Judson Brown, a Senior Secretary, along with Robert E. Speer, of the Presbyterian Board of Foreign Missions.

But in 1910, with the Edinburgh Conference, this form was to change. As the only worldwide conference of Protestants, it attracted a wider audience than those specifically committed to missions. Even some younger churchmen were there, along with Europeans and Americans who had wider interests as well. Out of this came eventually three continuing committees. The first, in 1921, was the International Missionary Council. Then came councils on Life and Work, and on Faith and Order, also in the '20s. They were very loose voluntary organizations but were places where common concerns could be discussed.

One of the common concerns was that of a continuing organization of Orthodox and Protestant churches. It had moved very slowly at first but it gained momentum and at meetings of Life and Work and of Faith and Order in Great Britain in 1937 the decision was made to appoint a committee to prepare for a World Council of Churches. The chairman was the Archbishop of Canterbury, and the secretary a young minister who was then General Secretary of the World Student Christian Federation, Willem Adolf Visser 't Hooft.

The International Missionary Council and its continuing committee was kept fully informed; in fact some of the same people were in both. But the IMC decided against joining with the others in forming WCC. This was in spite of the fact that some IMC leaders would continue on the Preparation Committee for WCC. This negative action of the IMC Committee was confirmed by the IMC Conference at Madras in 1938. The war intervened and the Preparation Committee continued until 1948, when the WCC came into existence at Amsterdam.

There were several reasons cited by IMC for not joining. Some were theological and some organizational. But it was not as simple as either of these. The Missionary Societies in Europe were the founders of the modern missionary movement. The members of these societies were interested and committed people who were church members and who founded these societies outside the church because the churches were not fully interested in missions. The societies formed themselves into National Councils which were still not of the churches. IMC was a council of such *councils* and not of *churches*. The societies could not entrust their sense of mission to their own churches. They therefore could not entrust themselves to a world organization made up of these same churches.

At the same time, with common membership, it was agreed that the WCC would always work within the IMC and vice versa. There was a joint committee to make sure this was true.

But now ten years had passed and one could see the pattern of the future.

The individual denominations among the younger churches almost unanimously joined the WCC. They were all equals there, even equal with the mother churches in the West. IMC also had solicited the membership of National Christian Councils in the areas of the younger churches. But these were weak councils. At the same time IMC was dominated by the older councils in the West, who paid the bills.

WCC existed without a missionary arm. This could not long continue. It was against the nature of many of its member churches. WCC had a Division of Inter-Church Aid, originally intended to care for refugees and to support rehabilitation after the war. But such help could not be confined to the older churches in Europe. The Division began also to help younger churches when they were in need. Leslie Cooke was the Secretary for Inter-Church Aid, and I remember spending a day with him in New York. It was in the early 1950s and he was seeking support for certain projects in Asia. One was for a seminary professor in Manila, a project we also were seeking money for in the Presbyterian Foreign Board. We called it mission and he called it Inter-Church Aid. In spite of all that could be done there was bound to be conflict between the IMC and WCC in such cases. In any struggle for the future the World Council had the edge. It had the pattern of equality and IMC had the burden of paternalism.

I did not know the World Council from the inside. I had attended some meetings at the Assembly in Evanston in 1954 with half of a ticket as a designated visitor, the lowest level of legitimacy. I was thrilled with the crowd at Soldier Field on the opening Sunday when our friend Marc Boegner opened the service with the call to worship: "Who are you who have come here?" "We are Christians." "Where have you come from?" "We have come from 160 churches in 90 different countries." "Why have you come?" "We have come to worship God." With Charles Leber I had attended the service on the night when IMC reported, and told him I thought that Charles Ranson had missed the boat by not challenging all these churches to be missionary churches.

I was prepared to support IMC becoming a Division of the WCC; I admired the relationship of equality. It was the same kind of relationship we were seeking. I was not afraid of the church. We Presbyterians had decided in 1837 that we would carry on mission as an arm of the church and not through an independent society.

The decision about IMC becoming a Division of the World Council was to be made at the Assembly of the IMC at Accra, Ghana, in 1957. This time I attended along with John Mackay, who was the retiring chairman of IMC. Winburn Thomas was with us as a representative of the church press. Christian Baeta, of the host church, was to become the new chairman. His sister, Mrs. Jagge, is now a president of the World Council. Two others I met for the first time were Shoki Hwang of Taiwan and Donald Coggan of England. This was my first Assembly in which I was a participant.

The issue of merger with WCC was thoroughly discussed. The opposition was well led and articulate. It consisted of missionary society people from Germany and England. My old opponent, Canon Warren, was one of its leaders. The vote was overwhelmingly in favor of integration by 1961.

At Ghana I also found that there were a few World Council people who were opposed to integration. They said they were getting along well as they were. The Division of Inter-Church Aid was becoming an outlet for mission and they could dispense with those "missionary types" who would come in with the merger. This was not true in general. Visser 't Hooft, for example, was a staunch supporter of the merger and of mission. But the opposition was there. I was confident that mission would thrive under the right leadership in WCC. On the IMC side we provided this leadership by electing Bishop Lesslie Newbigin of India as the new General Secretary for the period before us. He was a committed missionary and the intellectual equal of anyone in the World Council. Ranson was leaving to become Secretary for the committee that was being elected for the new Theological Education Fund. I became a member of that committee and of the IMC Administrative Committee.

The decision was a risk. Entrusting mission to the church is always a risk, but not to do it was to decide that the future of mission would be taken over under the pattern of Inter-Church Aid, or that the IMC would encourage little mission societies in all the younger churches. If mission people do not trust their own churches to carry on mission, they could not trust the new churches that they had established. For the present we had settled the issue, but for the long term the issue would still be raised, perhaps should be raised. Churches need to be reminded that there is another way to engage in mission if the church itself is not committed to doing it.

Interpreting COEMAR

Charlie Leber had not gone to Ghana, because of the negotiations in which he was involved in structuring COE-MAR. These negotiations continued until the General Assembly in May of 1958, and then for another year all of us were equally busy in actually working out the details after union. UPNA people moved into our offices at "156." The sixty-six members of the Commission had to be assigned to committees where their experience could be used but also where they could be exposed to the new dimensions of COEMAR. At the time we knew we would be moving to the Interchurch Center on Riverside Drive in the fall of 1959 and plans had to be made.

One of our first priorities was to try to explain to the churches the need for the change in name and structure. For several years we had said a "new day" was upon us. Now we could say it was here. Literature was prepared with the help of others in the church. John Mackay was our resource in defining "ecumenical," and Gene Blake was a tower of strength. As Stated Clerk and as an ex-officio member of COEMAR and its staff, his office carried the weight of the General Assembly in interchurch affairs, and he had the experience.

Some of this interpretation was done across the country by asking the Commission members to invite significant church leaders in their areas to a one-day consultation during which the meaning of the new agency was explained and discussed. This proved very profitable. Many staff members participated in these consultations. When I had the time I usually tried to make most of the following points:

1. There is really no theology of mission. There is Christian theology, which teaches us that everyone who believes in God through Jesus Christ has already become a "witness." Jesus told his disciples, "You shall be my witnesses in Jerusalem, Judea, Samaria, and to the uttermost part of the earth." In our time we are those disciples. This is why in the early days of foreign missions the Presbyterian Church

decided not to entrust mission to a special society of picked people but to the whole church. It is inevitably part of being Christian. We have only one choice. We can be a good witness or we can be a bad witness. We are stuck with being a witness. A good witness does not *impose* his faith on others. He *shares* his faith and *points* to Jesus Christ.

2. The Christian church in some measure has now been established in almost every major country. Such churches may still need our help but they must be trusted to be churches which are themselves missionary communities. They are not now our children. They are our sister churches in Christ and join us in being witnesses to the whole world.

3. The foreign missionary movement of our time has existed alongside the colonial era. In spite of its Christian motivation, it has sometimes been unduly influenced by colonialism. The missionary became a supervisor in the colony and the Foreign Board was referred to as the "Colonial Office" of the American church. The unplanned image and attitude has to change.

4. This means changing attitudes among some missionaries. Even younger people may be tinged with colonial attitudes and be unaware of it.

5. It means changing attitudes and habits in American churches. This is no longer "*our* mission," and we must be just as generous and friendly as when it was so conceived. We must pray for the leaders of churches abroad as we have prayed for our missionaries. And we must expect to listen and learn from them.

6. This means being ready for changes in structure which portray these changes in attitude and relationship. It will mean uncertainty for some of us. Sometimes it will mean we must pool our resources with other denominations.

7. The difficulties will seem very great, especially at the beginning, but the opportunities are also very great. Thus the church may finally appear as a worldwide *community* of Christians of various races and denominations. In our kind of world this can break down the barrier where Christianity has been labeled as a tool of colonialism and imperialism. The Holy Spirit is creating a new instrument for the proclamation of the gospel to the whole world in our time.

8. This can succeed if we all really are part of the mission-

ary community and are joined as partners with other missionary communities around the world.

At that time an old story kept coming back to me again and again. I often used it to close one of my speeches. I had a friend in Pittsburgh who was a lawyer and he had in his possession the diary of his father who came out of the Civil War a young lieutenant in the Union Army. He was twenty-two years of age and looking for a job. It was just when the laying of the Atlantic Cable had failed for the fifth time. There were many people who now believed that it was a physical impossibility to complete the Atlantic Cable. Some of them organized the Overland Cable Company with $7,000,000 in capital and started to build a telegraph line across Canada, Alaska, the Bering Strait, and Siberia into Europe—16,000 miles of telegraph line. They were looking for men who could go out to Asia and head up the building of this line. The young lieutenant took the job, left for San Francisco, crossed the Pacific, and went into Siberia. He was in charge of digging postholes in the area. He had twenty to twenty-four men working for him, but the ground was frozen so deep that at times they dug only three postholes a day. In the fall of 1866 the Atlantic Cable was finally laid. The Overland telegraph line could not compete with the shorter cable across the Atlantic and the company went out of business after spending $3,000,000. They sent word to their men in Asia to come home, but there was no way of reaching the young lieutenant and his men deep in Siberia in the winter, so for seven months, until the spring of 1867, they continued to dig postholes that would never be used. I am quite certain that if we do not change our actions and attitudes, we will continue to do the same thing.

Advisory Study Committee

In that first year of COEMAR, 1958–59, we began to think and plan for two longer-range projects. One was to secure a management consultant who would advise us about future structure as we got acquainted with our task and with each other. In fact we had interviewed our first possible management consultant by early 1959.

The other project was for an even longer range plan for an

Advisory Study Committee which would study all of our work and report on directions for the future. By the summer of 1959 we had tentatively selected a chairman and a secretary and made a rough draft of their mandate. Glenn Reed was to be the secretary. He was UPNA, and had been a missionary in the Sudan and then the General Secretary in Philadelphia. He had trained Don Black as his successor and then gone back to the Middle East as Foreign Secretary in Residence.

For chairman we were approaching an Asian whom some of us had met at Ghana in 1957. He was a native of Taiwan, a graduate of the best university in Japan, and held a theology degree from Cambridge, England. He was presently president of the Presbyterian Theological Seminary in Tainan. In the spring of 1959, on my way to the first meeting of the East Asia Christian Conference, I stopped to see our possible chairman, Dr. C. H. Hwang, whom we came to know as Shoki Hwang (Shoki was his Japanese name). He was interested, but I wrote to Charlie that I thought we could not get him. His family and seminary demanded his time, but he had a sabbatical the next year at Union Seminary in New York and we might fit this into his schedule. With the help of Pitt Van Dusen at Union we worked it out and Shoki came on board. With the help of Shoki and Glenn we began to fill out the membership of the committee with a list of first-rate people from across the world.

Kuala Lumpur, 1959

The East Asia Christian Conference meeting in Kuala Lumpur, Malaya, was the long-awaited result of the consultations we had had at Hong Kong in 1954 and 1955, and of the Bangkok meeting in 1956, where we decided to have another meeting in Prapat in 1957 of representatives of Asian churches, which in turn called for the formation of EACC and called its initial meeting for 1959. It had been long in getting born but it proved to be worth the wait.

It was the climax in the establishing of regionalism in Asia, an idea that has spread to the rest of the world. All of the Christian councils in Asia had responded, except China. The great majority of Asian churches were there. The theme was, "The Unfinished Task of Evangelism in Asia."

It was a very satisfying meeting from our standpoint, and I found many people interested in what we were planning in COEMAR. Bishop Newbigin was there as the new General Secretary of IMC. As the conference closed he told me this meeting had been more important to the future of the mission movement than was the 1952 meeting in Willingen, the last Study Assembly which IMC had held for its world constituency.

For me the climax of the meeting came on Sunday morning when a worship service was held in a soccer stadium on the edge of the city with an estimated 3,000 people present. Dr. D. T. Niles of Ceylon, the new General Secretary of EACC, was one of three preachers that morning. He came last but immediately commanded attention with his theme, "Bits of Change for the Marketplace." I do not remember the other sermons but I remember almost every word of his. Here follows his sermon in outline.

One day in India, Augustine Ralla Ram had come down from Allahabad to Madras for a church committee meeting. The train had no diner but stopped at three or four larger stations for a few minutes where snacks could be gotten. The five or six men in his compartment all got off, ordered some snacks and were eating them when the bell rang to go. They all paid but one man who had a ten rupee note; the counterman had no change and the others had to pay for his food. The same thing happened the second time, and the third, and the fourth. They arrived at Madras well fed, but one man had not paid at all, because his money was not usable.

Most of us Christians are like that. We have our faith in ten rupee notes that cannot be used in the marketplace. Let me give you some bits of change that can be used.

God made you. In the last analysis you are responsible to no one else.

God made you. *God loves you.* No matter what you have done. No matter where you are, God has sent the Elder Son into the far country to tell you that he loves you.

God Made you. God loves you. *Jesus died for you.* No man comes to himself until he stands at the foot of the cross, looks up and says, "I did that."

God made you. God loves you. Jesus died for you. *And when you die you will go to God.* For some that will be joyful. For some that will be terrible.

Here ends the sermon as I remember it.

Family Changes

The 1950s had been busy years in our family as well as in the Board and in COEMAR. In 1953 Floy had been threatened by angina. The doctor advised moving out of our two-story house into a house on one floor. We chose the church first and then built a house in the town of Mamaroneck, New York, some twenty miles north of New York City. The change was effective and Floy was soon active again in the Women's Association of the Larchmont Avenue Church and in Westchester Presbyterial. She had been a skillful driver of a car even before I had a driver's license. She now visited almost every church in the presbytery. On weekends we drove together to scout out the roads that led to the churches in Westchester County.

John, Jr., was married to a graduate of the College of Wooster in the summer of 1952. Barbara Polley Smith became a valued member of our family. John was trained in chemistry and soon was attracted to the patent activity in chemistry, graduated from Georgetown Law School and began practicing in Washington, D.C. He is an elder in the Saint Mark Church and on occasion serves the presbytery as its lawyer.

Louise also graduated from Wooster and then from Princeton Seminary in 1959. I got back from the May meeting of EACC in time to speak at the commencement exercises, using D. T. Niles's outline as my closing illustration. Louise received a master's degree at Yale Divinity School and then became the Assistant Director of the Westminster Foundation at Ohio University. A year later she was married to Rev. Laurence Woodruff, a young Presbyterian minister who was also a graduate of Princeton. It was good to have another minister in the family.

The Theological Education Fund

Both Charlie Leber and I were out of the country in July 1959. The World Alliance of Reformed Churches was holding its Assembly in Brazil. This was the first time that COEMAR would be the participating unit from our church. We had a good delegation, many of them members of COEMAR, and it was decided that Charlie would represent the staff this first time. He had been ill but his health seemed to have improved and he was able to go.

That left me free to attend a series of meetings in Europe. The first was a meeting of the Theological Education Fund committee that had been appointed at Ghana. Van Dusen and Ranson had planned for this fund and had asked John D. Rockefeller, Jr., for $4,000,000. After a survey by Yorke Allen, Rockefeller replied that if the churches would raise half the money he would give the other half. We got promises for our share and he paid his share. A first-class committee was appointed. The first meeting was in Montreal in 1958 and, to my surprise, I was elected chairman of the committee. With Pitt Van Dusen, John Mackay, Liston Pope, Gene Smith, and Alford Carleton at my side from America I was able to hold my own among the leaders of the other four continents.

Charles Ranson and I had clashed when he was Secretary of IMC, but he was an able theological educator with experience in India and was made to order for this task.

We started with two major projects. The first and easiest was to supply a minimum of major books for libraries of seminaries in Asia, Africa, and Latin America. We prepared listings of books for seminaries at the college level and then others for graduate-level schools. We offered a lump sum of money to each school which they could use as a credit with us for the books they needed. The first grant was small but it could be repeated if the institution demonstrated it was making good use of the books. We bought and shipped the books from England at a cheaper price.

All Protestant seminaries were included, even those not related to a mainline church. We were unique. It was the first committee I had ever sat on that had the money in the bank before it started. Actually, because interest rates on bank accounts were rising, all of our administrative costs were met by interest on the money. We were free to use all the money for what we regarded as the best projects without any regard to denominational affiliation.

Our second project was more difficult. We set out to select some twenty major schools who could best profit by a grant of up to $125,000 for buildings or program and thus become leaders of theological education in their geographical area. When Christian Baeta from Ghana realized what we meant at the first meeting he said, "You mean you are going to give all your cake to one boy!" And he was right. It was the theory that if we helped one to be best, then the others would scramble to match it. It often worked.

Later we started a third program, seeking to subsidize textbooks in various language areas by helping in making translations and in producing indigenous books by new authors.

This new manner of administration was so attractive that it was continued with a new mandate that did not depend upon grants of money but upon the value of sharing new ideas and expert counseling. At the suggestion of COEMAR the World Council established similar committees in the area of Medical Services and in General Education.

I personally was relaxed at such meetings. I was not troubled about raising the money for the projects and I had the best expert advice. At times our staff was supplemented by the best of young theologians who profited by their experience. Charles Forman at Yale was one of them, and two or three others from Europe were very useful.

The first committee meeting in Europe was immediately followed by the second and was composed of some of the same people. It was the Administrative Committee of IMC and was called to prepare for the integration of IMC with WCC at the latter's next Assembly in India in 1961. The friction that now existed between IMC and Inter-Church Aid would be in the family after integration. I had no doubt that it would continue, and in preparation I wrote several memos to Charlie about it. I remained confident that Visser 't Hooft and Newbigin would see it through.

Saloniki, 1959

I now turned to my third conference that summer, the World Council sponsored meeting on "Rapid Social Change." It was in Greece at Saloniki (Thessalonica). It was aimed particularly at Africa and its churches.

Colonialism was coming to an end in some countries and would be gone in many others in a few years. The question was, how could Christians prepare themselves to participate in the new countries that had come into being? They had no experience to guide them. They had kept themselves as free as possible from the colonial governments. But now they had a new obligation to participate responsibly as Christians in forming new nations.

The program was under the auspices of what we would call Church and Society in the WCC. Some two hundred people attended, many of them I was to recognize later as significant leaders among the growing churches of Africa. I roomed with Sir Francis Akanu Ibiam, a doctor from Enugu in Nigeria who later was a president of the WCC. There were plenary sessions with some important speakers but the discussion groups were most informative and sometimes exciting. I was getting acquainted with an Africa that was beyond the Africa I knew in the Cameroon. I was also meeting many leaders from Europe whom I had only known by name. One of my good friends was to be the Africa Secretary of the Paris Mission Society (Reformed). Pierre Benignus had been a missionary in Dakar and also knew the Cameroon.

One event at Saloniki was an evening session at which a French missionary from the Belgian Congo spoke, and was immediately translated into English. After the meeting I wrote a memo to Charlie, since it illustrated so well what I had been saying about possible friction as the IMC was integrated into the WCC. The following lengthy quotation gives the details:

We had an explosion last night. There has been a rather heavy program of speakers and, up to last night, of a high order. The emphasis has been on Africa, and three or four African political leaders and professors have spoken. One of them spoke last night from 8 to 9 and finished amid resounding applause.

The next speaker was the Rev. Dr. P. C. Tiureille of the Belgian Congo. He turned out to be a middle-aged fat Frenchman who for the last four years has been a teacher of religion in a secondary school supported by the government in Stanleyville. He spoke for an hour and a quarter in French, translated sentence by sentence by Robbins Strong. His speech was a hodgepodge, a "tossed salad" as one man described it. His theme, however, was clear. It was "The White Man's Burden in Africa," where women wanted babies at fifteen and became prostitutes if they had no dowry for marriage; where no man was ever seen carrying a bundle for a woman; and where anything fit to eat had to be imported from outside. It was a caricature of the missionary image of the last generation sincerely expressed and ending with an appeal to follow the Cross and love the African. If anyone had set out to portray such a missionary he would not have been believed. At first the Africans reacted strongly. One from the Cameroon called out, *"Non! Non!"* As it went on, however, it became more and more ridiculous. At the end the man from the Cameroon was cheering him on with a "Bravo!"

The speaker turns out to have emigrated from France to the United States ten years ago, to have been pastor of a French-speaking congregation in the Presbyterian U.S. Church, and then to have gone to the Congo from there. Poor staff work and misunderstanding at Geneva resulted in his being on the program. Even the most rudimentary inquiry would have revealed the kind of man he was.

Perhaps we needed to be reminded of the "pit from which we are dug," but the incident here has been most unfortunate. Most Africans here tend to overlook this as a mistake, but some others feel deeply about it. At the same time the missionary contingent here has taken it on the chin. This Frenchman is the only missionary on the program. Virgil Sly, a Disciples Board Secretary, speaks later this week but there is no missionary from the field. Some Europeans and Americans did not need this encouragement to look down their noses at the mission cause.

I had an exchange this morning with the WCC staff person in charge of the conference. He is defensive and after stating that it was a mistake, went on to say that after all this man did represent more than half the missionaries in Africa. My reply did not help matters much. I said that if this represents what Geneva thinks the typical missionary is, then this is what is wrong with Geneva. (We have since talked further.)

This, of course, is related to the comparative lack of sympathy by some people in Geneva for organized mission agencies. We are partly to blame, for IMC has stayed aloof from WCC, but this does not excuse such things as WCC ignoring the Near East Christian Council and other evangelical activities in the geographical area of the Orthodox Church, her scorn at times of missionaries, her acting at times out of ignorance when an inquiry would have corrected her, and the underlying assumption on the part of some that the day of the missionary and the mission agency is over. Now it is time the WCC took over and showed the rest of us how to do it. As integration takes place we have our work cut out for us. More than any other participating unit we United Presbyterians in COEMAR represent both Church and Mission. Our difficulty will be that we see both sides. But this can also be our contribution.

I am surprised at how many memos I wrote to Charlie from Saloniki. There was one that had three parts which traced the growth of Inter-Church Aid, its theological rationale, and the source of friction. Before I was through I decided to let Geneva call such aid "Ecumenical Diakonia" as long as I could call it "Ecumenical Mission." The EACC has done just that. They refused to enter the squabble in Europe where churches sometimes preferred to send their help through Geneva than to send it through the mission agencies. The East Asia Christian Conference was right. It did not matter what you called it, just so the work was done. EACC has a Secretary for Mission and Service and let it go at that. We could do the same while demonstrating by our work that those engaged in mission could be just as careful to respect the younger churches and their wishes as any WCC executive. I still had confidence in Visser 't Hooft and Newbigin, or rather that the Holy Spirit through such men would lead us all to do those things together which would advance God's Kingdom in our time.

Actually, Charlie Leber never read the batch of memos that I sent from Saloniki. He was gone before they could be typed and sent to him. Charles Arbuthnot drove me to the airport in Greece only a few hours before the cable came that shared the news of Leber's death in Brazil of a heart attack. I changed planes in Rome but the cable also missed me there. It was only at Idlewild after Floy and Louise had met me and helped me take my baggage to the car that they told me Charlie was dead. And then we cried and cried.

Chapter 9

General Secretary

NONE OF US on the staff knew that Charles Leber was seriously ill. For some time his heart had been affected by his diabetes, but usually he was strong and sturdy, or appeared to be. He could outlast most of us when meetings piled up on one another. After hours he never hesitated to spend more time if necessary. He was not one to share any physical weakness with us. I do remember that at the General Assembly in 1957 he was ill and needed daily attention by a doctor. I knew this only because he asked me to substitute for him at a General Council meeting. Another time he told me that he had blacked out while he was driving and had damaged his car. Otherwise I do not remember him being ill, so that at least to me his death came as a surprise. I have learned since that his doctor had given him a warning before he went to Brazil in 1959 and that he had shared this warning with a friend, who concluded afterward that it was characteristic of Charlie to go ahead with his task if he thought it was important.

Upon his death the Commission members along with the officers who were with him in Brazil immediately cabled the New York office, appointed Don Black as interim General Secretary, tried to find me, and then participated in a service for him which was conducted in São Paulo by the Assembly of the World Presbyterian Alliance. He was widely known as a friend among churches in the West as well as among the younger churches. Thus the service was a very meaningful one.

His body was sent back to New York by plane and a memorial service was held in the First Presbyterian Church on Fifth Avenue. Peter Emmons, former president of the Foreign

Board, presided; Dr. Eugene Carson Blake, the Stated Clerk, spoke for the church at large; and I spoke for the staff of COEMAR. I remember saying that we would pledge ourselves to follow the vision that Charlie had set before us but that did not mean we would do exactly what he had done. Even Charlie himself would not do that. He was always open to change and we hoped that we would be as open to the guiding of the Holy Spirit as he had been. The funeral service and burial were held in Baltimore, which had been his childhood home.

Immediately after the service I flew to Rio de Janeiro to take his place in a conference with Brazilian church leaders. This followed the Assembly and the centenary of the largest Presbyterian church in the capital.

The Commission appointed a committee to nominate Dr. Leber's successor. I know of no one, including myself, who was interviewed for the position or who applied. Dr. Leber had died the last of July. The last of September the Commission had its fall meeting. The morning of the first day Theophilus Taylor, the Commission chairman, came into my office and asked if I would accept election. I said I would, and I was elected that morning. Margaret Shannon, speaking for the staff, welcomed me as General Secretary, and Gene Blake in his remarks said that the people in Geneva would have been surprised if they had elected anyone else.

Up to the time of Charlie's death I had never expected to be General Secretary. Charlie and I were too near the same age for me to succeed him after ordinary retirement. I had shared the task with him but he still took responsibility, even for my mistakes. I was thankful that together we had gotten a year's start in COEMAR and that we had a good Commission and staff. I had confidence that I had come to the task without seeking it and that God would guide me if I would listen. Charlie had seen to it that I was properly trained. Now I think this was with his illness in mind. We would carry on what he had started.

Later we were to make several changes in staff when we were more fully aware of our various tasks and the capacity of staff. We made two changes, however, in the first few weeks. The Commission had elected Don Black to take my place as Associate General Secretary for Ecumenical Mission. We now abolished the office of Associate General Secretary for Administration, gave that task to the General Secretary's Office, and moved John Corbin from Interpretation to the General Secretary's Office to handle Administration. We then brought Winburn Thomas from the Chicago office to handle Interpretation. Both proved to be excellent in their new positions.

In the first year of COEMAR we had made initial preparation for two major projects. One was working with a management consultant, and the other was the Advisory Study. Proceeding with the latter was questioned by some on the staff who thought that we ought not to tackle this so soon. But by that time we had a better idea of what we wanted and part of the committee for it had been chosen. When Shoki Hwang found it possible to accept the chairmanship, it guaranteed that we would go ahead. The work on the Advisory Study Committee and the nature of the final report in 1961 is a separate story.

However, in preparation for this chapter I came upon a summary of a consultation that we had at Stony Point in January 1959. This was before Charlie's death, but it reveals the direction of our thinking as we prepared for the Advisory Study.

I have no list of the participants, but the consultation was surely made up of the Administrative Committee of the staff plus some resource people. Three of them were missionaries or people who had recently been missionaries.

The theme for study during the two days was "Community of Mission." It was one of the most important issues in our thinking. Remember that in COEMAR we were turning away from a foreign mission agency and seeking to establish ourselves as a link between churches abroad and in the United States. All were themselves missionary communities engaged in sharing the gospel in their own countries and joining together in sharing the gospel with people in places where Christian communities did not yet exist. This was based on the assumption that communities of believers were already or could become missionary communities where the mission of the church would have priority and not be lost in the multitude of other things that clamor for attention.

Charlie had designated me to be a kind of reporter in the consultation who would listen and then summarize what was being said. I presented it as "An Informal Personal Summary of the Discussion on 'Community of Mission.' " I remember that the discussion of the summary was very spirited and that probably I revised my summary to some extent after the discussion, but these became the main issues in our own thinking and in the charge that was later given to the Advisory Study Committee.

I must confess that until I found this summary I did not recall that we had gone as far as we did in raising these questions. The consciousness of our need was increased by the charges that some were leveling against the plan to make the International Missionary Council a Division of the World Council of Churches. The basic issue is as old as the missionary movement itself and is still with us. The alternatives probably need to be with us always and to stimulate periodic reexamination: "Can the mission of the church be entrusted to the church?" or, "If the church does not engage in mission, then should societies be formed for the purpose?"

Here are some quotations from my summary:

As an administrator in an ongoing mission organization, I have been interested in my own reaction to the discussion. It has veered from an instinctive defense of the status quo all the way to a tendency to think that our only way out is to scrap everything we are now doing and start all over again. Of course, neither of these extremes represent any hope for the future. We are what we are. We have what we have. We should not be defensive about it, but we have to start with what we have, recognize where we are weak, and set ourselves, under God, to serve the mission of the church more perfectly.

The central issue present to us here is this. We have believed in New Testament terms that Christ committed his mission to the whole body of believers and not to a particular section of that body. We are all witnesses. In like manner also the new churches founded overseas are to be bodies of witnesses. In our time the chief responsibility for witness is being transferred from our church to the new churches that have been established. We are the commission in our church which operates our relationships with churches across the world. Are the churches ready to be witnesses for Christ in lands overseas or even in the United States?

Is the church ready? When Richard Shaull describes a church in Latin America whose primary concern is with its own existence, my heart sinks. I know such churches in the United States and elsewhere, even whole presbyteries and synods, whose primary concern is their own continued existence, and whatever concern they have for mission is only fractional. And they are not all in Latin America or the United States. The conclusion must be that many, many churches are not now missionary communities.

But when Jim Alter speaks of churches in India or Charles Forman describes certain churches in Japan or Korea as "missionary communities" my heart leaps up, for I recognize that at least in part this also is true, and in this there is hope.

The obvious answer to the question of whether the church is a missionary community is yes and no. Sufficient examples can be given that indicate that the church at home and abroad is potentially a missionary community, though it falls short of the ideal and at times denies its very nature.

Therefore, we are also agreed that it is possible for God to use the present church, of which we are a part, for his purposes. In other words it is possible, under God, to become a missionary community. The difficulties are so great that at times we are tempted to turn back to the past and to pursue mission as separate from the church. At the same time, we are aware that opportunities are enlarged in our time. God is bringing the church and the missionary movement together. This cannot be without purpose. As Bishop Newbigin has put it: "The way may not be broad and easy, but it leads forward. We should undertake the costly but exciting task of finding out what is the pattern of the church's mission in the new day in which God has pleased to put us." The question that remains, then, is: At what points can we continue this exciting task of finding out what we do to further the mission of the church? Here are some of these points as I see them.

1. Let us set ourselves to discover what it really is that God seeks in a person when he commits himself to Jesus Christ as Lord and Savior; not how numbers are won to an institution, but how people are committed to a community whose purpose is the redeeming of all of life in relationship to God.

2. Let us continue to discover examples of churches which are missionary communities in the fullest sense and study what their characteristics are.

3. Let us share this concern with our sister churches from the beginning, that together we may learn what our nature is to be. Then let us make plain to our sister churches that the

primary concern of the Commission has to be the extension of the mission.

4. Let us examine our relationships with sister churches, especially financial ones, that we may contribute to, rather than deter, the church in its mission.

5. Let us, with our sister churches, examine the institutions we have established and which are now theirs. Do they truly represent that which best serves the church as a missionary community? If necessary, let us separate the sheep from the goats in this instance, continuing our relationship with those institutions which are truly part of the church's mission or may become so, and severing our present relationship with those who are or who are becoming secular in character. This would not preclude establishing a new relationship with such institutions—recognizing them for what they are and working in them in the same way that we work in relationship to other secular institutions.

6. Let us explore new ways by which the church penetrates the non-Christian world beyond the bounds of the church and its institutions, wherever they are.

7. Let us look at our own activities as a Commission. In view of the full sweep of our activities and of our limited resources, are we engaged in many "good things" that, after all, absorb our time and keep us away from adequate attention to the heart of our task?

8. With our sister churches, let us look at this same problem in regard to our personnel and funds from abroad. Does the balance in which they are used indicate that the church's primary concern is at the point of mission? It may be necessary to divest ourselves of certain responsibilities in order to get on with the task within our limited resources.

Management

Our experience of more than a year in COEMAR now led us to turn seriously to a search for a management consultant. We were fortunate in our choice of Frank Martin of Hayes Associates in Philadelphia. He had been an Episcopalian, now was a Quaker, had been the dean of a private secondary school, and had experience advising both business and church organizations. He himself became our consultant but had the advantage of the resources of the firm.

He began by getting acquainted with us. We were still a small staff of forty or forty-five, and he met with us in a staff meeting and then with each of us separately. He shared with us his general approach. He said a church organization needed to be businesslike and to be strictly accountable in all things. But a church was not merely a business organization; it was a combination of a business, educational, and governmental organization. As such the staff (faculty) needed to participate in policy-making, and, like government, we needed always to remember we had a constituency to which we were ultimately accountable and which had to be kept informed. He also said he could not and would not presume to tell us how to run our organization. He was not there for that. But he could do two things. He could ask us, "Why are you in business?" and help us clarify our answer so that everyone could understand the purpose of COEMAR. And then he could offer us two or three ways in which we could work toward achieving our purpose. We would have to choose a way and try it before he and we would recommend to the Commission that this was the way which should be accepted.

This process took time. Frank would come for several days, then not be back for a month. That gave a chance for his ideas to sink in and for us to have a reasoned opinion about them.

I was absent when the Commission adopted the structure, away at a meeting in Asia on the Advisory Study. But I had no qualms at all about it. We had finished the plan and used it in our daily work for more than six months before we presented it to the Commission.

The genius of the new structure was not in any new approach but in the fact that we had ourselves participated in planning and trying out procedures for administration. Frank once told us that if we were clear about our purpose and had a staff that was committed to it, we would eventually get the job done no matter what structure we had. He could help us pick an efficient plan and also teach us how to adapt it as we went along. We retained him as a consultant after the plan was adopted and consulted with him five or six times, until he told Don and me that we could do this as well as he did.

The major change made in the original structure of COEMAR was to abolish the two divisions of Ecumenical Mission and Ecumenical Relations. They had proved to be cumbersome and, moreover, in keeping them we were saying something we did not mean to say—that Relations and Mission are different and separate. Executives in Ecumenical Relations encouraged study and activities as though they were confined to the ecumenical sphere. They expected to be called in by the regional secretaries for that purpose, which left the regional secretaries acting as though they were not responsible for Ecumenical Relations. We now designated all executives as being responsible for both. We had needed the functional thrust at the beginning to get us started, but experience had educated us to see that we could do this together with resources available for both as needed.

One of the new features in COEMAR from the beginning was a Study Secretary. We started with Paul Verghese, an Orthodox priest from India who was studying at Yale and available to us for three months in the summer. We already knew that the new United Presbyterian Church was at work in Egypt, the Sudan, Ethiopia, Lebanon, Syria, Iran, and India, all countries where what we have come to call the Oriental Orthodox Christian churches are historically located. We all needed to know much more about them as we now met them in ecumenical relations. Later Harold Viehman was with us for two years, followed by Harold Nebelsick, a furloughed theological professor, and then by Margrethe Brown, who had European theological training. We expected the office to follow ecumenical studies and keep us informed, to alert seminaries to material for study, and to inspire executives and missionaries to study on their own. Personally I soon found that I was doing more reading of books in this area than I had done before I became General Secretary.

Salaries

In the old Board of Foreign Missions many of us had been disturbed by the differences between missionary salaries and Board executive salaries in New York. Missionaries all got the same basic subsistence salary plus housing, medical benefits, and allowances for children. The day Floy and I first landed in Japan we began getting the same basic salary as all other Presbyterian missionaries. Adjustments were made by the Board on the basis of different costs of living in other countries. At the same time, those who became executives received higher salaries, although they often were lower than the salaries in other agencies of the church.

The studies we were now making in management also gave us the opportunity to make changes in the salary scale. We had the help of a nonprofit consulting firm as we worked this out.

The base of all salaries, missionary and executive, became the median salary of ministers in the United States, as furnished annually by the Pension Board. Young people began with 90 percent of the median and were increased by 5 percent every five years up to 115 percent. Housing and medical insurance were provided, but no children's allowances except for possible scholarships in higher education. Cost-of-living adjustments were made between countries on the basis of Government statistics in State Department reports. All this improved the relationships of missionaries to their colleagues in American churches.

We then turned to executive salaries. The General Council had adopted a uniform classification for the executives of all agencies. This also provided high and low salary limits for all classifications. Working within these limits we applied much the same process for setting executive salaries as we had done for missionaries. After one or two years we found that in comparison with the other agencies COEMAR had the highest low salaries, the lowest high salaries, and the highest median salary. In addition we now had a rational explanation for the remaining differences in salaries between us and the missionaries. The details of the salary plan were known to all and we had diminished the discussion of salaries to a bare minimum. It became another feature of our collegiate administration.

Communications

From the beginning we had emphasized in the staff our being together. We continued to guard carefully the 9 to 9:15 A.M. period every working morning for a prayer service in the Leber Room. It was for executives and all other staff. It was not compulsory but we all knew it was there.

We also shared mountains of memoranda, beginning with the General Secretary's Office. I still wrote memos on my trips and meetings, sometimes reporting on actions as they were being taken. I could no longer write to Charlie but I wrote to

Don and Margaret, and to Dan Pattison, our treasurer—all members of the General Secretary's Office. The more important of these memos were shared with the staff and Commission members.

I wrote a letter after every Commission meeting to Commission representatives overseas and to absent Commission members. I had the help of John Corbin and Winburn Thomas for part of this, and soon after had help from Archie Crouch, whom we brought from the San Francisco office to head up Literature and Publications. He and I started the "Dear Colleague" letters which were printed and sent four or five times a year to all missionaries, Commission members, and synod and presbytery executives. We claimed the latter as part of our staff for interpretation.

We also brought all furloughed missionaries and staff and as many Commission members as possible to a conference every summer. We did it in three different places the first year, but then turned to a Chicago location for one single conference of several days' length. We planned carefully to make this important and relevant to all who participated in all that we were doing.

Purpose

At a staff conference at Stony Point, Frank Martin again put the question, "Why are we in business?"—this time to me privately. I told him I thought our staff knew, having in mind the statement we had made at Lake Mohonk on Christian mission, revising it from "foreign missions" so that it included our related churches overseas. He told me then that he would ask the staff members individually that day, "Why are you in business?" He did so, and that day at dinner he told me the results. He convinced me I might be wrong. I called a meeting for the evening and we all decided we did not have a clear common purpose. What we had did not fit COEMAR, though its wording in some mission situations was still valid.

So we began a long process, involving all members of both staff and Commission, with a joint committee to supervise the process. We revised the Christian mission statement and then added our responsibilities in "relations." As COEMAR, we found we had to begin by first stating the purpose of the church. We used the statement of "The Great Ends of the Church" as a beginning, and then added some paragraphs on reconciliation from the Confession of '67, which was in process of formulation at the time. Everyone joined in. At several points I still can name the person who suggested the exact word that we chose to use. I consider it, along with the Advisory Study, as the greatest contribution that COEMAR made to the United Presbyterian Church and to the wider Christian community. Here is the final wording as adopted in 1967:

The Commission on Ecumenical Mission and Relations is an agency of the United Presbyterian Church which, as a member of the one Holy Catholic Church, is empowered by the Holy Spirit to go into the world:
    —to make Jesus Christ known to all men as fellow man and divine Lord and Savior;
    —to enter into the common life of men, sharing their aspirations and sufferings, striving against inhumanity, and healing the enmities which separate them from God and from each other;
    —to encourage all men to become Christ's disciples and responsible members of His Church.

We proceeded to use this statement in many ways. It was an interpretation piece; it was on the table when we interviewed candidates for missionary and executive service; and one year we used it as an outline for our budget, checking how we were spending our money against what we had set out to do. This was extremely good for us. I recommend it.

The Advisory Study

We had not planned it that way, but our study of management had led us to begin our study of purpose, and this now accompanied the Advisory Study.

As I reread the memo that I wrote in January 1959, which was used in establishing issues for the Advisory Study, I asked myself the question, "If we did so well in stating the issues, why did we not proceed on our own to get the answers?" We did not ask ourselves that question. We might have gotten most of the answers ourselves, but that was not the point. We were no longer in that kind of game. If we wanted our related churches overseas to study the issues and come to answers themselves, we could not begin by our stating the issues and suggesting the answers for them as well. That day in mission was gone forever. We were one body, one family, and we must together state the issues and together seek the answers.

So from the very beginning the Advisory Study Committee was planned as independent of the Commission. It had a qualified Asian Christian as chairman. It had a secretary who had been an executive overseas for the Commission. Of the fourteen other members three were Commission members, two were missionaries, and the other nine were men and women who were leaders in related churches in other parts of the world. We had made sure that the thinking in this study would not be dominated by those who had called for the study. The complete membership was as follows:

C. H. Hwang, chairman (Taiwan), Catherine Alexander (Iran), Mrs. Howard Black (United States), Rafael Cepeda (Cuba), Esdras Borges Costa (Brazil), Robert Gibson (United States), Francis Ibiam (Nigeria), Richard Davies (United States), Fayez Fares (Egypt), Wadad Jeha (Lebanon), Pyung-Kan Koh (Korea), Philippe Maury (Switzerland), Matthew Ogawa (Japan), Richard Shaull (Brazil), W. S. Theophilus (India), and Glenn Reed, executive secretary (United States).

The committee had three full meetings, the first in 1960 at Stony Point, New York, the second in the late spring of 1961 at Asmara, Ethiopia, and the third near Chicago in September 1961. On the way to and from these meetings the members of the committee visited various churches related to us, two or three of them taking assignments that were set up by the whole committee. At Asmara they met in conjunction with a meeting of sixteen Commission representatives and tried out some of their conclusions before they wrote their final report. COE-MAR in no way determined their assignments or the items on their agenda. We had insisted that the committee be competent but also that it should be free.

That September we were meeting at McCormick Seminary both in a furlough conference and as a Commission. The report, entitled *An Advisory Study*, was ready in mimeographed form and became the major item on the agenda of both groups. It was approximately one hundred pages long.

After a reasonably thorough reading and discussion, one of the officers of COEMAR moved that we adopt the Advisory Study as our own and begin to implement its recommendations. This would have been disastrous, for it would have meant that COEMAR was imposing its own conclusions on all our sister churches. The motion was withdrawn and a substitute motion accepted the report for study by COEMAR and by our sister churches as a basis for making plans for the future. *It was an Advisory Study.*

The report was of such a nature that it lent itself to such study. To quote from the report itself: "The first unanimous conviction to emerge within the committee concerned involvement of the 'related' churches in study of the nature and mission of the church in our time." And again: "The mind of Christ, as revealed in Scripture, in past and current history, and the contemporary experience of the ecumenical church, can be known only by those who diligently seek to know."

The Commission's reaction to the report was encouraging. In addition, others in similar mission agencies were impressed. Some of the comments were as follows. One called it "an extraordinarily valuable report." Another said it was "the most effective of all such studies." A third person remarked: "It contains more sharpened and more decisive thinking than I've seen anywhere else." Dr. Kenneth Scott Latourette of Yale said that the Advisory Study's first section on theology was "the best brief statement of mission theology" he had ever read.

None of us believed that such study would be easy. The first section of the report dealt with Biblical and theological truth in a fresh way, but still at considerable depth. The second section dealt with the situation at that time, and the third dealt with the problems we faced in our plans for the future. These last were easier, but we were warned by the Advisory Study Committee itself that the Biblical and theological basis was its own starting point, and that the rest could best be studied after digesting the first.

I was impressed especially by two things. At its first meeting in Stony Point, the committee had started with Col. 1:14–20 (NEB):

He is the image of the invisible God; his is the primacy over all created things. In him everything in heaven and on earth was created, not only things visible but also the invisible orders of thrones, sovereignties, authorities, and powers: the whole universe has been created through him and for him. And he exists before everything, and all things are held together in him. He is, moreover, the head of the body, the church. He is its origin, the first to return from the dead, to be in all things alone supreme. For in him the complete being of God, by God's own choice, came to dwell. Through him God chose to reconcile the whole universe to himself, making peace through the shedding of his blood upon the cross—to reconcile all things, whether on earth or in heaven, through him alone.

I took this to mean that once the Christian assumes that this is the starting point, then the need to share this faith with the world follows naturally.

The second thing was the explanation of the report that all people live within circles (*oikoi*, houses, environments) with other people. They may participate in various circles—family, community, church, nation, and universe. The Christian's business is to live in each circle as a Christian. If it is a circle of Christians, then we have the assurance that God will give the gifts of the Spirit that will enable them to be witnesses in their time and place.

I was quoted as saying that I thought this last was the key to the report. If these gifts are recognized, cultivated, and used, they will be adequate. The church is not an institution or a bureaucracy, but a living thing. We are a worshiping community meant to be witnesses wherever we are.

Such ideas could stimulate churches abroad and in the United States to a new sense of their responsibility under God. We must study this together now and ask him to lead us.

Follow-Up of the Advisory Study

Planning for this study was the most complicated thing I have ever been involved in. We printed the report and sent it to all missionaries, related churches, commissioners of General Assembly, etc. But little would happen just by distribution.

We began at home. The Commission studied it and individuals reported on what they found. Some said this could remake their own churches. Staff studied it. The report did not deal with all the practical things that we faced, but it did deal with many of them, and we set up a task force for each major item. What does this mean for the way we help with money? How do institutions fit into this picture? How can seminary students be trained for this at home and abroad? What does this say about our relationship with the Orthodox churches, with Roman Catholics, with conservative evangelicals? How can candidates best be recruited, trained, and used? What is the place of COEMAR in all this, and how do we avoid the mistakes?

Participating in the study with sister churches was more complicated. In many instances it involved mission agencies of other denominations in the United States and in Europe, even in Australia. We solicited Presbyterian U.S. cooperation and together studied the Advisory Study report in a Latin-American meeting of churches. In Africa we involved the World Presbyterian Alliance and the All Africa Conference of Churches in a study consultation.

Asia offered the most complex situation. But the East Asia Christian Conference was holding a preliminary consultation at Bangalore just before the World Council of Churches Assembly at New Delhi in December 1961. I attended and listened as they planned Situation Conferences at three places in Asia for early 1963, which all churches would be invited to attend for study. The issues were the same in most cases and, after all, Shoki Hwang was an Asian. The Advisory Study became one of the documents for the Situation Conferences, and I attended all of them. We profited from the fact that the Advisory Study was already well known by reputation. Translations were made in a selected number of languages. This action at Bangalore was based on the value of the Study itself and not at our request. Bishop Newbigin and others considered it the best that they had seen. Let me quote from D. T. Niles's summary of what we all hoped to get done in the Situation Conferences.

We want churches in Asia and related mission agencies to look together at:
1. Frontiers we must hold against attack.
2. Growing edges of the church which we must strengthen.
3. Things we are doing which should be got rid of.
4. New things we should be doing.
Then we should look at how best to use all the resources we have in order to get these things done.

The nitty-gritty, of course, was the effect of this study on the things that were being planned by related churches and ourselves. We pushed it down to this level at every opportunity. For example, at the World Council Assembly in New Delhi I had about one hundred copies of the report with me. For at least one or two meals a day I invited representatives of related churches to sit with me and talk about the Advisory Study. I informed them we were studying it and then hoped to talk with them about what they thought. No one can judge the final result. I'm sure that some ideas got across and that at points it made a significant difference.

One place where we failed was in the United States. Many COEMAR members believed the Study would help American churches. We advertised it at the General Assembly and gave every member a copy. As far as I know nothing happened, except where some member of COEMAR got busy on it. I showed the Study to another General Secretary of a Presbyterian agency and asked him later what he had gotten out of it. His reply was that these things might be significant overseas but were of little or no value in the United States! Whether he ever read it or not I do not know. Recently a former Secretary of another agency at that time told us the Advisory Study was one of the best documents the church ever produced.

In the mid 1960s many parts of the church got involved in long-range planning under the auspices of the General Council. Because of the Advisory Study and the insistence of Frank Martin that we state our purpose, we were a step or two ahead of the others in long-range planning. One of our Commission members was a planner and he recruited others for a committee and helped train a staff member for us. The study was done well and was published in 1967. We included our statement of purpose and objectives. They showed the force of the Purpose to guide us in the "middle axioms" that governed. We had already selected seven objectives upon which we would give priority emphasis in the next year's program.

One must remember that alongside this study in COEMAR and in other parts of the church, a General Assembly committee was working on the Confession of '67. I consider the latter a remarkable document that freshens the articulation of our faith. There are times when we need to do this for ourselves and not remain locked in the statements of the past.

Any student of these materials will soon note some similarity between the Confession and COEMAR's purpose. We did not write our purpose because of the Confession, nor did the committee write the Confession to suit our purpose. I believe it was the result of the Holy Spirit speaking to all of us through the things we were studying. God in his providence was preparing us to stay together and work together in the days of the '60s, which were to bring the challenge of change in so many directions.

Throughout 1963 and beyond, our major COEMAR concern continued to be the follow-up of the Advisory Study. During the year, we completed our conferences by regions and began the bilateral conferences in each country. Don Black prepared a brief statement on the Advisory Study which proved to be very useful. He and other staff members participated in conferences in Africa and Latin America.

I spoke to the Pre-Assembly on Mission and Evangelism in the Presbyterian Church U.S. and to the General Assembly of our own church. Among other things I said:

> By far the most important single thing in which we have been engaged has been the follow-up of *An Advisory Study*. You will remember that the report itself is ninety-four pages long and is a working paper on the policies and program of COEMAR, prepared by fifteen people, most of them from outside the United States.
>
> Let me now report that 12,000 copies of this book in English have been distributed, some of them given away but most of them sold. In addition it has been translated into Arabic, Chinese, French, Japanese, Persian, Spanish, and Thai. Portuguese, Amharic, Urdu, and Korean translations are in process.
>
> The extent of distribution and sale outside our own church has been phenomenal. In the United States, organizations that have bought anywhere from 30 to 285 copies include the National Council of Churches, American Bible Society, Presbyterian Church U.S., Reformed Church in America, Evangelical United Brethren, Disciples of Christ, United Church of Christ, American Baptist Convention, and the Episcopal, Methodist, Brethren, Mennonite, and Lutheran Churches.
>
> In Canada the United Church, the Presbyterian Church, and the Anglican Church have bought copies. And in similar manner churches have bought considerable numbers in Great Britain, New Zealand, Australia, the Dominican Republic, British Guiana, India, Indonesia, Taiwan, Malaya, the Philippines, South Africa, and the Netherlands.
>
> The World Council of Churches, the Lutheran World Federation, the East Asia Christian Conference, and the All Africa Conference of Churches have used the Study in quantity.
>
> We ourselves have just completed regional conferences on

this Study in Latin America, Africa, the Middle East, Asia.

We are now faced with the crux of the matter. Next Monday, the 27th of May, we begin in Beirut the first of a series of country-by-country consultations in which the total program in which we participate will be looked at in the light of our common study.

The Advisory Study has taught us to focus on the central question for all the churches in our time. For the last hundred years the critical question has been concerning the vitality of the foreign missionary movement. The growth and strength of the Christian movement around the world depended primarily upon the recruiting and support of Western missionaries. At General Assembly in such occasions as this, we were likely to say that the future of the church depended on more people and more money from America.

Now the critical question has been enlarged. It has become, "Are each of the churches, both younger and older, really witnessing communities, ready to assume responsibility for the mission of the church in their part of the world and to assume their part of the responsibility for the unfinished task to the ends of the earth?" This is now the basic question for all of us. It is followed by still other questions:

What is the purpose of the church as a witnessing community?

How can the congregation best be structured?

Is the minister alone the driver of the bus which is the church?

Are the laymen at best only back-seat drivers?

How can missionaries and their money best be used?

Where are the growing edges of the church?

What kinds of things should the church give up in order to be free to support the growing edge?

Where should denominations cease, and we begin to do things together as one people of God?

These are thought questions, and the answers will be hard to arrive at. But we assure you that it is our intention and the intention of the churches with which we are related to ask them now in every country where we participate. There will be difficulties, we will doubtless have some failures to report, but the result ought to be a fresh look at all we are doing and a release of energy for the central task of the church.

This study has also driven home to us that the issues

raised in the Advisory Study are the same issues which churches in the United States must also face. May God help us all.

The Advisory Study, within a short time, began to prove the wisdom of its insights and its directions. Let us turn now to the Christians of Asia to garner proof that our study and labor were not in vain.

Situation Conferences

On April 17, 1963, I was able to report that I had attended five conferences held outside the United States. Three of the conferences were Situation Conferences, following one another successfully: Madras, Amagisanso in Japan, and Singapore— all held under the auspices of the East Asia Christian Conference. Each conference lasted seven full days and the pattern was very similar in each. Between 65 and 75 grass-roots representatives of the East Asian Churches were present and were active and generous in sharing their views and sometimes their grievances. At each conference there was a sprinkling of celebrities such as Lesslie Newbigin, Leslie Cooke, D. T. Niles, Alan Brash, Ronald Orchard, and Hans Margull representing both the World Council and the East Asia Christian Conference. For the most part the participants came to the conferences well prepared, having studied and pondered the questions sent to them from the committee. At the same time they came prepared to present their respective points of view, each group mindful of its own environment and cultural, social, political, and economic conditions, as well as the particular kind of Protestantism which had been imposed from abroad. The following paragraphs from my notes convey something of the impact of the conferences:

> The leaders of the Christian church in Asia are realistic about the evils of their dependence upon foreign money. . . . A Lutheran pastor whose funds were cut off from Germany by the war in 1940 stated that this experience was a blessing and the major source of the church's strength today. He then turned to me and said: "I ask you to make us suffer. It will be good for us."
> The Christian leaders also are sensitive as to the burden of

institutions, not because institutions are wrong, but because they often distract the attention of the church from its major task. Several of the Asians are saying: "You set us free to do as we please, but you left us a pattern we cannot break. You will have to help us break the pattern."

Yasuji Ichikawa, pastor in Osaka, . . . stressed self-support. He closed with this illustration. A young pastor who had been a member of his church became pastor of a small but old church. It had about 100 members who gave on the average of 50 yen each month (less than fifteen cents). They had been helped for a long time by the United Church and by the offerings of a missionary who lived in the community. Their only suggestion to the young pastor was that he might not need all of the old manse and part could be rented to help pay his salary. The young pastor began by telling them the minimum offering should be 500 yen (ten times the old standard). Then he shocked everybody by telling the missionary he should give his offering somewhere else. After two years of hard work the church became independent and had a healthy life.

The first of the eight questions which the Advisory Study had submitted was to this effect: "What are the positions on the frontier which must be held at all costs?" Our Asian Christians had difficulty with the question and rejected the terms "positions," "frontier," and "at all costs." They recast the question to read, "What are the things which a church must be free to have if it is to be missionary?" And to this question they answered, "We must be free to worship, to belong to the body of Christ, proclaim the gospel that people may believe for themselves, establish homes, train children, strengthen one another, support all people, and make Christ relevant to all of life." My notes continued:

Shoki Hwang [speaking in Japan] thinks that we ought also to have a conference in Northeast Asia that will include Formosa, Japan, and Korea on theological education, bringing together the presidents of seminaries . . . and really spending some time in looking at the problem of theological education.

Bishop John Daly, an Anglican from Korea, is here as chaplain. He assisted in the [Holy Communion] service and invited all to partake. But he also announced that since this is

Lent there will be an Anglican Communion service every morning at 6:30. He continues to say that all are invited to [audit] these services but he had no authority to invite other Anglicans to partake. [All of which obliges me to ponder, who gave the authority to include us at the Lord's Table at one time and exclude us at another? What a curse our confessionalism, our denominational structure can brew!]

The Madras conference discussed four areas which did not come to the serious attention of the conference in Tokyo. I am not critical of the conference in Tokyo, because at certain points it was not ready to discuss these four areas, and because it made such progress in other affairs that the loss need not be serious.

The first area was a question of institutions. The Madras conference made some statements about the relationship of churches to institutions that should be significant for us in our study in any one of the countries across the world with which we are specifically related. The question of institutions in Japan is not at the same stage, nor is this question in fact at the same stage in any of the countries that were represented here. There was no similarity of approach to the problem in any case.

The second area was the area of confessionalism. This was introduced into the Tokyo conference but never was seriously faced. Madras faced it, and made a separate statement, but this was probably because it had more time, since there was no need to become acquainted with one another, no need to make statements as to the actual situation in each of the countries, and no need to hear lectures on various subjects.

Madras did discuss the question of missionaries and the pastoral care of missionaries. Tokyo did not face this. I suspect that this was because the churches were getting acquainted with the other churches and thus were self-conscious about discussing funds and personnel from abroad when they were posing as independent and sovereign churches in their own right. This was not done consciously, but I wonder if this is not the explanation that arose out of an unconscious inclination. EACC is taking this question seriously and is inviting a group to come together at Rangoon at the second Assembly, to be held in March 1964, at which time they will talk together about missionaries and the frustrations that they face. They expect to invite a selected list of younger missionaries, who are going through these experiences, and expose the problem to the leaders of the churches who will be brought together for this consultation.

In Madras we discussed the necessity of mission agencies taking more initiative in relation to matters in that part of the world. Tokyo did not discuss this question. It was mentioned once or twice, but people went on from there without seriously looking at it.

This conference already reveals the evidence of vitality in the Indonesian Church. It has been handicapped by the language barrier . . . and it has been handicapped by lack of university education. Both of these are being overcome and 3,000,000 "Reformed Churchmen in Indonesia will be heard from."

In Indonesia it was again evident that we are at the most critical period in the modern history of the church. The missionary movement has conceived of the mission of the church as an extension of the base from Europe and North America into Asia, Africa, and Latin America. That day is at an end and we are glad of it. Now the mission of the church belongs to all of us together. . . . The basic question is, "Are the churches in the East and the West themselves really missionary communities capable of carrying on the mission in their own areas, and to the ends of the earth?" Putting it another way, the question becomes, "Are Christian communities in our countries vital and flexible enough to carry on the mission in the world of our time?"

One of the most interesting men here is Major General T. B. Simatupang, who is only a little over forty and is a retired general of the Indonesian Army and on the staff of the Indonesian Council of Churches. He was a leader in the revolution against the Netherlands and recently was chief of staff. He now is giving most of his time to the church. He is able and vigorous, reads Barth and Niebuhr, and uses German theological terms. He is a symbol of the Indonesian church's emerging importance. General Simatupang said, "In Indonesia we are not a ghetto Christian community. We have fought for our freedom and our Christian dead are buried alongside all others in our military cemeteries."

One of the most searching of questions confronted us again and again in the East Asia conferences: "Where is Jesus?" Jesus is, to be sure, present in his body the church. But is he present in other religions? And does he make himself known outside and beyond the embrace of religious structures or organizations? In response to this question there were many and ever-conflicting opinions.

D. T. Niles was convinced that Christian mission in its ecumenical dimensions "moves toward an end, a predetermined end. It is prolonged but is going somewhere. Christ will come in glory. But until the Kingdom comes we have the task of being involved with him. . . . We show forth the Lord's death till he come."

Conference on Confessionalism

As a direct result of the Situation Conferences in Asia a conference was held in Geneva in October 1963 on the issue of "Confessionalism" that had risen in Asia. What Asia means by confessionalism might better be called "worldwide denominationalism," particularly as expressed through worldwide denominational organizations.

There were thirty-five delegates present at the Geneva conference, with every major group represented. Shoki Hwang led off and D. T. Niles supported him. They particularly attacked confessionalism because it has produced churches that are divided, and also because their denominational relationships on a world scale sometimes effectively prevent their joining other Christian churches in their own countries in church union efforts, or in most common efforts to support programs. Their loyalty to the world denomination prevents their coming closer to their own Christian neighbors.

Lutherans and Anglicans often lead the way in this, but all of us are tempted to do this at times. When an interdenominational challenge comes we cannot find the money to participate, but when the same thing is proposed on a denominational basis we somehow manage to find the money. Niles called this confusing the bloodstream in the body of Christ. He pleaded that the bloodstreams that are growing in younger churches in a given area, as they seek to become the body of Christ, be allowed freedom and not be hampered by restrictions from outside.

At that conference, I think, the case was adequately presented. In the long run, however, the decision must be made on the basis of the urgency of the things that we do together.

My appreciation of the Presbyterian approach to this was enhanced. We do have a world fellowship of Reformed churches. It is stimulating both in fellowship and study of our heritage, but it does not take the place of the wider ecumenical fellowship. It means very much to younger churches who are not ready for the wider fellowship, and it preserves the particular contribution that all can make to the wider fellowship. Thus far we have succeeded in resisting the temptation to become more than that. It was true once and may still be true that wherever there is a United Church and Congregationalists and Presbyterians are in that country, most of them are in the United Church.

The Timeliness of the Advisory Study

The end of the colonial era was traumatic for many. Even some Western Christians thought that it was also the end of the missionary movement. Some said that with the end of colonialism in Africa the African churches would also suffer, because Christianity was the colonial religion and could now be discarded.

Both Catholic and Protestant statisticians soon had an answer for that. They told us that in 1900, 85 percent of all Christians were still in Europe and North America and only 15 percent in Asia, Africa, and Latin America. In 1965 the 15 percent in the Third World had grown to 37 percent, and it was estimated that by the end of the century there would be more Christians in the Third World than in the West. Among the reasons for this prediction was the steady growth of the churches in Africa.

At the same time, because of population growth, there were now more people than ever in the world who did not know Jesus Christ. The task was still there with all its urgency. The difference was that God had provided more Christians for the worldwide task.

The wide use of the Advisory Study indicated that both the older and the younger churches were beginning to face this challenge together.

Chapter 10

The World Council of Churches

FOR THE Commission on Ecumenical Mission and Relations (COEMAR) a major responsibility in Relations was the United Presbyterian connection with the World Council of Churches. We nominated to our own General Assembly those who should represent us at WCC Assemblies. We had to clear the names of those people in our church whom the WCC wanted for service, and we interpreted the WCC to our constituency. It was a new experience for most of us—all but Ralph Lloyd and Gene Blake, who had been members of the WCC Central Committee since 1954. For most of the rest of us, our first exposure was through the International Missionary Council and its plan to become part of the World Council of Churches.

Edinburgh, 1960: Church and Mission Reunited

The 1910 World Missionary Conference at Edinburgh had been the seedbed for the International Missionary Council. It was also the seedbed for the Faith and Order movement and the Life and Work movement, which decided in 1937 to merge and create the World Council of Churches. It was natural for both IMC and WCC to celebrate the 50th anniversary at Edinburgh in 1960. The celebration was preceded by meetings of the WCC Central Committee and the IMC Administrative Committee, both of which met at St. Andrews, Scotland. Ralph Lloyd, Gene Blake, John Mackay, and Pitt Van Dusen were among those present. It was especially helpful to have Dr.

Mackay along, both as the former chairman of the IMC and as a Scotsman in his own right.

I had seen the WCC Central Committee in action for a day at a meeting in New Haven a year or so before, but this was my first view of the longer session. My chief participation, however, was in the IMC. We had had an ad hoc committee to prepare for merger and it met first. Then came the Administrative Committee itself. In addition to IMC members, there were several members from the WCC committee on Evangelism. This was to be the Division of World Mission and Evangelism, which emphasized the fact that its program would be directed to all countries and all member churches.

We soon found that there was to be some foot-dragging, this time primarily from the British Isles. It started first on money. British churches could not contribute much and did not want a budget in which they could not carry their share. The treasurer was from Great Britain and he proposed that the budget be limited to that approved at Ghana by the IMC in 1957 and held at that level until the next Assembly on Mission, which would not occur until 1963. A new division of the WCC would hardly thrive on that. The motion was defeated. The next question was the location of the office and the home of the Secretary. It was then in England and it was proposed that it stay there. It was cheaper than Geneva and the officers could fly to Geneva for meetings. The ad hoc committee was split down the middle on this one. I then raised the question about whether we could decide where a main office and the residence of the Associate General Secretary of the WCC should be. The WCC should see to that. We therefore registered a majority for Geneva and left it to the WCC to decide. This kind of discussion led some to say we were moving forward grudgingly. But when the final decision came in the Administrative Committee it came with fitting seriousness and the knowledge that we were participating in a historic decision.

The final vote on integration with WCC came on August 15 in the morning. There were three final speeches, one by a Church World Service man raising some questions but accepting, one by Bishop Chandu Ray welcoming the action for Asia, and one by Visser 't Hooft stating that this action will help to keep the WCC straight. Unity must be for mission. The vote was unanimous and John Mackay led in prayer.

The anniversary celebration in Edinburgh was impressive. It was in St. Giles' Cathedral with the fanfare of trumpets and the presence of the city dignitaries, as well as addresses by several IMC and WCC leaders. The reception at the castle where the Queen stays when in Scotland was also impressive.

The meetings lasted all of three weeks and I remember most of all the new friends that I made. I saw and talked with my first two members of the Secretariat for the Promotion of Christian Unity at the Vatican. And on several occasions I talked with Father Makari of the Coptic Orthodox Church in Egypt. Dr. Mackay introduced me to him, for he had been a student at Princeton. We talked about many things, including our relationships in Egypt. He later became Bishop Samuel, and then acting Patriarch of the Orthodox Church, and still never forgot the things he learned at Princeton about the West. (In 1981 Bishop Samuel was assassinated along with President Sadat in Egypt.)

Some of us roomed in a dormitory that overlooked the clubhouse and the first hole of the St. Andrews Golf Course. A few played some golf on the main course. There was also a putting course, and one evening four of us played nine holes there. I made a hole in one. I liked to tell the story, naming two of my Japanese friends and a Secretary at the WCC who made up the foursome. Then I would add, "I made a hole in one at St. Andrews"—and, after a pause—"on the putting course."

Asmara, 1961

Our relationship with the Orthodox developed naturally because of our relationship with them in the Middle East. At Asmara, Ethiopia, in the spring of 1961 it became evident that the Commission representatives believed that COEMAR had a special challenge in regard to the Oriental Orthodox. Strictly speaking they were not Eastern Orthodox, i.e., those who respected the Ecumenical Patriarch at Constantinople as supreme. They had separated after Chalcedon and the breach had never been fully healed. The theological difference, however, was no longer greatly significant. The difference was cultural as much as anything. The Eastern Orthodox were in Europe primarily, with some refugees in the Middle East. The Oriental Orthodox were in Egypt, Ethiopia, the Middle East, and India. In at least four countries we also were present as a missionary group.

Our people had often regarded them as superstitious and fit objects for evangelism. The Orthodox regarded us as proselytizers. There was no love lost between us. But now we were all members together in the World Council, and the former mission agency had become the agency of relationship with the WCC and all of its members. This was the place where our new Christian responsibility began. Paul Verghese had helped us at the beginning. Now Hal Viehman was leading us. Kyoji Buma, through the Youth Department of the World Council, got the first opportunity to break the ice in Ethiopia. He had had a work camp experience in Addis Ababa with some Ethiopian theological students and they had given him a recording of their Eucharistic service in Geez, the ancient language of the country. He found that the Swarthmore, Pennsylvania, Presbyterian Church choir director appreciated the music. When they learned I was going to Ethiopia in early 1961, they had me come to preach at a Communion service, recorded the music, and sent copies of the music with the recording along with me to give to the abuna or archbishop of the church. Glenn Reed supervised my plans. I went up from Asmara to Addis Ababa for a day or two during our meetings with the Advisory Study Committee. That evening in a meeting with missionaries, someone asked me if I was going to see the Abuna. I inquired why they asked and the answer was, "Everyone wants to see the Abuna now. They do not want to see us." I asked them what they would think if a friend of theirs came to see the Abuna and never called on them. They would not like it. I had met the Abuna. He was a fellow member of the WCC. I would make an appointment now and come back later to keep it, but a missionary and an Ethiopian Presbyterian must go with me. It worked out that way and the gift of music was delivered. Kyoji had taken the first step. I now took the second. At New Delhi and later we went farther. Glenn Reed was a good go-between in this, as was Norman Horner later. We learned a great deal about the Oriental Orthodox and, although we often did not agree with them, we came to regard them as fellow Christians and to work with them on projects. In Ethiopia we even worked at evangelism; all who were baptized became members of the Orthodox Church. We also helped train students at the seminary in Addis Ababa. Our major work was in the primitive areas in the interior, so that geographic competition was not always present.

New Delhi, 1961

December 1961 was the date of the Third Assembly of the WCC, held at New Delhi, India. In WCC Assemblies all member churches—now more than three hundred—are represented. Delegates are chosen by the churches themselves, and the number for each is in proportion to the size of the church. The United Presbyterian Church U.S.A. had fifteen at New Delhi. There were also observers, accredited visitors, and members of the press present. Study papers were sent out ahead of time. The theme of this Assembly was "Jesus Christ— the Light of the World." Instructions for Bible study were also supplied as preparation went ahead. Thus all those who came had been prepared after a fashion to understand and participate.

Bible study began in small groups but was extended also into the plenary sessions. Every delegate was assigned to a section for Bible study and for reports on various business.

Most delegates had arrived a day or two ahead of time and were prepared for the first session, which was a formal worship service with the delegates coming from all over the world.

The first morning I stood at a window on the second floor of the Vigyan Bhavan and watched below as the first half of the procession slowly moved into the great tent where the opening service was about to begin. The delegates who watched with me remarked that probably I was not moved as much as they, since I had attended such services before, but they were wrong. Such a scene never fails to move me.

The procession moved by countries—Australia, Brazil, Cuba, France, Germany, etc. One recognized personal friends among them of various denominations, of different races, in colorful robes and in business suits. One by one they added to the completeness of the world Christian community.

And then those of us on the second floor began to move— delegates from India, Japan, Korea, the Philippines, the United Kingdom, the United States of America, and the Union of Soviet Socialist Republics. Perhaps it had special significance that these last two brought up the rear and moved into the service together.

That afternoon the Assembly continued with opening addresses by Bishop Lesslie Newbigin and Dr. Visser 't Hooft, and would continue for almost three weeks. The three sub-themes of Witness, Service, and Unity would be fully discussed.

In such a setting, the reading of the Scriptures, the prayers, the reciting of the Creed, and the singing of the hymns took on new significance. Two that were particularly meaningful to me were these:

> O come, O come, Emmanuel,
> And ransom captive Israel,
> That mourns in lonely exile here
> Until the Son of God appear.
> Rejoice! Rejoice! Emmanuel
> Shall come to thee, O Israel!

> Jesus shall reign wher-e'er the sun
> Does his successive journeys run;
> His Kingdom stretch from shore to shore,
> Till moons shall wax and wane no more.

Thus began the first Assembly to be held in a land where other religions dominate, and the first Assembly to include the mission of the church at its heart.

I have already reported that at New Delhi I spent my free time discussing the Advisory Study report, entitled *An Advisory Study*, with leaders of our related churches. I distributed or promised to send at least three hundred copies for study. Our request for study was reinforced by the fact that the only statement on the cover in addition to the title was "A Working Paper for Study, not to be interpreted as the Policy of the Commission."

One free evening we invited the full delegation of the Ethiopian Orthodox Church to dinner with our delegation. We had a private dining room and were careful to observe protocol. Nevertheless, it was what the Japanese would call a "warm meeting," meaning warm in fellowship if not in temperature. The spirit of the meeting was to support our relationship for many years to come.

For the purposes of the merging of the International Missionary Council with the Evangelism committee of WCC as the new Division of World Mission and Evangelism of the World Council, the Assembly's section on Witness was of special importance. Our old friend Rajah Manikam of India was chairman. I had been assigned, however, to the section on Service as a secretary and was kept busy with the discussion of Inter-Church Aid. In addition, I was in a small group from the International Missionary Council that informally kept tabs on IMC interests in the merger.

As a delegate for the first time, I was one of those who had to get accustomed to the process followed in the plenary sessions. We were too big an assembly for all to be able to hop up and ask for the floor. Reports were mimeographed and distributed. Then when these were presented by a representative of the committee that prepared them, there was time for questions, discussion, and amendments. However, a delegate who wished to participate had to send up a written statement to the chairman stating who he was, what he wanted to discuss, and whether he wanted to make a motion, and if so, in what form. The chairman would not shut off debate, but he could arrange the persons speaking and the material to be presented in a more orderly fashion.

When the report on the new Division was released I was dissatisfied, not with the new Division itself but with the setting in which it was presented. I wanted to strengthen the statement at the point of its introduction. I was rooming with two other men, and early on the morning of the discussion one of them was leaving before dawn. We all three got up and continued discussing the issue while our friend Kishi got ready to return to Japan. Then Harvey Perkins of Australia and I decided to try to write this out briefly. We chose a place in the first or second paragraph to make an addition by amendment. Here is the full text of the amendment:

The program of the new Division is not here finally described. It will provide a new frontier, a new dimension of the World Council. We have made a general outline of its task. We cannot know or define all its deeper meanings or the extent of its activities. Only the experience of working together can teach us these. Our temptation will be to think of the Division simply as a continuation of the interests of the International Missionary Council, with emphasis on Asia, Africa, and Latin America. We must resist this temptation. This is the Division of World Mission and Evangelism of the World Council of Churches.

We are concerned not with three continents but with six. In cooperation with every department of the World Council, and with the full resources of the Christian community in every land, we would help the churches to confront men and women with the claims of Jesus Christ wherever they live. We now prepare to venture forth. We pray that we shall be sensitive to the leading of the Holy Spirit, as He begins to use the structure that has been created.

That morning I took the sentences to Newbigin, who listened and studied them carefully. Then he said they were good and should be added, but suggested I go to Manikam, who was presenting the report, and see if he would not accept them as an amendment when I presented them. This I did. Manikam agreed and I presented them as an addition which would spell out more clearly what was really intended in the report. Manikam accepted them and they were included. Newbigin picked up these words the next year in his first annual report and they later became part of the theme of the first Division assembly.

No one envies the members of the nominating committee at a WCC Assembly. They are busy far into the night. They are to nominate to the Assembly the six presidents of the WCC and its Central Committee members, all of whom are to serve until the next Assembly, probably seven years. The Central Committee really runs the World Council, its actions being subject to review at each Assembly.

At New Delhi we elected 80 Central Committee members. Since then the number has risen to 120. All the member churches cannot be represented, but denominations and confessions and nationalities and races must be reasonably satisfied. Once a denomination has one or two or more members on the Central Committee, it is hard to reduce that number. Hence the size of the total WCC grows.

Ralph Lloyd and Gene Blake had been our two members because of the positions that they held in the church. Now Ralph's committee was part of COEMAR. Would his place on the Central Committee go to COEMAR, and if so, would it go to a staff member or to a Commission member? I never consulted with anyone and no one consulted me. But the day before the last day, which was the day of elections, Visser 't Hooft stopped me in the hall and asked if I could stay an extra day for the meeting of the Central Committee, to which I was being nominated. I have never asked why, but have always suspected the deciding point was the need for the IMC to be adequately represented on the Committee. I am reasonably sure that Newbigin would push for some of his people. He got three of us on the Committee from mission agencies in the United States—Bishop James K. Mathews, Alford Carleton, and myself.

The Central Committee met briefly and elected Franklin Fry as chairman and Ernest Payne as vice-chairman. They had served since Evanston and were well liked. The only question in the Central Committee was whether we should not reverse the order and make Payne chairman.

Dr. Thimme, later Bishop Thimme, of Germany led the devotional service on the First Sunday in Advent and closed with the description of what was happening in homes in Germany that morning. It was a good description of the Advent wreath and the lighting of the first candle. I was impressed. Coming from the UPNA, which had inherited some of the features of the Covenanters and the Seceders, I had never seen the candle lighted and placed within the wreath.

I had never been in Lebanon and Syria and we stopped there on my way home from Delhi. One day we set out from Beirut by car to go through Damascus up to Homs, where we were to meet leaders of the Protestant community in Syria. On the way we stopped at the desert town of Nebek. There was a Christian hospital there, founded by the Danish Lutherans. It was now part of the work of the Syria-Lebanon church. It was almost dusk when we arrived and it was getting cold. The Arab Christian doctor and one of the Danish nurses met us at the gate and we were taken to see the hospital. Then in the dark we went to the nurses home for tea. We took off our coats in the living room and turned to the dining room, where the table was set. There on the table was the Advent wreath with two candles shining in the darkness.

West Meets East

Bob Cadigan, the editor of *Presbyterian Life*, had said at New Delhi that he was not writing much about the Assembly. He would write later when he had absorbed something of what was said and done. That was true of all of us. Such Assemblies are often too massive and too complex for us to really understand and sort out the important things that are happening. That is especially true for a person who is attending for the first time.

I could understand that it was the first Assembly in Asia, so that our saying that Jesus Christ was the Light of the World had new significance. I could also understand that the instantaneous translation and communications equipment made this the first assembly since Pentecost where when one man spoke, everyone heard him in his own language.

Dr. Kenneth Miller, an old college friend who had been at the first two Assemblies, remarked that "this Assembly was certainly more mature." It was not a "show" where you saw new and curious things. "The excitement of just being together was not sufficient, and people were anxious to talk about the serious things that were common to the Christian faith, wherever people lived."

Increased participation of Asia had begun at Evanston and was continued. But now the voice of Africa was also being heard. In a mature Assembly, however, this means Asia and Africa will have to have something to say. Up to now for a non-Western voice to be raised was unusual. Now it is usual, and more and more all voices will be judged on their merits.

New Delhi was more of an activist Assembly. At Amsterdam, theological debate was the background of the Assembly, often between Europeans. At Evanston the debate was between Europeans and Americans, often over the main theme of the Assembly and its eschatological significance. Here such debate had a secondary place. Asia and Africa joined the Americans in insisting that something must be done in making the Christian faith relevant to the situation in which they live.

New Delhi was not dominated by leaders or great speakers. Its strength lay in its sections and its subcommittees where everyone had a chance to express himself. The result is that many of the best things will be found in the reports, which will need to be "mined" if we are to get the best out of them.

We adopted a new basis of membership, which strengthens the emphasis on the Scriptures and the Trinity and says we "confess" our faith, not just "accept" it.

We approved the admission of the Russian Orthodox Church, with few dissenting votes. This move had been studied seriously and admission meant that we believed they were sincere Christians. Later, in the Central Committee, we had a debate over whether we should admit another church that had less than 10,000 members. One of the Russians commented that a church of less than 10,000 members might very well be a real church with a full understanding of the gospel, and we should be hesitant in excluding such churches lest someday they be the larger churches and the larger churches be the smaller churches!

We also approved the membership of two Pentecostal Churches from Chile. When they were questioned in the press conference as to why they had not come before, they said they had been misinformed. When asked then why they had decided to come now, they said the experience of the WCC relief program in Chile had helped them to understand, and that they then asked questions and learned that they had been misinformed. Then one reporter asked them who it was that had given them the wrong information. Carl McIntire was in the press conference and so the Pentecostal replied, "Everyone in this room knows where we got the misinformation, and everyone in this room knows that that man is present."

During the next two years and more, some of us were kept busy explaining the meaning of all this in several places. For example, I spoke on "The Missionary Movement in the World Council of Churches" to the North American Section of the World Presbyterian Alliance, and later at New Brunswick Seminary and Princeton Seminary. There were times when I felt I was in a bit over my depth, but I carried on. It was not that I knew it all, but I did have a part in it and it was worth sharing. One fact I emphasized over and over again:

> We cannot understand the spread of the Christian church in the last century and a half, from a base in Europe and North America out across the world until it has a foothold in every country, unless we understand that this was also the period in secular history of Western expansion in which Western civilization moved out in discovery and exploration, and sometimes in colonial control. I am not suggesting that the modern missionary movement is simply another expression of Western expansionism, but I am suggesting that in God's providence this period of Western expansion has been used in order that the churches might be stimulated and the gospel might be preached to the ends of the earth.

But that period is over now. The new nations of Asia and Africa may be in disagreement on many things, but they are in agreement on one thing. Colonialism is at an end. The control by the West is at an end. I think it can be said with the same emphasis that the period in which the Christian church can move out from a base in Europe and North America in expansion in Asia, Africa, and Latin America is also at an end. Therefore secular history and church history have already begun to move into a new era. You and I as Christian people will need to examine this situation carefully to discover the framework in which we are now called upon to live and to work.

I am not a prophet or the son of a prophet, but I think I have begun to discern the general outline of the historical era into which we are moving. It is trite to say that we belong to "one world," but it is nevertheless true that in the secular world this is the greatest single new fact of our time. We are one world of interdependent people. It is significant that when we in the United States 185 years ago secured our independence from a colonial government, we immediately asserted our sovereignty by saying that we would have no entangling alliances with any other nation. But now when the nations in Africa secure their independence from colonial government they accompany their assertion of sovereignty by an application for membership in the United Nations. In other words, in our time the symbol of sovereignty and maturity for new nations is their membership in the family of peoples.

These words were written seventeen years ago. Today I would add one comment. The newly independent churches in Africa have flocked to Geneva to apply for membership in the WCC. This is their symbol of maturity. In this and similar ecumenical gatherings, like the Billy Graham-sponsored World Congress on Evangelism at Berlin or the Second Vatican Council at Rome, Christians will meet one another as equals and join in airing plans to work for Christianity in the world. This is no accident. In an interdependent secular world, God has been preparing the instrument of a world community of Christians to carry the responsibility of sharing the Christian message with all people.

Committees Meet in Europe

The first Central Committee meeting after New Delhi was held in the summer of 1962. The time between meetings is twelve or eighteen months, but this time the gap was only eight months. It was preceded by meetings of the Theological Education Committee at Arnoldshain and the Division of World Mission and Evangelism Committee in Paris. Between meetings I visited both East and West Berlin.

The Theological Education Fund was approaching the end of its mandate with the larger share of its work done. A blue-ribbon committee was appointed to study its results and recommend its future. It seemed sure to continue in some form.

The DWME Committee started with a report from the Director, Bishop Newbigin. He began with our much-quoted paragraph. I had been a bit discouraged after New Delhi, but this time I was encouraged. At an early meeting the Division discussed with evident enthusiasm the setting up of a central fund from which we could respond to missionary and evangelistic opportunity in any part of the world without regard to denominational affiliation. It was an old idea, but it had been defeated by the IMC. Virgil Sly and I proposed it now in the light of Inter-Church Aid's ability to reply to physical need. We found support, even from Germany. I wrote back to COEMAR, "I am sure Charlie Leber knows this, as he knew it certainly in anticipation."

Such meetings almost always produce stories. Here is one from Bishop John Sadiq, confirmed from another source by Newbigin:

"A Hindu, who was the head of the India delegation at the peace conference in Moscow three weeks ago, spoke at the last session of the conference along these lines: 'I am a Hindu. I will probably remain a Hindu. At least I will not become a Christian because someone tries to persuade me. But you and I know that the only answer to this problem of peace is in Jesus Christ.' "

Newbigin adds: "An English delegate went up to the Indian and thanked him, saying, 'I'm an ordained clergyman, but I did not have the courage to say that.' "

The report of the DWME Committee to the Central Committee was an encouraging one. There was a freshness about it, an openness to the learning process combined with a commitment to the sharing of Jesus Christ with the whole world by all Christians. It also faced the handicap of a past structure built on the base in the West. The whole report indicated that the Committee was ready to plan a new program related to the rest of WCC and employing the resources of the whole Christian community.

Most Central Committee members were members of subcommittees and had been meeting in Paris as I had been meeting with DWME. We now came together for the larger meeting. In addition to the 80 members and the staff, there were visitors and press—some two or three hundred people all together. It was presided over by Fry and Payne, with one of the six presidents occasionally assisting. Fry was the leader, genial and exact. Payne was the parliamentarian. Forty percent of the membership was new, as new as I was.

One was almost immediately struck with the fact that there was a Council that worshiped and studied together, as well as discussed issues and made decisions. My experience up to then with ecumenical bodies had principally been in the NCC in the United States. By contrast, the NCC did not often worship together or take Communion, its Bible study was for brief worship services only, and its discussion of theological issues was so rare as to seem almost forbidden. I later found that this was intended from the beginning. The NCC was formed in the period when it was believed that action unites and theology divides. The WCC had been born at a different place and a different time. Theology and Bible study together were important and Communion services were always held, even when two or more services were needed to enable all to partake. The differences in NCC were less than in WCC, but WCC overcame them better.

Each Central Committee meeting had a theological theme, with papers and official commentators on the papers. Then there was discussion, reference to committee, and a report. At Paris the theme was "The Finality of Jesus Christ." There were papers by John Marsh and Paul Verghese. The discussion was long and often spilled over into private conversations. It was interesting that no one questioned that Jesus Christ had the final answer. The How was debatable but the Fact was not.

There were reports in Central Committee from its divisional committee, but then the reports and the issues were referred to new committees, where they were examined afresh and recommendations were made for the approval of the Central Committee.

Gene Blake was the chairman of the Committee for Inter-Church Aid, the one with the largest program and budget.

There was great interest in this Central Committee in the fact that it was the first in which the Russian churchmen were participating freely. One of the issues was the admission of the Baptist churches in the Soviet Union. Fellow members from the same country are always consulted. Metropolitan Nikodim was consulted and he spoke highly of the Baptists, saying they were evangelistic and active, sometimes even proselytizing among the Orthodox. He approved their activity among unbelievers, but when they were active among the Orthodox, then he must strengthen the activity of the Orthodox in that area. There was a pause, and then Dr. Fry said, "A bit of free enterprise, eh!" Nikodim joined heartily in the laughter. The Central Committee accepted the invitation received from the Vatican Secretariat for the Promotion of Christian Unity to send one or two observers to the Second Vatican Council. Invitations had gone also to a number of the confessional groups and most had already accepted.

About the only thing I contributed to my first Central Committee meeting was the fact that I happened to be on the steps of the building after dinner one evening and recognized Prince Alexander Desta coming up the steps. He was the favorite grandson of the Emperor of Ethiopia. I introduced him to Visser 't Hooft and he introduced the prince to the committee.

Mission and Evangelism

The first Assembly on World Mission and Evangelism, held under the auspices of the World Council's Division (DWME) was in Mexico City at the end of 1963. The theme was "From Three Continents to Six." It was in the series of missionary conferences that began in the nineteenth century and continued at New York in 1900, Edinburgh in 1910, Jerusalem in 1928, Madras in 1938, Whitby, Ontario, in 1947, Willingen in 1952, and Accra, Ghana, in 1957. It was to be a test as to whether this series could continue with integrity in the new structure.

It included delegates from former "sending countries" who represented national missions as well as foreign missions. It focused on the problems and opportunities for the Christian message in every country in the world. I believe that DWME met the test with flying colors.

In retrospect I am pleased that the thrust which we anticipated at New Delhi had come to the fore in Mexico City. The message there became a challenge to all the churches to move forward in a new missionary movement. The enlargement of the pattern established by the Theological Education Fund was exciting and the manner in which all supported the plans to join in new areas of mission, including unreached geographical areas, was gratifying. This included the Orthodox delegates, who were the new boys in all this.

The Bible study and its application to the areas for discussion were remarked by many. Some of us had just come from an assembly of the NCC in Philadelphia and the difference was very evident. I had had a new experience at Philadelphia. I was now a vice-president of the NCC and Chairman of its Division of Foreign Missions. As such I was on the message committee for the Assembly. The president of a theological seminary had drafted the message, with the help of NCC staff, and I thought it was inadequate. I prepared an amendment with something of Christian hope and the challenge for people to believe. It was considered but voted down in committee. That evening the draft message was distributed and all were invited to a hearing the next afternoon where it could be discussed. I tried to recruit two other denominational people to go to the hearing and support me but they were busy. I went but had very little hope. This time, as usual, the Lord knew better than I, for as the hearing began, Archbishop Iakovos of the Greek Orthodox Archdiocese of North and South America came with his flowing robes and his staff. I had met him first in Ghana and then as a president of the WCC. When the hearing was opened for discussion, the Archbishop said that in this draft there was nothing that he could preach on Sunday morning. What could he say out of this to his young people, and what could he say to Oswald? (It was just after the Kennedy assassination.) This impressed the committee and finally the chairman said that the Smith amendment had something to say about this, so it was resurrected, improved, and adopted by the committee and then by the Assembly.

At the next NCC Triennial Assembly in Miami Beach in 1966, I was again on the message committee and this time the first draft was prepared by an Associate General Secretary of the NCC. Members of the committee got it on Saturday as they arrived for a General Board meeting and the committee itself was to meet on Sunday afternoon. Again I did not like it and this time tried to write a new draft of the whole message while in the General Board meeting. (Charlie used to say I could write a memo while standing on the corner of Fifth Avenue and 42d Street.) I was sitting with Presbyterians and shared what I had written. They liked it and encouraged me. Sunday morning I preached at Winter Haven and read my "message" to the congregation at the end of the sermon. There was a good response. I got back in time for the committee meeting where Charles Taft was presiding with some dozen people present. I read my draft as a possible substitute for the proposal before the committee. Robert Marshall, Fry's Lutheran successor, moved that they start with my draft as the base of the committee's work. We did so, and its basic elements survived the committee, the hearing, and the Assembly. Some said it was the most substantive message we had had for a long time.

The above indicates to me that we American Christians in the NCC could break out of the prison of the past if enough people were determined to do it. In my time there was no real resistance. It never occurred to the majority that this was a place to study the Bible or to discuss theological subjects. Many of the same people would attend WCC meetings where the Bible was studied and would be pleased.

Rereading the reports from the 1963 Mexico City assembly of the WCC's Division of World Mission and Evangelism, and the things reported to the NCC's Division of Foreign Missions, I am impressed with the progress that was made in the early '60s concerning mission theory. Most denominational leaders knew we had moved into a new era and were in general willing to consider new relationships. The real danger was to be whether they would support new forms of mission action and financing and whether the local congregations would understand and support them. Judging from fifteen years after these reports, I have to tentatively conclude that our performance in the "new day" has not measured up to our vision.

Nominating a General Secretary

The choosing of a successor to Dr. Visser 't Hooft as General Secretary of the World Council of Churches was to prove more difficult than any of us had imagined. He had warned us in 1962 that he would retire at sixty-five in 1965. This would complete 27 years of service, ten with the Committee preparing for the formation and seventeen after the formation at Amsterdam. He was known, respected, and honored all over the world. How could we possibly do without him! But he insisted we must, and so we began the process of finding a candidate.

The 1963 Central Committee meeting was at Rochester, New York. Floy and I both drove up for her first Central Committee. We were housed at Colgate-Rochester Seminary and we stayed in a student apartment.

We had a close friend in Rochester, Mrs. Harper Sibley. She and her husband were prominent Episcopalians and committed to the ecumenical movement. She was chairman for ten years of the Women's Committee of the Japan International Christian University Foundation, in which Floy also served as a member of the Executive Committee. She entertained us and sometimes came to sit in the balcony with Floy. I had an Episcopalian colleague also. My seat in the Central Committee was beside that of Nathan Pusey, president of Harvard University.

The theme for study at this meeting was, "What does it mean to be a member of the World Council of Churches?" and the major paper was prepared and read by Dr. Visser 't Hooft. Even such a practical theme had its theological implications before the paper was finished. In brief, his answer was this: "It means that we recognize one another as Christians and worship together, we *listen* to one another, and we agree that, if the Holy Spirit leads us, we will be willing to *change*."

As soon as the paper was finished the meeting was open for discussion. The first to speak was an Orthodox theological professor from Athens. He said: "If we had known that was what it meant, we would never have joined. My church does not know I'm here and I will not report to them." There was laughter. But no doubt he expressed for all of us our own reluctance to change.

The Executive Committee of the Central Committee, through its vice-chairman, proposed to the Central Committee that it appoint a special nominating committee to select a nominee for General Secretary. It should have an adequate number of members so that geographical and confessional representation could be satisfactory. This nomination would be made at the next Central Committee meeting, in the spring of 1965.

The only discussion about the committee arose when the Bishop of Winchester questioned the cost of a special committee. One meeting would cost $5,000 and there might be two or three meetings. He concluded that since the Executive Committee itself had adequate numbers and was representative, the Executive Committee should become the nominating committee. This was approved, in spite of the vice-chairman's misgivings.

The Executive Committee has meetings every six months; thus there would be two meetings between these Central Committee meetings. At the first one a tentative nomination was agreed upon and the potential candidate given some time to discuss it, think about it, and reach a decision. After two or three months he decided he was not ready for this task. He was a member of staff and a good one, but he believed he was too inexperienced about other parts of the World Council outside his own Faith and Order Commission.

At the second meeting in the summer of 1964, the Executive Committee was pushed to make a quick decision. It chose another staff member from the same commission, who was less well known than the first choice. He was brought to the meeting from Geneva and in a few hours agreed that his name might go forward as their nominee. The name leaked to the press and was soon widely known. My good friend Eugene Smith was *elected* at the same meeting as Secretary of the United States Office of the World Council of Churches. *The New York Times* put the pictures of these two men side by side in one edition of the paper. It was easy for some people to become confused and assume the choice of a General Secretary was complete.

Inevitably there were rumors. One was that the staff at Geneva was not at all satisfied with the selection. There was at least one attempt to organize resistance against the election, an attempt that failed. Nevertheless it became apparent that the choice was not widely regarded as a happy one.

The Central Committee met in the spring of 1965 at Enugu, Nigeria. Our host was Sir Francis Ibiam, who was now governor of the province of which Enugu was the capital. The first major item of business was the election. The proceedings began in the first afternoon session with Payne in the chair and Fry presenting the nomination of the Executive Committee. Then the time for questions and discussion began. It ran through the afternoon. This was what we could call an "executive session" and what Europeans call a "closed session." It was really closed. Visitors, staff, and press were excluded. Two or three translators stayed and Norman Goodall was selected as secretary for the minutes, with the understanding that at the end of the session the minutes would be *sealed*.

At the end of the afternoon it was clear we were not ready to vote. We adjourned for dinner and returned for a second closed session. This was equally futile. I kept track of the number of speakers and listed 25 in the two sessions, 13 who appeared to support the nomination and 12 who seemed opposed. We adjourned for the night to meet again in the morning. We were cautioned not to give any reports to either staff or press, but one can imagine the guesses that were being made as people watched our faces.

There was little or no discussion among us that night and there seemed to be no plan for anything but to continue the discussion leading up to a vote. So the next morning in the third closed session the discussion continued, although by that time it seemed everything had been said. One or two members of the Executive Committee were irritated by the reluctance of the Central Committee to accept the nomination and suggested that failure to do so would be a vote of lack of confidence in the Executive Committee that would make it difficult for its members to continue to serve.

I had not spoken the day before and had no intention of speaking that morning, but it suddenly occurred to me that there was a possible way out. I thought it through carefully but conferred with no one. I asked for the floor and was recognized. I also asked for the privilege of making a statement before I made a motion. That was also granted. I said something like this: In Pittsburgh, where I had been a pastor, committees of congregations that were seeking a new pastor often were uncertain whether the candidate they were presenting would get an affirmative vote. They therefore did not ask the congregation to vote on the man but asked them to vote on whether they were ready to vote. If the vote was negative, then they must search again, not necessarily eliminating the candidate they had been ready to present. This freed them and did not expose the man to possible defeat. From the discussion I had listened to in the three meetings I was concluding that this "congregation of believers" was not ready to vote. Therefore I was proposing three motions: "I will read all three before making the first one so you will know what will follow if you approve. (1) I move that we take no action upon the nomination of the Executive Committee. (2) I move that we ask Dr. Visser 't Hooft to serve for another year. (3) If these are passed, I will move that we seek another way of getting a nomination for the next meeting of the Central Committee."

I then made my first motion and the discussion began. The American president of the World Council of Churches moved as a substitute motion that we vote on the nomination of the Executive Committee, but Jim Mathews rose to a point of order. He had been reading the rules and noted that a substitute motion which had the effect of restoring the original motion could not be allowed. The chairman agreed with Mathews and said that if we wanted to speak, it must be to the motion of "Coventry Smith." The discussion did not continue long before a motion to close was made and we voted. The vote was 40 to 37 in favor of the motion. A change of two votes would have reversed the decision. Someone said later that it was a shame the candidate lost by such a narrow margin. I replied that he would not want to win by such a narrow margin.

The second motion was passed quickly and the implementation of the third motion was referred to the nominating committee of that Central Committee meeting. They returned to the fourth closed session with a recommendation that each member of the Central Committee select the names of 10 members whom they would like to see on the new nominating committee. The committee would take these votes into consideration in selecting 18 names, balanced confessionally and geographically, whom they would then present as the new nominating committee. This was done before the day was over.

The new committee met under the chairmanship of Bishop John Sadiq of India during our sessions in Enugu. A German was selected as secretary and we interviewed Fry, Visser 't

Hooft, and one or two others about the sort of leadership we should now be looking for in the light of what had happened at Enugu. The advice was that we should look for mature and well-known leadership that also knew the World Council and could serve for at least one term of five years. I awakened the next morning with the thought that this might be Gene Blake.

All the names that the Executive Committee had had before them were given to our committee and we solicited suggestions for still other names and decided to meet in Geneva early in the summer to make our nomination.

I never discussed what I had done with anyone at Enugu or asked for comment. I did hear that Gene Blake had said I had made "some useful motions." Years later I asked Payne what he thought when I made the motions. He replied, "I thanked God for the International Missionary Council." Franklin Fry remained friendly as always, but the American WCC president took longer to get over it.

Support for the motion had come from Europe and the Third World, which felt that they did not know the candidate. The three Americans who voted for the motion all had had missionary experience. The opposition centered in the Executive Committee and among the Orthodox. It was a standing vote.

The meeting in Geneva was called to order by Chairman Sadiq in the evening of its first day. We were given the names of 50 people who had been suggested. We ruled out any names of those who were on the committee. We began discussing each of the names and sharing information about them.

The next morning we continued to discuss the names one by one and finished the list by noon. Then Bishop Sadiq suggested that each of us take a blank sheet of paper and put down five names he would like to discuss further. The votes were not to be signed and no nominations were to be made by individual members. After lunch the chairman and secretary gave us the results of the voting: names, and numbers of votes. There were 16 names and we discussed them all. At teatime we voted again, this time putting down three names we wanted to discuss further, and as a result our list was reduced to eight. The discussion each time was more thorough, but no one chose sides in the discussion. We then took another vote and reduced our list to four names.

That evening we discussed the four names as thoroughly as possible. Then the chairman asked us to take a blank piece of paper once again and put *one name* on it. The result was that every member of the committee voted for Gene Blake as his first choice. We did not proceed to make a second choice. The chairman had led our worship service at the beginning and asked God's guidance. Now he led us in thanksgiving that the choice had been made with complete unanimity. We could not have wished for any better solution in the selection of leadership for the World Council of Churches at such a critical time in its history. It guaranteed that the failure at Enugu would not haunt us.

John Sadiq called from Geneva and got Gene Blake at his home in Stamford, Connecticut, that night. He told him of the selection and I added my word. John asked that Gene consider it, ask questions if he wished, and send us his answer if it was no, so we could meet again. If it was yes, he was to keep quiet. We could guess but no one could say it was settled. Our last meeting would be just before the Central Committee met in the winter of 1966.

The Central Committee met at Geneva the last of January. The nominating committee met just beforehand. We had Gene's official reply that he would accept if elected. One or two members who had not been present at Enugu heard the details of the Geneva meeting for the first time and were amazed. John Marsh of Mansfield College said he had never heard of anything like it.

John Sadiq presented our nomination to the Central Committee. There was discussion before the vote, overwhelmingly favorable. One man questioned whether a citizen of one of the great powers should serve the World Council of Churches as General Secretary. Bishop John of the Russian Church spoke to that and said, "We think of Gene Blake as first a Christian and then as an American."

I was and am very happy about that outcome. I could not press my support in the committee; none of us was doing that. It was as fair a committee as any in which I have served. The process was making that possible. At every step of the way I felt that we were being led. I was exceedingly happy about the selection and glad my colleagues agreed with me unanimously. But I think that at the time I could have accepted another candidate if that had been the decision arrived at in the same way. I'm reasonably sure that every other member of the committee felt somewhat the same way. We were there as instruments and not as advocates.

I've tried this process several times under varying circumstances and recommend it as a very useful process in making a nomination.

We were under no illusions about the difficulty that Gene Blake faced. No one could really fill the shoes of Visser 't Hooft. Moreover, Blake now started a year late in preparing for the Fourth Assembly of the World Council of Churches. But we were sure that he had it in him and that he would seek God's guidance as we had sought it in selecting him.

There is one basic characteristic of Eugene Carson Blake which was very seldom discussed but which was consciously and unconsciously behind the unique unanimity in his election: Of course he was an American and skilled in the processes of assemblies and in administration. He was the right age and he knew the World Council from its beginning as very few knew it. He was open to change. (This last could be against him as well as in his favor.) But after all these years I think the fundamental reason was that he articulated his faith in basic New Testament terms and could be trusted to steer a course guided by these principles. It was most important that Europe and the Orthodox recognized this and followed him.

At this point Blake was most like Visser 't Hooft. Behind the vision that both men had was the faith that God in Christ had set before us a plan for the salvation of the world. In spite of everything they never deviated from that faith.

Ecumenism, a Movement in Christ

To get to that Central Committee meeting that elected Gene Blake in 1966 I had flown all night from New York to Geneva in order to be present for the opening of the Committee of the Division of World Mission and Evangelism, which met before the Central Committee. Charles Arbuthnot met me at the airport and we went over my schedule for the day as we rode back to the city. I was to present a paper to the Committee before lunch, participate in discussion afterward, go to dinner with Leslie Cooke, and then attend a meeting on Latin America.

The paper was on the internationalization of mission and

had been prepared by Don Smith and Don Black of COEMAR. It had been asked for by the DWME at its meeting in Mexico City and contained the results of a conference Don Smith had attended in Asia. The paper proposed a way by which DWME could be a center for finding personnel for mission service in special cases where the sending and receiving churches were unable to supply a person. It had been authorized in Mexico City and our paper was only on the way to implement the policy.

It was a somewhat surprising experience but perhaps one I should have anticipated. We were the innovators in this area and resistance was very strong. The policy itself was attacked: It would make the WCC a "super church." It seemed to imply that "internationalization" was a good thing in itself. We ought to wait until the churches themselves initiated this. The opposition came from Germany, Sweden, France, Switzerland, and the Netherlands. Japan, India, the United States, and New Zealand supported me. Inter-Church Aid said they were ready to do this. But the DWME was not ready and voted only to circulate the paper to member councils. The criticisms were in good spirit and those who objected were apologetic to me over coffee.

The evening meeting was more tense. The month before, I had seen Theo Tschuy of the WCC staff in New York and shared with him the concern of Gonzalo Castillo that UNILAM, the provisional committee for regional unity in Latin America, was moving too fast and with WCC support was in danger of dividing the evangelical community in Latin America. Bishop Newbigin had gone back to India as Bishop of Madras, and Robbins Strong was interim DWME Secretary. I shared my fears with him by letter and suggested we might get together in Geneva. Strong had circulated my letter to staff and invited people to meet me and talk about it. We met for two hours, about a dozen of us, including David Stowe, Jon Regier, Paul Abrecht, Leslie Cooke, Robbins Strong and Visser 't Hooft.

I explained that we were in favor of regionalism, and had supported it in Asia, Africa, and the Middle East. We had hoped for a committee in Latin America and supported UNI-LAM as "provisional." Our fears were that we might unintentionally rush into recognizing UNILAM alongside Asia and Africa as representing all of Latin America in the WCC and thus polarize the ecumenical concerns around a small fraction of the evangelical community and leave the rest no choice but to rally around another center.

Some WCC people were blaming such mission agencies as COEMAR for encouraging conservative antiecumenical attitudes in Latin America. One said: "We must choose to support the avant-garde of young rebels we have trained. They are the only hope of the future."

I ended by saying that for WCC to choose the avant-garde as the part to support was to be as paternalistic as any mission board. We must trust the church, including conservative hierarchy and avant-garde, to resolve its differences and move toward unity.

In the midst of this, Visser 't Hooft came over to my side and UNILAM remained provisional, pending the widening of the base in Latin America.

(An article in *The New York Times* had just said that for twenty-four hours after crossing the Atlantic by air a man's judgment is not to be trusted!)

At our DWME committee meeting we nominated to the Central Committee our choice as the new secretary of DWME, Dr. Philip Potter, a Methodist from Jamaica whó had been chairman of the World Student Christian Federation, and was now the Africa Secretary of the British Methodist Missionary Society. He had been the Bible study leader at both Ghana and Mexico City and was well known to all of us. The Central Committee elected him as Associate General Secretary of the WCC, to take office at approximately the same time as Gene Blake assumed the duties of General Secretary.

The theological theme of the Central Committee meeting in 1966 was "The Ecumenical Way." The draft of the paper on the theme had been prepared by the staff of the Faith and Order Commission and four members of the Central Committee had been selected to present brief papers, fifteen minutes of comment on the draft. The commentators had had a draft of the first paper before coming to Geneva, and by the time of presentation everyone had drafts of all the papers with translations where necessary. The commentators were Karula Jacob of the Church of South India, Bishop Hanns Lilje of the German Lutheran Church, Archpriest Borovoy of the Russian Orthodox Church, and myself.

I had brought a draft with me and had Paul Frelick, an

excellent theologian, check it for glaring errors. I was participating with some trepidation.

I criticized the draft theme paper on two counts. It was a
Faith and Order paper which did not include mission, scarcely
even by implication. I had been brought up by John Mackay
who believed that mission and unity belonged together. "You
can't have one without the other." Experience had confirmed
my conviction that this was true. Secondly, the paper reflected
the belief that the World Council of Churches was *the* Ecumenical Way. Membership seemed to be the test of both. I could not
agree. The Ecumenical Way was a movement in Christ. Membership in a particular organization was not the one test. The
Second Vatican Council, a local council of churches, a conservative evangelical group, even a confessional group, could be a
step toward ecumenism for some people. And maybe it was
the step they should take now. I had learned this particularly in
Latin America, where I could not write off my brethren just
because they had not joined the WCC.

Again my support came from the United States and the Third
World. Europe was against me, which meant the old-line
ecumenists were for playing ball in their own family. Robbins
Strong put it this way: "This Ecumenical Way is like running
around a closed track which has been traveled often by most of
the runners. Sometimes they are bunched together, sometimes
strung out, and evidently it is a long race, for occasionally the
runners have time to glance out to the world outside the track.
The need today is for an Ecumenical Way which is like a cross-
country race, up hill and down, across streams and over
unanticipated hurdles and with unknown dangers."

The theme at Enugu had been "Conversion." It seemed not
to get far that time around, but it was to be embodied in the
theme of the Fourth Assembly. Maybe the Ecumenical Way
would have another chance. In the Christian Way there are no
"closed tracks."

The thinking that had been stirred in me by the theme at
Geneva and my response to it had a fresh exposure near the
end of the year at Berlin. This was the scene of the World
Congress on Evangelism held under the auspices of the Billy
Graham and *Christianity Today* organizations. There were 1,000
voting delegates, 200 observers, then press and others. Half the
delegates were North Americans, the other half from the rest of
the world.

The Congress was really the home of my friends the conservative evangelicals. Many were there. One of them insisted on my coming to breakfast with him one morning, where he introduced me to a score or more of his friends. He told them he wanted them to meet a man who was on the Central Committee of the WCC who did not have horns.

The leadership was very much aware that they must free themselves from the image of Carl McIntire and from the attitude of being anti-WCC and they largely did so.

Also many of our friends from the Third World were there. I met them everywhere. I would judge that half of them would have attended a conference on evangelism that was called by the World Council.

Chapter 11

Ecumenical Relations, Evangelism, and Social Witness

THE OFFICE of COEMAR at 475 Riverside Drive was kept busy. We were engaged in time-consuming business, but it was exciting and we felt we were part of a most important activity of the church. We maintained our collegiate relationships and tried to give serious consideration to new ideas from anyone. The Chicago furlough conferences were an avenue to missionary participation. Archie Crouch's "Significant Papers" and the "Dear Colleague" letters kept us aware of areas of new thinking. Stanley Rycroft researched our facts. Dan Pattison kept the budget balanced, and John Corbin kept the ship in good shape. Winburn Thomas lived in Larchmont and rode back and forth with me every day that we were both in the office. There was no uncertainty in his interpretation.

Gradually the General Secretary, the two Associate General Secretaries, and the Treasurer became a "General Secretary's Office." We met once a week regularly. Each brought his agenda and we stayed until we were through. Each took assignments, and when one went to a meeting he spoke for all. Margaret Shannon left to run the office in Church Women United and Ray Kearns came to take her place.

A good share of our strength lay in the members who were elected by General Assembly to the Commission to which we were accountable. We worked carefully with the nominating committee of General Assembly in voicing our needs. We had able pastors and laymen, both men and women. At one time we had Jim McCord from Princeton, Art Mc Kay from McCormick, and Charles Forman from Yale. We did not suffer from lack of expertise that could be called upon for help on almost any occasion.

Our home in the town of Mamaroneck, New York, was increasingly a joy to us. We could entertain our family and friends, some of them from abroad. Floy was at home in the church and in the Presbyterial. In 1961 our daughter, Louise, was married to Larry Woodruff in that church.

Also in 1961 Floy faced another illness. She had had a bout of phlebitis and was in the hospital for a checkup when they found the beginning of Parkinson's disease. We got the best treatment there was at the time and held the disease somewhat in check. She could still drive her car for several more years. We had planned for her to go with me on one or two trips abroad; we even had passports and reservations at one time, but she was not able to go. She finally had to use a wheelchair for meetings in New York and for trips to the General Assembly in 1966, 1968, 1969, and 1970. By that time L-dopa was available and helped her greatly. Even when she was not able to go she kept up her interest in all the activities in which I was engaged. She helped furnish an office for the Division of World Mission and Evangelism when it was moved to Geneva, and we entertained Newbigin and Niles and Hwang when they were in New York.

Stony Point

In 1948, within the first two months of our residence in New Jersey, Floy and I visited the most recently acquired property of the Board of Foreign Missions. This was the Gilmor-Sloane House at Stony Point, New York, given to the Board by a family that had used it as a summer residence for many years. The house itself is about a mile outside of the town, located on twenty-seven acres of land. The house was originally two stories in height but later it was raised and a new first floor built under it. It is attractive and can house more than a score of people for meetings, usually over weekends. There were already a farmhouse and a stone barn as well as another, larger barn and two or three outbuildings on the property.

The house was full of furniture and knickknacks, but some of these brought a good price at an auction and we soon had a useful property. Charlie Leber gloried in it as a meeting place for staff and sometimes for picnics.

John Corbin installed the Ernie Mosers in it as houseparents and we began using it for retreats for congregations interested in overseas mission. It also still served for important meetings of staff.

Soon other uses arose and grew. The first was Readers' Service. This had been begun by Dr. and Mrs. J. Stewart Kunkle at 156 Fifth Avenue in a small office. Dr. Kunkle had been a seminary professor in China and decided to spend the rest of his life collecting books and distributing them to individuals and institutions overseas. His office was bulging at the seams, so he moved to the farmhouse at Stony Point and soon increased the status of the post office there. He built another home on the property and we built a home for Readers' Service, later enlarged. It is still there, served by a succession of retired missionaries and mailing upwards of 50,000 books a year.

When we had experimented with a training school for missionaries, first at Hartford and then at a summer hotel in New Jersey, we were encouraged to build the Ecumenical Training Center at Stony Point with homes for the staff also on the property.

We had originally tried to interest other denominations in joining us but failed to do so. However, they together pursued the idea of locating on the campus of an educational institution but came to the same conclusion we had, that this was not suitable. I remember well the day that Jim Mathews, the chairman of the interdenominational committee, called me and asked, "What conditions would you require of us if we decided to come to Stony Point?" My reply was: "There are no conditions. Let's form one committee with all of us on it, study on the basis of our experiences what we want at Stony Point, and then take what can be used and together add to it." And that is what we did. Our dream of preparing together in order to work together on the field had come true.

In later years when the numbers of new missionaries dwindled, there was no longer need for the Center. In 1976 the Program Agency bought out the other denominations and Stony Point is now a United Presbyterian center for study and for the use of churches in the area. I was fortunate enough to be present at the meeting of the United Presbyterian Foundation at which, for legal purposes, it was acting as "The Commission on Ecumenical Mission and Relations" and deciding to buy back the property.

For several years, beginning in 1959, COEMAR transformed the barn into a summer playhouse which not only served the New York area with entertainments of religious drama but trained people from all over the world in the use of drama in the mission of the church. The Barn Playhouse is now closed but its results still are evident in many parts of the world.

Protestant–Roman Catholic Fellowship

When COEMAR was formed we anticipated that the new relationship between Mission and Relations would open up more adequate understanding between churches and develop new opportunities for action together in mission. This proved to be true at many points. Direct relationship between sister churches often improved when they were looked at with the context of the larger Christian community. But one of the major gains was totally unexpected.

By 1961 the calling of the Second Vatican Council afforded an opportunity for the Roman Catholic Church to invite observers. This began with the WCC but similar invitations were sent to world confessional groups. The World Presbyterian Alliance was one of those invited to send observers and immediately accepted. This was not just a gesture. It was an opportunity to develop and express a new attitude and relationship. At this point the best story I have heard out of Vatican II was told by a Belgian cardinal at a public meeting in New York. A Methodist bishop had been an observer and one day found himself in a small meeting which included Pope John XXIII. He asked Pope John how long he thought it would take for true unity to come. His Holiness replied, "As far as you and I are concerned, it has already happened." It was this spirit of unstructured unity in Christ that encouraged Roman Catholics and Protestants to seek other opportunities to express their fellowship. I remember that on our way to Enugu, Nigeria, in 1965 our plane stopped to take on other passengers at Rome. Among them were Visser 't Hooft and others from Geneva. We welcomed them and found that Bishop Willebrands of the Secretariat for the Promotion of Christian Unity had come down to see off his friend Visser 't Hooft.

The first thing that happened to me personally was a call that came one day to Church World Service at 475 Riverside Drive from two or three Jesuits in an office in New York who were wondering how they could get in touch with us. They wanted us to come to lunch. Two or three of us accepted and we had lunch in a dining room over which Emily Post once presided. One of our hosts was Daniel Berrigan. Later we invited two or three of them to lunch at "475," among them a priest from one of the Catholic orders who had been an observer at the Vatican Council. As they were leaving, the priest said: "I'm glad to have met some mission agency people. We know now that we owe a debt of thanks to the missionary movement for helping start the ecumenical movement."

After Vatican II, in the United States the National Conference of Catholic Bishops sent invitations to major mainline denominations suggesting that they form bilateral committees to discuss future relationships in the context of what had happened at Rome. For some denominations this caused an awkward wait. Who would respond for their church? For the United Presbyterian Church there was no awkward waiting. COEMAR had been formed for the occasion. Plans went ahead carefully and swiftly.

Our first meeting was in the summer of 1965 in Washington at the Georgetown Presbyterian Church. It was cautious but friendly. There were a dozen to fifteen people on each side. On their side were a number of scholars and professors, including one younger priest who had studied in Switzerland and had written his Ph.D. thesis on the life of John Calvin. We had two or three scholars, Robert McAfee Brown and Norman Horner among them. But we also had a cross section of the church, including some women and laymen and some mission agency people. They were quick to see this and at our next meeting their representatives included a wider variety of people.

The first day we got acquainted and appointed a joint committee to plan a worship service for the next morning. That was an inspiring occasion. We also appointed a committee to plan the next full meeting. Ray Kearns was our secretary for all this and William Baum represented the Roman Catholics. Bishop Unterkoefler was the Roman Catholic cochairman.

The next meeting was at the Krisheim Study Center in Philadelphia in the fall of 1965. We began studying joint worship services for the local level, both in homes and in churches, questions of marriages and funerals where both were represented, and the whole question of how this attitude and material for discussion could best be shared with all the people in our congregations.

I had not been able to go to the Krisheim meeting, but I learned that there the Roman Catholics had asked if they might not have Mass on one of the mornings. Permission was granted and all were invited, though the Protestants could not receive the elements.

The third meeting was at Fordham University, on Roman Catholic "turf." As preparations went forward for the meeting Ray came into my office one day with the schedule which the hosts had suggested to him. It provided for a joint worship service on the first day, a Mass in the chapel on the second, and on the third day we Presbyterians were to be in charge of the worship service. We began to wonder if this meant they were suggesting we could have a Communion service if we wished, and then we wondered if we wanted to do it. We asked advice from some of our members and replies varied. We decided we would first find out if we were free to hold such a service at Fordham. We called Bill Baum and posed our question to him. He thought the hosts might be suggesting it. We then asked what we had to do to pave the way for it. He said we should call Bishop Unterkoefler and, if he thought it was a good idea, he would call Cardinal Spellman, in whose diocese Fordham was, and seek his permission. We decided we would try. Unterkoefler approved and Spellman approved. John Middaugh of Baltimore was on our committee and had had experience in a joint television program with a Catholic priest. He prepared the service and conducted it. In our turn we asked St. Augustine Presbyterian Church in the Bronx for permission to hold the service in their area, and their pastor, Edler Hawkins, and one of his elders assisted in the service. The second elder was a woman who was a member of our committee.

The Mass in Fordham Chapel was conducted by the bishop. He asked us to choose the hymns and we were all there, participating in the prayers and the hymns. The next morning the altar in the small chapel became a Communion table and we conducted our Reformed service. All our friends came and read the prayers with us and sang the hymns. As is our custom, we invited all who believe in Jesus Christ to receive the elements with us, but they could not. But the spirit of the service was excellent. I had the brief homily and Floy said I spent more time on it than I had done with other sermons. After the service two priests came into our room where we were and one of them said: "Now I have an answer when some of my parishioners say that Protestants do not believe in Jesus Christ. I can answer, I have seen them." It had never occurred to us that if we had failed to hold the service it could have been interpreted as meaning we did not believe. We never knew whether our Fordham hosts had intentionally opened the door for us, but we were very glad we had the experience together.

At about the same time, approaches were being made for a relationship with the NCC. I remember Monsignor Joseph Gremillion speaking at a meeting of the General Board and Roswell Barnes making sure that I met him. We had him later at a board meeting of COEMAR and at a furlough missionary conference. One day he called me and said he wanted to bring Cardinal Silva of Chile to see me. The cardinal spoke little English. We had someone interpret for him as we talked and had tea. I had a picture on the wall painted by a Frenchman which was entitled *The Missionary*. It was a picture of a missionary in a black robe seated among several priests in brilliant robes, one of them a cardinal, and he was reporting to them while one sipped tea, one played with a dog, and one napped. Cardinal Silva was interested in the picture and I explained it to him. I said we thought of ourselves as the hierarchy and the picture reminded us we must listen. The cardinal remarked, "It does not do much for cardinals."

Joseph Gremillion was one of those who initiated an inter-American conference which was held every year for fellowship and discussion among Catholics from North and South America. I attended once in Chicago for several days. The "good" Senator McCarthy (Eugene J.) was there, as were three cardinals, Cushing from Boston and two others from Latin America. One evening we had dinner together. Father Joe was originally from Louisiana. As a young priest he visited Latin America and was shocked by some of the churches that he saw. He set about interesting North Americans in these churches and their problems.

Later I was at a General Board meeting of the NCC in the Midwest when my secretary called me and said that Cardinal Spellman's office had called and they wanted me to have lunch with the cardinal the next Monday. It had something to do with Church World Service and the Secretary of CWS was also invited. I agreed to go and tried to find out what the meeting was about. Ros Barnes told me to call Father Joe, who was on the staff of Cardinal Spellman. I called and he had not heard of the meeting but said he would find out. The next morning he called and said: "Be careful. His Holiness has given the cardinal the tiara he used at his installation as a token of his appreciation for what Catholics and other Americans had done for world relief. The cardinal wanted to find a way by which they could use the occasion as a way of arousing more interest and more money for relief. He thought we might have a joint television program and receive the tiara, then appeal for gifts to be sent to post office boxes, one for Catholics, one for Protestants, and one for Jews." He said that Lutherans would also be at the luncheon.

I reviewed very carefully what I wanted to say in reply. Then I tried it out on Father Joe and on the CWS Secretary, and I went. Spellman was courtesy itself—met us at the door, took our hats and coats himself, talked a bit, and then showed us the tiara on a pedestal on the balcony above the dining room.

The luncheon was beautifully served and we enjoyed the fellowship. The idea of doing something together was presented and the Jews replied first. They were having a fund-raising dinner in Washington and they wanted to display the tiara there and refer to the gift in the context of their meeting. The Lutherans said they would think about it. I was next. I said we were thankful that His Holiness had remembered us in the giving of the gift. We expected to talk with (Roman Catholic) Bishop Swanstrom, through Church World Service, about other ways in which we would cooperate in the future. But he should understand that some things he could do might cause us trouble if we did them. Using the tiara might be one of them. Our parting was cordial and we never heard of it again.

I received another invitation which I could accept. There was a meeting of Roman Catholic organizations interested in mission in Washington and I was invited to speak and I did so, finding out later that the Maryknoll order had printed my speech in some of their literature.

Conversations between the NCC and the National Conference of Catholic Bishops resulted in a joint committee there also. At first it was just getting acquainted and I had the impression that the Catholic members were those who volunteered to go. William Baum was the secretary, Archbishop

Carberry was cochairman with me, and we met about twice a year for two years. Then suddenly it became serious. The General Secretaries from each side were added; Avery Dulles, a canon lawyer, joined the group. Carberry, now a cardinal, was replaced by a more active bishop and we were told to explore from both sides the question of possible membership in the NCC by the Bishops Conference. We were involved in this for more than two years. Once we almost quit. I protested, saying we ought to continue, and even if we had to scrap what we had and start over again together on what we now believed we both needed, we ought to be ready to do it.

We started again and we did produce a document. Avery Dulles was the principal drafter on the Roman Catholic side. It suggested many things but its main thesis was that we joined in the statement that there were no doctrinal or ecclesiological reasons why the Roman Catholics should not join the NCC. This document was printed, was received by both national groups for study and is on the shelves for future reference. Possibly other groups at local and state level have used it as the basis for their broader relationships. Some state councils of churches as well as city councils do include all of us together. Doubtless ten years ago we were too far ahead of our constituency, especially the Roman Catholics in several areas. And perhaps the National Council of Churches needs to be a better council with a greater interest in the Bible and in spiritual things before it becomes a fit instrument for such united effort.

I know that William Baum felt that the Catholics would never feel the full force of the need for reconciliation until they faced the conservative evangelicals. I once invited the Roman Catholic scholar on Calvin to one of our conferences at Malone College. He accepted but the weather was bad, his plane was grounded, and he could not come. I reported the invitation to the group and was told I should not do it again. I retired soon after that. I have always wondered if they would have rejected him if they had had a chance to know him.

Our missionary force was greatly interested in the development of dialogue with Roman Catholics. In most instances it fitted into what was happening to them on the field. In one or two instances the exact opposite was true, especially in Latin America. In Brazil some leaders of the Presbyterian Church used this as an added reason for breaking off some of their relationships with us. In that country the situation had taken a curious turn. Many of the Catholics were social liberals and opposed some of the things the state had done. Presbyterians, at least these leaders, were conservatives in both theology and politics and supported their government at the same points.

At the Fourth Assembly of the WCC in Uppsala in 1968 I was anticipating seeing Joe Gremillion, who by that time was attached to the Pontifical Commission for Justice and Peace and was with the delegation of observers at the meetings. Actually he found me before I found him. We had just taken our seats in the Presbyterian section when he came up to where I was sitting with Bill Thompson, now our Stated Clerk. We talked a bit and planned to see each other again. It occurred to me that seven years before in New Delhi our delegation had given a dinner for the Ethiopian Orthodox delegation. Would it be possible now to have as our guests for dinner the Roman Catholic observers who were about the same in number as ourselves? I asked Bill and he thought it was a good idea. I set out to find Joe. He was standing in the balcony talking with Lady Jackson (Barbara Ward), who was another of the Roman Catholic observers. They thought it was a good idea and Bill and I set Ray Kearns to work making the plans in a small hotel nearby.

Several nights later we had the dinner, about 35 people in all. No set program. At the beginning we had self-introductions. As Moderator that year I welcomed our guests and Bishop Willebrands replied. Then Jim McCord spoke from the standpoint of the World Alliance of Reformed Churches, and Lady Jackson spoke briefly. Then anyone who wanted to chimed in. The dinner hour was over and we stayed on, missing the evening meeting. Gene Blake missed us from the auditorium but most of us believed we were better employed. Several said that one evening was the highlight of the Assembly and worth crossing the ocean to be present.

Membership in the WCC for the Roman Catholic Church is a different question than joining the NCC. Would it be a set membership for the Catholic Church in each country, or would it be one great membership for all? Either one would be difficult. At least for the present the Catholic Church will cooperate fully in many things but refrain from membership. We now know many of its leaders at least as well as we know some Protestant leaders. We are becoming one family, although the structure for the family is still incomplete.

At least in some places this all has resulted in strong local ecumenical bonds between Catholics and Protestants. In January 1978, on the Sunday evening of the Week of Prayer for Christian Unity, I had been invited to preach for a union ministerial group at a Roman Catholic church in Levittown, Pennsylvania. We had had unusually deep snow—at least twenty inches—and it was a cold night. There were some 20 ministers present to march in together and a congregation of 500 people, about half Roman Catholic and half Protestant. A choir of 160 people led us. (They had practiced two or three times that week and they wanted to sing. That partially explained the attendance.) An older priest had built the new church but the associate, a younger man committed to the new relationship, was in charge of the meeting. It went well. When it came time to speak I could feel the interest in those present, the kind of congregation of believers that helps the preacher do his best. They even laughed at my humor, sometimes when I did not expect them to. I am putting away this night alongside of the one in Uppsala as a foretaste of heaven. After all, we will all be there, won't we?

Meetings with Conservative Evangelicals

In the early days of cooperation among missionary-minded churches there were voluntary groups that met in addition to the more formal Foreign Missions Conference of North America and, later, the Division of Foreign Missions of the NCC. Membership was by invitation and I was privileged to be a member of two of them.

The larger group was called "Lux Mundi" and met three or four times each year for a weekend to talk about issues before the missionary movement. Papers were assigned before each meeting, with two or three members assigned to comment on the papers after their reading. The papers were expected to be good. Kenneth Scott Latourette was a member and he was on the *International Review of Missions,* so that some papers might eventually end up in being read all over the missionary world community. This personal relationship between us also strengthened the ties that bound us together when the same people met to plan and act in the Division of Foreign Missions.

The second group was smaller and was called "Praise and

Prayer." Members met once a year for discussion and prayer together. Between times we circulated prayer lists among the group with all periodically contributing suggestions. This had been started in the very early years by John R. Mott and Robert E. Speer among others. We valued membership in this very much, especially because it furnished a link with the past, with the early beginnings which led later to the world organizations.

In our own times some of us started a new informal group. The stimulus, I think, came when the door to fellowship with the Roman Catholics opened. Eugene Smith of the Methodists was our leader in this, together with a Southern Presbyterian who had been a missionary in China, Moderator of his church, and then secretary of the Missionary Research Library, which was located in Union Seminary in New York.

We all had some relationships with conservatives in missionary activity who were outside the NCC and the WCC. Our name for such people was "the conservative evangelicals," and I suppose they called us "the ecumenical evangelicals." The three of us believed that just as we now had fellowship with Roman Catholic mission groups, it would be less than ecumenical on our part to refrain from fellowship with those outside the usual ecumenical circles. We determined to try it as a kind of semiofficial committee of NCC. That did not work. A few were interested but they could not at all persuade their fellows.

After a year or two of failure a small group from both sides who met at Fuller Seminary hit upon a solution by which a group might be brought together. The basic issue was the question of who was inviting people to come. They decided no organization or group of people should do this, as this would arouse suspicion. But if six of us, after consultation, should each as single individuals invite some of his friends, we might get a response. A meeting was planned for the summer of 1961 at Lake Forest, Illinois. Papers were assigned, one to each side of an issue about mission; commentators were also invited on each paper, and each of the six of us sent out invitations. The concentration was upon people related to foreign missions, but they were not invited because of their position but as friends.

The plan worked. We had 18 or 20 people for three full days. At first people were cautious. One man later said he had been scared; he had never met anyone related to the NCC. Another who had been cautious was the first to say on the last day, "When do we meet again?"

We set up a core group of four or five that still was informal but could plan meetings and invite people. We began meeting at Malone College in Canton, Ohio, during summer vacation. We never invited the same group, at least not entirely. We met for ten years in all and discussed a variety of issues. We soon discovered that when we took sides, sometimes we found conservatives and ecumenicals on both sides. World Council people were welcome and Norman Goodall, Bishop Newbigin, and Philip Potter were at times our guests. Paul Hopkins, Bill Thompson, and I were regular attenders among Presbyterians.

The only year we missed was 1968. We found difficulty in getting our quota and called it off. Gene Smith was the acting secretary for the first five years and then I became secretary.

We never gave any possibility of publicity about our meetings or who was there. Once there was a hint of this in the papers and we had questions asked, but it did not cause real trouble. I was sometimes asked by my own United Presbyterian friends who knew about it, "What do you aim to get out of this?" My answer was: "I don't know, but these persons are Christians who are in the same work we are engaged in and God is leading us to consult together. Whatever the future shall be is in the hands of the Spirit of God. When the time comes we'll know."

At the meeting in 1970 I resigned as secretary and a man from Fuller Seminary took my place. I lost track of the meetings for a time but now understand that the Overseas Ministries Study Center at Ventnor, New Jersey, with a permanent staff and many of the same people and interests, is doing the same things on a much wider basis than we did at Malone.

I now know that those ten years of association were a balancing influence in my personal life as well as in my work as a missionary executive. I do not belong to the "conservative evangelicals," at least not under that name, but I believe myself to be an evangelical and I can learn from many of my friends who do belong.

I am beginning also to believe that when mainline churches become more evangelical and "evangelicals" are more concerned with social witness, we may together lead the church in renewal of mission to the whole world.

Evangelism Recommended

As General Secretary of the Commission on Ecumenical Mission and Relations, I was ex officio a member of the General Assembly Council on Evangelism. Part of the council's task was to arrange for a pre-Assembly conference on evangelism every year. I usually was on the docket in some capacity. I remember one of the presentations with considerable clarity.

In 1966 the Presbytery of Cuba, which had started and remained as a part of the Synod of New Jersey, was freed by the Assembly to become the Presbyterian Reformed Church of Cuba. The Moderator and Stated Clerk were sent to Cuba to officiate at the ceremony and I was also sent to represent the new relationship we would have with that church.

The Cuban church had an excellent high school called La Progresiva, with a committed Christian as its principal. He knew the need of a good secretary and had asked for one from the Board of National Missions. A young woman in their offices volunteered and went to Cuba. After Castro took over she stayed in Cuba to help at the school and soon was helping also in Christian education and music in the presbytery. We could readily see the importance of what she was doing.

One or two years later this woman returned to the United States to visit her family. We had a chance to talk with her one morning at "475." It was our first chance to talk with a person who could report firsthand on how the Cuban church fared under Communism. I remember she told of how they had decided in the presbytery to have certain years of emphasis. One was on Christian education, and now they were entering a year of emphasis on evangelism. Knowing the restrictions the Communists would place on the advertising of meetings and on the holding of special meetings themselves, I asked her how the presbytery did this. She said it was not an activity of the presbytery itself but of the Christians as individuals. She gave an illustration about one of the teachers and then one about herself. This was hers: In spite of all the other work she had to do, she now went to help the laborers at the time of the sugar cane harvest. It was unusual for a person like herself to do this and the more unusual because she was an American. It raised many questions. When they asked her why she did this for them, she replied that it was because she came to know Jesus Christ and therefore had concern for all people who need help. With this opening she could talk about serving Jesus Christ.

That year at the General Assembly I told this woman's story and remarked that here was a small young church, restricted by Communism, that engaged in a year of evangelism. We were losing members in our churches but we did not plan to have a year of emphasis on evangelism.

The United Presbyterian Church had lost 10,000 members in 1966, the first loss for many years. However, the yearly gains had been diminishing and our research department had told us in 1965 that we would lose 25,000 members in 1967. We lost exactly that. Now we were told that we would lose 35,000 to 40,000 in 1968, and that the total loss in five years would be 250,000, with the annual loss five years from now at 70,000.

When the Stated Clerk reported this first loss, the secretary of the Council on Evangelism prepared a draft of comment. I saw the draft. Much of what was said was true but the total was quite inadequate. The explanations sounded like excuses and rationalizations; indeed, the draft ended up almost saying that the loss in membership was a sign that the church was succeeding. I sent my comments to the secretary, suggesting that he reduce his explanations and add a call for examination of ourselves as witnesses to the Good News. Nothing ever came of it.

In all this I understood that the climate had changed since the 1950s and that the church would naturally have a more difficult time. That is all true, but my irritation arose because in this critical time we were not doing all that was possible to study the situation and to advise about new and more vigorous approaches. Times were changing, but for the most part we seemed like observers looking at the change but not doing anything about it.

The Scriptures and Unity

In 1966, at the time of the World Council of Churches Central Committee meeting that elected Gene Blake, Visser 't Hooft made his last address as the General Secretary. Part of it answers the questions I have been asked as to why I seem to be more inspired by World Council meetings than I do with meetings of the National Council of Churches in the United States. In the midst of his address Visser 't Hooft made this statement:

I should like to call attention to another lesson we have learned in the ecumenical movement, namely, that its health depends on the place it gives to the Holy Scriptures in its life. Already in 1926 Adolf Deissmann said at the Life and Work meeting in Bern, "The secret of the force of the ecumenical movement is to be strongly rooted in the Holy Scriptures." In the following decades that truth was strongly confirmed. For the drawing together of the churches in the thirties and forties, the finding of so much common ground at Oxford, Edinburgh, and Amsterdam could not have happened if in those years there had not been a renaissance of Biblical theology in so many different places and if that theology had not produced a remarkable consensus on many essential points. It was affirmed with remarkable unanimity that, although the Bible was a collection of writings of great diversity, as critical scholarship has shown, it was at the same time characterized by a strong unity in that it is the record of God's redemptive activity, as God in history, having its center and goal in Jesus Christ.

It is this same basic conviction which has given its substance to the dialogue between Roman Catholic and other theologians. The secret force driving us together has been the Biblical kerygma that we have heard again in a new way on both sides.

It is interesting to note that the first to draw the obvious consequence that common Bible study would therefore have its regular place in the ecumenical meetings were the youth movements. The World Christian Youth Conference of 1939 is especially memorable for this. And we have seen in many later meetings that the Bible is and remains the reliable link between us and the force that obliges us to enter into deeper unity with each other. So when in New Delhi we added the words "according to the Scriptures" to our Basis we were not simply making a pious gesture, we were recognizing with gratitude what we owe in fact to the Bible in our common life.

Hattiesburg, 1964

Like the nation itself, the church was caught up in the civil rights movement. Our full participation began in 1963. The Board of Christian Education had a committee and staff on race relations, but the General Assembly of 1963 was faced with the need of enlarging its concern. This started in a pre-Assembly meeting and finally resulted in the establishment, by the Assembly itself, of a Council on Religion and Race in which the three major boards participated.

Gene Blake's involvement and arrest at the park in Baltimore occurred early in the summer of the same year. Later in the summer, while the WCC Central Committee was meeting in Rochester, Gene participated as a speaker in the mass meeting in front of the Lincoln Memorial at which Martin Luther King made the famous speech about his "Dream."

The opening of the voter registration movement at Hattiesburg, Mississippi, came in January 1964. My selection as the United Presbyterian spokesman came out of a General Secretary's conference the week before.

The account that follows is part of a report I made after going to Hattiesburg.

Sometime early in January the Commission on Religion and Race of the United Presbyterian Church was invited by COFA, a combination of four civil rights organizations in Mississippi, to participate in demonstrations on "Freedom Day in Hattiesburg." The National Association for the Advancement of Colored People was a member of COFA, as were other civil rights organizations, but in Hattiesburg the actual arrangements were under the direction of the Student Nonviolent Coordinating Committee (SNCC), which had a strong nucleus in the city.

"Freedom Day in Hattiesburg" was the beginning of a program arranged by the civil rights organization in Mississippi for voter registration emphasis all over the state. About 4 percent of the Negro population in Mississippi who were of voting age were registered, and about 70 percent of the white population. The civil rights organizations believed that this was the one place of priority in civil rights demonstrations and had been preparing over several weeks for demonstrations asserting the right of Negro citizens to register. They had also been preparing Negro citizens so that they would be able to register. This involved getting them to decide to do so, as well as to be familiar with the process.

The Commission on Religion and Race responded, as did the special group of the Episcopal Church that is concerned with this issue, and the American Rabbis Conference. There were smaller numbers from other denominations.

Freedom Day in Hattiesburg was set for January 22, and by that morning 51 ministers had arrived, 31 of them from the

United Presbyterian Church. The night before there had been a mass meeting in one of the Negro churches. I estimate that 350 to 400 people were inside the church and 150 or 200 outside standing at the windows or doorway. The meeting lasted from two to three hours, with the combination of a number of speeches by Negro and white leaders and songs by the audience. Speeches included instructions on the voting process. Lawrence Guyot, the field secretary in Hattiesburg, was in charge and spoke briefly. John Lewis, the national chairman, and James Forman, the executive secretary, were also present as was Charles Evers, Medgar Evers' brother and representative from NAACP, and Aaron Henry, the Freedom candidate for governor. This indicates that the Negro leadership was concentrated in Hattiesburg for this day. Layton Zimmer, Episcopal rector from Swarthmore, Pennsylvania, spoke for the Episcopalians, Rabbi Ungar spoke for the Jews, and I spoke for the United Presbyterians. Rabbi Ungar's prayer was a very moving one ending with the petition that we might have "the guts to march."

The songs that were sung were variations on the old spirituals: "Go Tell It on the Mountain," "Let My People Go," "This Little Light of Mine, I'm Gonna Let It Shine." They also had yells that were like cheers at football games. One began slowly: "Freedom now, freedom now, (faster and faster) freedom now, now, now, now." Another, borrowed from Africa and Tom Mboya, was simply "Freedom" lengthened out, and "now, now, now, now." The most moving song was "We Shall Overcome." I had never been impressed by this previously, but as it is sung by an audience of people who feel it deeply it is tremendous. "Deep in my heart, I do believe, we shall overcome some day."

Here are some comments from speeches made that first night. One said: "If I worked for $10 and when I got through my employer said 'I will give you $2 now and then some more later,' I would not stand for it. The white people are lucky we don't grab all our rights right now."

Another cautioned: "We must be both Christian and American in our efforts to get our rights. We love our country and are confident that it will act under the Constitution. Let us never lose faith in our America."

A third spoke as follows: "Medgar Evers, my brother, freed me when he was killed. He took me the length of his body, six feet two inches, closer to freedom. We must now lose our own fear of consequences." Charles Evers had also started with the Twenty-third Psalm and ended with the plea that men and women give their lives to this. "We were born to die sooner or later, as Medgar did and as Kennedy did." He also said the last time he was in Hattiesburg, the fire department came out and tried to drown out the singing. He added, "There is a fire going on now, but water will not put it out."

Hattiesburg had been selected by these civil rights organizations both because it was a sizable city of some 35,000 population which had registered very few Negroes as voters and because it was likely to be a little bit responsive to the movement for registration. However, there seemed to be no outward sign of this responsiveness because the registrar, a Mr. Theron Lynd, had during his first two years in office succeeded in evading registration of any Negro. According to a report from the Mississippi Advisory Committee to the Commission on Civil Rights of the Federal Government, Forrest County—in which Hattiesburg is located—had 7,400 Negroes of voting age in 1961 and 12 of these were registered voters. This did not increase until 1963, when Lynd was summoned to federal court and was held in contempt by the federal court until he had registered 43 names which he was holding and until he gave assurances that more adequate facilities would be available. He had registered this 43 and from September to December 67 others had applied, and it was estimated that something under 100 out of 7,400 Negroes were now registered voters in Forrest County.

The evening meeting was intended to be a stimulus to the community, to eliminate reluctance, to instill courage and determination, so that people would not only demonstrate but would actually register. Meetings were held every evening through the week. They were held to train leadership among the young people as they participated in the meetings, as well as to keep up the spirits of the people.

My own deep impression was that the Negroes preparing for this demonstration and for registration were moving against fear. Even the song "We Shall Overcome" has one verse that indicated this. We do not sing, "We are not afraid, we are not afraid," unless we are afraid. In addition, a special Freedom

Day song had been prepared. The first verse went as follows:

> Freedom Day in Hattiesburg
> We took a final stand
> Conquering our trembling fear
> We stood in silent might.

After the evening meeting was over, the ministers met for a brief time to go over the preparations for the next day. We were to march with a number of Negroes in a picket line in front of the courthouse beginning at 9:00 in the morning. We had been told before we left home that we should come prepared to be arrested. We were assured this evening that no civil rights demonstration in Mississippi had ever lasted more than fifteen minutes. We were instructed in the nonviolent ways by which we should deal with policemen when we were arrested. We were told to put some money in our shoes, not to carry pencils or pens as they would be regarded as possible weapons, and to be prepared to insist upon the right for one telephone call before we were actually imprisoned. This is guaranteed by federal law.

The Negroes who were going to march with us were not prepared to pay bail. In fact, part of their psychology was "Jail without bail." Some of the ministers also were prepared to go to jail without bail for a period of ten days to two weeks. The rest of us expected to stay in jail some three or four days and then to be bailed out. All had come prepared to get bail, if necessary.

Most of the ministers were assigned to Negro homes. Some few stayed in motels and hotels. Four of us stayed in a farmer's home on the edge of Hattiesburg. It was a very fine modern home equipped with all modern conveniences. This black farmer was sixty-eight years old and very cordial in his reception of us.

We dressed in the morning very much the way some of us dressed on the morning of December 15, 1941, when we knew we were going to internment camp in Japan. Everything in our pockets was carefully weighed as to whether it belonged there if we were going to jail. We had breakfast together, joined in a brief devotional service, assembled at the headquarters near the center of town, and then drove in cars to the courthouse. By this time it was raining buckets, but we did not expect to be very wet before we were arrested. We did not come to be arrested; we hoped it would not happen, but we had been fully convinced that it would happen. In fact, the last word at breakfast had been: if you are not arrested, that in itself will be a great victory.

Bob Stone and I were in the first car and were in the first group of pickets. Bob was the staff person in charge of the picket line and coordinator with SNCC. I had been selected as one of the two spokesmen along with Rev. Pierson from White Plains, who was a son-in-law of Nelson Rockefeller. There were about 75 of us all told, perhaps 40 ministers and 35 Negroes from Hattiesburg. Other ministers had been especially designated not to picket at the beginning because we needed people outside of jail to help us if we were imprisoned.

Some five minutes after we began to picket, 32 policemen in squad formation marched down the street "hip, hip, hip, hip." They were dressed in slickers, but you could see the billy clubs and guns as well. They cleared the streets in front of the courthouse on one side and then stood in the street with their backs toward us as guards against any possible attack from townspeople. We marched for an hour and a half and there were no arrests. All of us were wet to the skin. Few had come prepared for marching or for the rain. Newspapermen and cameramen were in evidence, but there were no interviews and very little reporting was done. As the *New York Times* man reported, "In such situations blood and guts are news and there is no blood and guts."

About 11 o'clock the picket line had increased from 75 to 200 or more. Negroes who were hesitant about picketing and not prepared to be arrested now came out and joined the line. At the same time the number coming up to register, crossing the line, and going up the steps of the courthouse had increased, and some 25 Negroes were standing on the steps waiting their turn. Some time after 11 o'clock more than 100 Negroes, young people who were in the picket line, assembled on the courthouse steps and began to sing. They sang some of the songs we had sung the night before, ending with "America." It was one of the highlights of the whole experience. For here was a group of people that felt themselves inferior and fearful but now were asserting themselves and calling for their freedom in terms of Christian hymns and of a patriotic song. Try to sing "America" under these circumstances and you begin to understand what a revolutionary song it is.

Shortly after 12:00 we broke up and went to lunch. Ministers were fed in one of the Negro churches, where we had a chance to dry out a bit. There were one or two who suggested that maybe we had made our contribution and we did not have to march any more, but a great majority believed that we had to stick to it, which of course was the wisest decision. We went back on the line in the afternoon and marched somewhere between five and six hours that day. We left the courthouse at 5:00, assembling on the steps for a brief prayer before we broke up. As I led the line from the steps of the courthouse down to SNCC headquarters, I passed in front of the officer in charge of the police and I stopped and thanked him. He was surprised and automatically said, "You are welcome."

The only time of fear, apart from the first hour, was late in the afternoon, about 3:30, when school was out and there were more people on the streets. The police began to allow traffic to pass and people to enter the stores on the other side of the street and turned their backs to the street and faced us instead. The tension mounted, but no violence occurred.

That evening we attended another rousing meeting. This also was in a church far away from the center of town. The larger Negro churches were not available for these meetings and their pastors did not appear in the meetings. They were under pressure from the white community. Two pastors did appear. I think the most we had were three at any one time. There were 15 or 16 churches in the city for Negroes. The second evening was more informal than the first, and at least a dozen young people participated. It was like a testimony meeting or a Methodist camp meeting with people asking for the floor and then saying how afraid they had been and how glad they were to overcome their fear to register or to march in the picket line. There were three or four hundred people there. I was told by one of the pastors that at a meeting the week before there had been 27 present. He indicated that our presence strengthened the will of people who had been afraid. Words such as "when it gets too thick we thin out" were spoken and the young people's witness began to turn to the older people. They said, "Some of us are trying to believe the stories you taught us." (They referred, of course, to the stories of the Bible.) One minister got up and said he was ashamed of himself and he would now exert more leadership. I suggested to one of the young white ministers that we might speak about our also being afraid and he did speak, bearing witness to how afraid we had been.

Larry Wong of California, making reference to Charles Evers' statement about his brother, said: "My leader fell 2,000 years ago and He has set me free."

Lawrence Guyot made a very interesting comment: "Redemption is an experience that recreates only those who wish to be redeemed." (I told him later that this was a theological statement.) He ended his speech by saying we have now arrived at the moment of truth whether we like it or not.

The next morning we started marching as before. There seemed to be no particular strategy, though we were determined that we would support the people who were coming to register. There had been 35 the day before, which equaled the previous highest day in the history of Hattiesburg. That had been the day after President Kennedy had been assassinated. It had stimulated the Negro community to come forward. On our second day 40 made application.

The registration was a very interesting one to us from the North. Lynd had registered as high as 160 people a day who were white but had never registered more than 40 who were Negro, even though there were far more waiting outside. He slowed down the process and asked all the possible questions, insisted that they fill out the forms in detail, did not give them any advice, and if they made a mistake by leaving out a middle initial, thirty days later he would tell them they had failed.

Thursday it still rained and we took some chairs up on the steps of the courthouse for the Negroes to sit in while they waited. I talked with some of them. They were most appreciative of our being there, for they indicated time and again they would never have had the courage to come and register if we had not been there. We heard this from others as we walked in the streets of the Negro section on Thursday also.

Curious people often stood and watched us as we picketed and some at the ends of the line would call dirty names at us. At times when we left the line—for we rotated off that second day—we would get names called to us also. "Nigger lover" was the most common, but I became known as "the grandpa Nigger." I had worn a hat in the early hours of the first day, but finally decided to abandon it. I suspect I was the oldest man marching and, therefore, was the butt of a considerable amount of derision. However, there was no violence and no indication in that direction. Even when two of us helped some Negroes up the street and across the line into the courthouse after they had turned back because of fear, no one interfered with us.

Thursday morning when I rotated off the line about 10:30, I started down to SNCC headquarters. It was a very busy and active place with anywhere from 30 to 150 young people in it off and on. As I was coming down the street a car came up beside me and a man leaned out the window and asked me if I was not one of the leaders of the group. I said I was one of the 51. He said he would like to talk to me about juvenile delinquency as he was the officer in Hattiesburg and he was concerned about some high school students who were marching in the picket line. I told him I would be concerned also if they were out of school, though there is no compulsory school law in Mississippi. I said I hoped that he was also as much concerned about improving the schools and getting better facilities for Negro children. He replied that this was not his business. He asked if there was someone down at SNCC headquarters to whom he could talk, and I said yes, and as he turned back to the car the man driving the car said, "If you wouldn't mind riding with the chief of police, I will take you down to headquarters." I got in the back of the car and we went down the street.

The first man went in to see Lawrence Guyot. I stayed to talk with the chief of police. On Wednesday morning a man by the name of Oscar Chase, a young white student from Queens who graduated from Yale Law School in June but who had been working with SNCC since the summer awaiting his call into the Army, had been arrested. He was driving a car, brushed against a Ford truck that was parked with no one in it, got out to see if any damage had been done, could see no damage, and went on. An affidavit had been filed by someone who saw the accident and Chase had been arrested about noon on Wednesday. He had been kept in jail. Through the night two others were put into the cell with him, one partly drunk and one who had been in a fight. When they discovered that he was a white man who was working with the "Niggers" they beat him up. There were bruises and cuts all over his face and blood on his shirt. At 7:30 A.M. he was released and had come down to us at SNCC headquarters. I told the police chief that I wanted to hear his side of the story. His side was essentially the same as I have reported. I asked him if he had made any inquiry when the affidavit was made as to whether any damage had been done to the car or to an individual. He said this was not his business. He protested that he did not have any idea that the two men that were put in the cell would beat up young Chase and that he had gotten him out of the cell and given him medical attention as soon as possible. I discovered that he was a Southern Baptist so I said to him that I thought Christians ought to be able to settle these things between them. His reply was, "We will never settle this issue." I said, "You are a Christian and you believe in God; you cannot believe that we will never settle this issue." He said, "It will be hundreds and hundreds of years; maybe Khrushchev can settle it."

I went into headquarters and found the juvenile delinquency officer talking with Guyot and threatening to close the head-quarters, intimating that we were responsible for young people who had left high school to march. I assured him that I knew of no one who had encouraged high school students to leave school and march. I had never heard this and if he had any evidence of this kind, we would be glad to listen to it. Otherwise what he was saying sounded like a threat. He replied that in spite of the lack of a compulsory school law he was responsible for juvenile delinquency and that failure to attend school and thus contributing to that delinquency could be prosecuted under the law. He said that the law could be interpreted very loosely and that the police department would accept whatever interpretation he gave.

The trial of Oscar Chase and a young Negro graduate of Harvard University, who was working with SNCC and who had been picked up on the street by a police officer when he had not moved as fast as the officer wanted him to, was to be held in the city hall, which was three blocks away from the courthouse. The decision was made to picket the city hall with one half of the picket line. We picketed in front of city hall, which also included the police station! At the same time a group of ministers and Negroes had gone into city hall court-room for the hearings. They were not organized, but they sat down together. When the marshal asked them to separate, Negroes on one side and white on the other, they did not do so. Later the judge, who was a woman, requested them to separate and they did not. She ordered them to do so or to leave the courtroom, and the marshal reinforced this by saying if they did not do so they were under arrest. Jack Pratt, the

National Council of Churches lawyer, who was one of the two lawyers with us, asked for a recess so he could confer with the people in the audience. During the recess the county attorney conferred with the judge, and she announced that though they had been segregated for 100 years, she would allow them to sit together for this court session.

Oscar Chase was found guilty of leaving the scene of an accident and fined $75. Forty dollars of the fine was given to the owner of the car. Robert Moses, the young Harvard graduate, was fined $200 and sentenced to four months in jail for "loitering."

The next day Jack Pratt, the National Council lawyer, called me before I had had my breakfast and suggested that it would be wise for Layton Zimmer and myself to meet with the Coordinating Committee at 10:00 A.M. and try to set forth some principles that should guide us in the light of our experiences during the last two days. We did meet at 10:00. We gave strict instructions to those who were participating in the picket line not to engage in any activities that would leave room to be regarded as picketing "illegally." This meant they must stay six feet apart, they must not sing and must not expose the line to unnecessary attack. We also set apart a group to visit in Negro homes and confer with prospective voters, helping them to prepare and encouraging them to register.

In the process of the conversation Jack Pratt reported that he had heard, in the discussion at court the day before, that the chief of police, a man by the name of Herring, had remarked that he had met this man Smith and "he did not seem to be such a bad guy." We decided that this might be worth following up. I suggested that three or four of us might go to see the mayor. Two would be Negroes and two would be ministers from the North. A group was selected, and the four of us decided we would try to make the first contact by telephone. I asked one of the girls at the desk to call the mayor's office. His number was not in the phone book and when she called information, the information girl did not understand her. I picked up the phone and asked information for the mayor's office and she said, "The mayor has an unlisted phone and I am not at liberty to give his number to you." We decided, therefore, that instead of calling upon him unannounced I would try to make an appointment through the chief of police. By this time the four of us were in a car cruising the streets and determining what we wanted to say to the mayor if we had a chance to say it. The Negro pastor among us had made an appointment for this group to meet with a white Methodist minister at 12:30 and I was let out of the car to go to the police chief's office while they visited the white minister. When I arrived at the office, after having tried to see him where he usually eats lunch, I found that he was there, and when he took me into the office there were the mayor, the former mayor, and the county attorney. The mayor's name was Pittman; the former mayor's name was Pope, and the county attorney's name was Zachary. Zachary had prosecuted the cases in court the day before. Whether or not they had been alerted by someone that I was on the way I do not know. I suspect they had. They were prepared to talk, and later I found out that they would not come together again to meet with the others. Therefore, I continued alone with the opportunity that had been given to me.

The chief of police first asked me if I had a transistor tape recorder on me. I said I did not and offered to be searched. They didn't search me. I then apologized to the mayor for coming in this way but said I had tried to call him on the phone and Information said she could not give me his number. I went on to talk about something else and the mayor interrupted me to say, "This is strange." The county attorney said, "Preacher, if you weren't a preacher, I would call you a liar." Then taking the police chief's phone he dialed information and asked for the mayor's number. We could hear enough over the telephone to confirm the fact that the girl said, "The mayor has an unlisted number and he has asked me not to give it to anyone." The mayor interrupted to say he never had done so. I remarked, "Who is a liar now?" The county attorney persisted with Information and finally got a number through which he secured the mayor's office. Then he turned to me and said, "See, if you had persisted, you would have got the number." I said, "When Information tells me that she is not at liberty to give me a number I hang up." He said, "You heard what you wanted to hear," at which I replied: "If this is the way you are going to start, there is no use in our talking any longer. I came as a Christian to talk to Christians, but if you accuse me before I begin of not being sincere, there is no use continuing our conversation."

I personally think that this was probably the best way the

conversation could have begun, for this cleared the atmosphere and the mayor asked me to continue. I was able to present, with some interruption and comment along the way, the things that we had agreed in the conference to talk about. I first talked about our purpose in being there, namely, to encourage voter registration. I gave the figures from the Mississippi Committee's report and was told that they had no idea whether their figures were correct or not because they kept no figures as to Negro voters. I suggested that it would be a good thing for them to do so, for then they would know how few there were and would have their own plan for encouraging such registration. They said there are adequate Negro schools. If Negroes go to these schools and are not prepared to register, it is not their fault. I said yes, but you have about the same number of white students as you have Negro students and you spent 81 percent of the funds for the white students. They replied that these figures were for the whole of Mississippi and that Hattiesburg was somewhat better.

I then brought up the subject of intimidation and cited the arrest of Oscar Chase. They insisted that arrest by affidavit of one person without investigation of the charge was common all over the country in the case of leaving the scene of an accident. I said I was no lawyer, but I did not believe this was true. I did not believe that beating of people by fellow prisoners was common, and I still believed that their release of the prisoner after the beating was intended to intimidate the community.

Then I moved on to the larger question of the fear of the Negro community. They denied that this existed. They said their race relations were very good in Mississippi. I replied that race relations were not good in the North and I did not think they were good in Mississippi. I gave illustrations and told of several conversations I had had with the registrants which indicated that there was a deep-seated fear and I suggested that the mayor of such a city should welcome leaders of the Negro community to come and talk to him about ways by which voter registration could be carried on and fear could be eliminated. The mayor said his door was always open. Negroes came to talk about a Negro cemetery and funds for Negro churches. I said that was not what I was talking about. I said I could give him the names of people who would be glad to come and talk to him about deep-seated needs. I indicated that I knew it would be impossible for him to do this now, for politically it might be thought to be done under pressure, the pressure of our demonstrations and our visit, but he should be prepared to do it within a few weeks.

The police chief played very little part in this conversation. Zachary, the county attorney, turned out to be the man who was in charge of police activities. He had been a federal officer and therefore could avoid infringing federal law. Pope, the former mayor, was a man whom all of us could like. He was married in Riverside Church in New York. He had been in Riverside Church the Sunday before. He said he had heard a Negro preach there and a white woman had walked out and said she would not listen to a Nigger. I said that is true, but you wouldn't even have a Negro preach in your pulpit. He said, "We would have before the Kennedys tried to make us." Pittman, the mayor, did not say much, but I had the impression that Pope was there by his invitation and that Pope's readiness to listen to what I said was some indication that the mayor was also ready to listen.

I left the office after about an hour and forty-five minutes. The mayor had missed his next appointment in order to stay with me. We agreed not to have any press conference as a result of our conversation. I inadvertently used the word "negotiation" at one point and immediately withdrew it.

I walked back to SNCC headquarters and talked with the ministers a bit, reporting some of our conversation, and also made a report to Lawrence Guyot. But before I could get any lunch, word came down from the courthouse that Mr. Pope and Mr. Zachary wanted to see me right away and I went back. Mr. Pope met me at the door. He said a woman had come in just after I left, reporting that her daughter had left school in order to march in the picket line and they wanted me to hear her story. Pope said, "We had the impression you didn't believe anything we were saying." I said I believed them and I would believe whatever they said this woman said about her daughter. He said he wanted me to hear it directly, so we went downstairs. Both Zachary and Pope were somewhat concerned when they discovered that this woman and her daughter were already being interviewed by the prosecuting attorney. His name was Finch. Pope called him out and introduced us. He said we were both Presbyterian. Finch was an elder in one of the local congregations. Finch immediately said, "I don't belong to your church, I belong to the rebel church." He refused to grant Pope's request that I sit in on the examination of the girl and her mother. He said he had only one thing to say to me. He would explain the Constitution of Mississippi concerning our contributing to juvenile delinquency. I said I would be glad to hear this and then would hope in the spirit of our discussions at noon to talk about the Constitution of the United States. He said: "I don't care for the Constitution of the United States. I did not take an oath to uphold it." I told him I would wait, for someone was bringing me a sandwich since I had had no lunch. He said he had had no lunch. I suggested we might eat together. He said, "Thank you, I will wait for dinner."

My sandwich did arrive. I had my picture taken by the police photographer, who tried to photograph me with Mr. Pope, but Mr. Pope ducked behind the wall. Mr. Lynd, the registrar, came in and I met him. He weighed 340 pounds and was shaped like a very fat bowling pin, narrow at the top and narrow at the bottom. He did not look me in the eye; in fact, I had the impression of a rather mediocre personality who had been put in this job to hold the line.

I think it was after Lynd left that Zachary remarked, "We think the Federal Government is interfering too much with Mr. Lynd." I said we thought the Federal Government was not interfering enough; this was one of the reasons we were here.

The two ministers who brought me my sandwich also brought a small package of fruit for Robert Moses from his wife. Zachary immediately blew up. He accused them of wanting to see Robert Moses when he already had too many visitors and that the gift of fruit intimated that he was not being fed well. He calmed down a bit and I said no one was asking to see Mr. Moses but simply asking that the fruit be sent in to him. With regard to the fruit, I had been in prison some months and even if I was well fed, the fact that my wife would send me some fruit would be greatly appreciated. Finally the interview with the woman and her daughter was over and Mr. Finch consented to bring the woman out, but not her daughter, saying that she was all mixed up and there was no use in interviewing her. He asked the woman what her name was and she said "Olny." He asked her where she worked. She had two jobs and one of them was as a maid for a Presbyterian pastor, who incidentally was Mr. Finch's pastor. He asked then what her complaint was. She said she had been having trouble with her daughter, who was thirteen years old. She had a mess of children, but this was her oldest. This trouble had come to a head the day before when she had stayed out of school and been in the picket line. She had not come home until 11:00 at night after the evening meeting. She was then asked who had persuaded her daughter to do this and she said, "Some white men." I asked her who they were and she said she did not remember their names. Finch said that he had some names. The only one he gave me, however, was the name of Samuels, a name that I couldn't document among our group or anyone related to the demonstration.

When I spoke to the woman I asked her again what her name was. She said, "Olny Kerr," and thereafter I addressed her as Mrs. Kerr. I assured her that none of the ministers would have persuaded the girl to leave school in order to march. Undoubtedly this girl, who already was a difficult child, had been influenced by other people who were marching and encouraged to go with them. I said that if we had in any way unintentionally contributed to trouble between herself and her daughter we apologized. Mr. Finch broke in to give his assurance to Olny that they would care for her in any of her difficulty and then asked her, "Olny, are you afraid of me? Are you afraid of Mr. Pope? Are you afraid of Mr. Zachary? Tell the preacher you are not afraid of us."

After he had assured Olny again of their willingness to listen to her anytime she was in trouble, I also spoke, addressing her as Mrs. Kerr, and assured her that she had other friends who would try to help her if she needed help. This infuriated Finch, who said, "I know what you are trying to do, but we will not change our way of life." I said, "The reason you won't change is that you really don't believe that these people are human beings." I added, "We are created equal." He said, "You didn't create them." I said, "No, but God did." He said, "He did not make their bodies equal." I said, "He made of one blood all people who live on the face of the earth." He said, "Preacher, don't you try to preach to me," and walked out.

Somewhere along the line I brought up this question of his loyalty to the Constitution of the United States and both Finch and Zachary denied that he had said he did not care for the Constitution. They said, "You said that." I then asked him, "All right, what do you think of the Constitution?" I got no reply.

Mr. Pope stayed and talked with me for another fifteen or twenty minutes. He said that they knew they were in trouble in Mississippi. They had lived here on poor land for 100 years and Negroes and whites must have compassion on one another. Someone coming in from the outside and saying things caused them to want to hit him, and then they knew that they had to think more calmly about these things. Pope hoped that the men being trained in the universities and some of the men in the theological seminaries now would help them.

All of these men, except Finch, were Southern Baptists. At the end of the conversation with the mayor, I told the mayor and Mr. Pope that I had a special concern because I had been a foreign missionary who was now the secretary of an agency that supported 1,300 missionaries overseas. I referred them to *Christianity Today* of January 17, to an article by Ros Coggins, Director of Communications for the Christian Life Commission of the Southern Baptist Convention, in which he says: "Racial tension in your hometown exerts a seismic effect on world missions. Our missionaries around the world describe our racial discrimination as a veritable millstone around the neck of Christian missions." They agreed that this was true, but they said, "Why don't the other countries say the same thing about Russia and her racial discrimination?" I said, "Jim Robinson taught me the answer to that: Russia does not pretend to be Christian."

I think that I should say, however, that except for the conversation with Finch, which at times got pretty harsh, most of our conversations were held in good spirit. We had begun by saying that we were Christian, that we wanted to talk within the spirit of our Christian faith, and most of the time the conversations were on that level. Both the mayor and the former mayor kept it on that level. The county attorney, Mr. Zachary, could be as forceful and overbearing as Finch, but underneath he was a rational man and could be appealed to on the basis of reason. He was likely to end by saying, "Well, I can understand how you hold this viewpoint, although I can't agree with you."

At one point near the end of the first conversation I told them I couldn't have said these things to them if I had not been there and marched in the picket line, and I didn't think they would have listened to what I had to say unless I had marched. All of our conversations were remarkably free from charges that we were outsiders who could not understand the business there. On the Negro side there was insistence that we were not outsiders, we were Americans; we had been invited to come by a sizable portion of the population and we belonged.

Saturday morning when I woke up I began going over, in my mind, the conversations of the day before and one statement came back very clearly. The county attorney at one point said to me: "Preacher, don't you know what you are doing? You are lending dignity to what they are doing." We mulled over that one quite a bit. Essentially I think he was correct; that was part of our purpose in being there, although there is an innate dignity emerging among the Negroes as they take courage and assert themselves. At the same time the methods do not detract from the essential dignity of the white citizens.

Friday evening some of us had a long session with the FBI. The continuing harassment by the police afforded the occasion for this. A Negro minister from Staten Island had been threatened twice by the police; they would arrest him if he appeared on the street again without his draft card. He was fifty-three years old and, like most of us, had not seen his draft card for many years. He was pretty scared and appealed to his congressman by telephone and the congressman got in touch with the FBI and they sent two people to see us. They assured us, of course, that there was no federal law by which we could be arrested for not having our draft cards and that the police were entirely out of line. The occasion, however, offered further opportunity for discussion with them. I learned how careful the FBI must be as an investigating agency, turning over their evidence to other divisions of the Justice Department and letting them prosecute. The Justice Department was also told, and we talked with one of their representatives on two different occasions. They were photographing all the applications in Theron Lynd's office and were putting the pressure on him as much as possible. They fully expected to have a second case against him in the very near future.

I had one very interesting opportunity to talk with three students from the white high school. They represented the student paper and were referred to me. Our conversation took place on the courthouse steps. They were asking the right questions; they were listening to what was said. They seemed eager to understand. Our conversation was interrupted by an older man on the steps who felt we had talked too long. But they later came back and talked to me and to another man at the hotel. One got the impression that the younger generation would be more open-minded.

A good many, myself included, left during Saturday. I had come down to Hattiesburg, and now went back, with Metz Rollins, a black pastor from White Plains, New York. We changed planes in Atlanta. The presence of large numbers of white people in the airport scared me and I walked close to Metz for protection.

Though some of us returned home, a considerable number stayed and additional men were invited to come. We did not believe we could come into Hattiesburg, stay for a week, and then leave. Too many things were going on, too much expectation had been aroused.

The Negro leadership of the protest movement had very little sympathy for the religion of the white churches. I would not blame them if out of their experience in Hattiesburg they were to conclude that the Christian church there was one of their major obstacles. The white churches were numerous and strong. The great majority of the people went to church. There were Sunday evening services as well as prayer meetings through the week. The Negro churches were also strong, but many of the prominent churches were not involved in the civil rights movement, mainly because of fear of losing white financial support. Before I left I spoke to Guyot about our wish to work with him at the points where we agreed. He said he could not think of himself as a Christian in the old sense. I responded that I was not surprised, and then tried to share with him some of the theological concepts which compelled the church to work in the changes that affect men's lives in our time, and I tried to point out to him that some of the things that he was saying were really theological statements.

At the same time it is quite clear that as yet the civil rights movement is within the framework of the Christian faith. It is truly a movement of laypeople, with some ministers included. They are determined to use Christian methods. It is still possible for Christians in the South to solve their problems within the context of the Christian faith.

At the end of two weeks of registration 300 new black voters had been registered, multiplying their number fourfold.

The church participation continued in Hattiesburg and other cities in Mississippi for at least six months, with many ministers taking part. Along with them were also many missionaries and members of the COEMAR staff. There was a spontaneous desire to do this. The cost was borne by the participants themselves and others of the group who could not themselves go. Money came from many parts of the world. There also came letters from some of our related churches. For example, both Mexico and Brazil identified themselves with us in this participation, thanking God for this opportunity for us to express support together.

There was often evidence in this participation that the missionaries brought a special dimension. They had themselves crossed racial and cultural lines before, and without thinking about it they knew some things that were needed. Later, missionaries on furlough and on leave were used in presbytery projects in race relations in the United States.

The Vietnam War

I had been a staunch supporter of American participation through the United Nations in the defense of Korea. I had been there. I knew that Syngman Rhee was the choice of the people in their first adventure in a democratic government. I knew that the South had been able to defend themselves from attempts at guerrilla warfare. I knew that the attack was from the North without any legitimate reason and must be resisted if democracy was to survive. But I thought going North was a mistake.

Some of my friends may have been surprised when I criticized the Vietnam War. I had concluded that Ho Chi Minh was the popular leader against the Japanese and then against the French. He was the George Washington of Vietnam, just as Syngman Rhee was in Korea. He asked for our support and got no reply. Instead we supported the puppets that France left behind. They may or may not have been more democratic than the North but they could not suppress rebellion in the South and did not have popular support. We tried to do it alone or with the allies we could buy. The rest of the world did not offer to help resist what it did not regard as aggression. The farther we went the worse it got, until finally we had a half million men involved and were mired in an Asian war our leaders had always cautioned against. From this distance it all seems like a bad dream.

I was also made very much aware by conversations with my Christian brethren around the world that this was a war they were not happy about. It seemed that a bully was trying to beat up on a smaller person and the farther he went the worse he became. I was present at the NCC General Board meeting in Madison, Wisconsin, in the fall of 1964 when the first strong actions were taken raising questions about the war. I was involved and then asked Gene Blake to help us in drafting the preliminary paper. That was finally adopted after a discussion that went well past midnight. This action set off other actions by denominations.

Early in the summer of 1965 Gene Blake wrote a letter to Secretary of State Dean Rusk, with copies to Robert McNamara and Adlai Stevenson, calling attention to the fact that all three of them were Presbyterians and it might be well for church leaders to talk with them. Rusk set a date for us and we met in his offices. Blake, Moderator Thompson, William Morrison, Kenneth Neigh, myself, and James Stewart, Rusk's pastor, were present. By that time Adlai Stevenson was dead. However, George Ball also sat in with us, for Rusk and McNamara had to be away for a time just before lunch. I have learned recently that Ball might have been our ally.

Blake opened the discussion with the simple statement that he was finding it harder and harder to defend American foreign policy as he spent time abroad with other churchmen. He called on Neigh to speak about the Dominican Republic and for me to talk about Vietnam.

Our hosts were very gracious, made their replies which we had anticipated, and Rusk stayed with us through lunch in his office. McNamara had to leave again just at lunch, and said as he left that we could do nothing about the foreign policy. That was the President's prerogative. Why did we not spend our time on domestic problems about which we might do something constructive? I could not let this pass and when he passed me I said: "We are not just American Christians. We belong to a wider Christian community which is disturbed and we cannot keep quiet." He must have heard me, for a week or so later I had a call from the Defense Department asking me if I remembered what he said and what I had said. I did remember and I told them again.

The NCC by this time was trying to get a date with Rusk, and I went with them when the time came, some three weeks later. This meeting was less cordial. Questions had been requested ahead of time and we got formal replies. Not much more than that.

In January 1966 the State Department sent for NCC people. They were explaining a shift in policy and wanted us to know. Rusk met us alone; it was the fifth anniversary of his taking office. Edwin Espy, Gene Smith, and Bob Bilheimer were also there for NCC. Rusk was not at his best. I remember Gene saying to him that our foreign aid to developing nations needed to be increased. Rusk replied that we were the most generous nation in history. Gene reminded him that that may have been true at one time but more recently we were far down the line in proportion to gross national product. Rusk was also defending some of our air strikes as retaliation for what the North had done to us. I pointed out that the North would then strike us again because of the air strike and we would continue in a vicious circle. I asked him if we could not do something to stop this. His reply was, "Yes, we can kill them."

Our General Assembly now began a series of annual actions on Vietnam. Some thought these were planned from the beginning. I can assure them they were not. Each Assembly has a great majority of new people. If the church did not like what the Asesmbly had said about Vietnam, it could stack the next Assembly against further action. This never happened. In 1970 a group tried to head off action by asking that Nixon send a cabinet member to explain his policy to us. He came and spoke, and then we voted an even stronger action. In the 1968 Assembly I spoke from the floor in support of the action. I was Moderator and knew I could answer one charge that was made. Bill Thompson was at my elbow, saw I wanted to speak, and suggested I turn the chair over to the Vice-Moderator and take my seat in the Pittsburgh delegation, from which I could speak. I did so, but we lost the particular point I was trying to make.

No one I knew in the churches ever conferred with President Johnson on the question of Vietnam. This continued under Nixon. The resistance to the war was getting stronger and stronger but no message was getting in to Nixon. I said as much at a prayer service one morning at "475." Some of my Republican friends asked if I would go if they could get me an appointment. I said I would. The appointment that came through was with Melvin Laird. I had met him at the annual Communion service for congressional members in 1969. I talked with him a bit and he remembered me. The luncheon was a weekly affair in his offices. Mayor Walter Washington was there, also the president of Rockefeller University, a woman newspaper reporter, and Mr. David Packard. Laird introduced me as his pastor and asked me to say grace. His father was a pastor and he is an elder. We started on Vietnam as soon as we sat down. Laird listened. He finally said he had heard most of this from his son, who had marched in the protests in Washington. I was impressed with his openness. He did not shut us up, nor did he give in, but I felt he heard us and was open to suggestions.

By this time I was nearing retirement at the end of 1970 but I was still a president of the WCC and could speak in that capacity. Blake wired me from Geneva after the Cambodian incursion. I tried my opening to Laird and got an appointment. I took a United Church of Christ man with me, Howard Schomer, and between us we saw Senators Mike Mansfield, James Fulbright, and Adlai Stevenson III, and then Laird. All seemed open to us. When Laird discovered that my UCC friend had taught in France at a school where many Vietnamese came and that he knew some of them, he wanted to know what he thought. He ended by saying that he was greatly interested in the peace talks, and if we had any suggestions about them, we were to see him again. He gave me telephone numbers that would reach his appointments secretary.

Several months later Gene Blake, Bob Bilheimer, and I used this channel and spent some time with Laird. Bilheimer had written out their suggestions. I know Laird heard. Some of Bilheimer's phrases appeared in a White House statement on the negotiations.

In the midst of this there was a Moratorium Day in Washington. We went to the service in the Washington Cathedral, where Blake spoke, and then to the Presbyterian meeting in the National Presbyterian Church. It was primarily for those who had come from some distance. They got to meet friends there. Bilheimer spoke and I presided. It was a good meeting in spite of the fact that the church had at first refused to have us. Bill Thompson had to remind them that after all they were the General Assembly's National Presbyterian Church. One elder who was a retired Army officer expressed appreciation for the meeting. He said it was a Christian meeting. I have wondered what he thought we were going to do.

On the day of the Moratorium, Alan Brash was in town and flew down with me to Washington, where his son lived. He was then the Deputy General Secretary of the WCC. He remarked that he admired very much the way in which the churches were expressing themselves and the lack of violence in the protests. He thought there was no other country in the world where this sort of protest could be carried on.

The closed door of the Nixon Administration to any contact with the mainline churches had forced us to use the lines we could find in various offices. With Nixon's resignation and Ford's inauguration we tried immediately to open the door again. Direct approaches failed the first time around and I was asked to see if Laird could help with Ford. He was out of office but was willing to try, and may have helped. At least we succeeded shortly after he tried. Ford was very gracious, stayed with us more than the allotted time, and recognized we were from both WCC and NCC. He also began opening doors in his administration for our approaches.

1966 General Assembly

After Blake became General Secretary of the World Council of Churches, the 1966 General Assembly chose Bill Thompson to succeed him as Stated Clerk. Nomination procedures were carefully followed. The General Council set up a representative nominating committee, which spent long hours in coming to the recommendation of two candidates. One was Bill Thompson. The General Assembly then elected its own nominating committee, which received the two names, made its own study, and came up with another name as its single candidate. This nomination was made to the Assembly, Bill Thompson was nominated from the floor, and the Assembly then voted for Bill. Bill was a lawyer, past president of United Presbyterian Men, member of General Council, and the immediate past Moderator. He did not need much training except in WCC matters. He took Gene Blake's place on the WCC Central Committee and we worked there together.

The Middle East

In 1967 the Six-Day War left us struggling to find ourselves in its aftermath. The Christian community, including its leadership, was utterly unprepared for the questions that this raised. We did not have a clear theological position about the Jews, the foreign mission wing was sympathetic with the Arabs, and the national mission wing had friends in the Jewish community and tended to side with them. Add to that the immense complexity of the Middle East problem and we were in confusion.

The NCC appointed an overall committee to deal with the problems that arose. I was chairman and I learned a lot. We had a subcommittee on drafting and we met with both sides. We are now more familiar with the issues than we were then and we had to learn what the issues were about Sinai, the Gaza Strip, the West Bank, Jerusalem, and all that. We finally made a statement which satisfied neither side. We knew we might have to do it again.

That summer the WCC Central Committee met in Crete. Its principal business was to prepare for the Fourth Assembly at Uppsala. But it also had to deal with the Middle East problem.

I was on the Committee of Reference, which dealt with structural problems and Bill Thompson was on the committee where the Middle East would come up. I asked to visit that committee when the Middle East came up and was granted permission, not an unusual thing. At the end of the first session I summarized the items we must deal with. It was no great accomplishment after my NCC education, but it resulted in my being made the chairman of the drafting committee.

The WCC had the struggle right within its own membership. There were several Arab Christians on the Central Committee, and there were several people from Europe who were vigorous, even rabid defenders of the Israeli position. At least one of these was on the staff of the Commission of the Churches on International Affairs. When he discovered that I intended to write my own draft, he said that if the staff did not agree with me they could release their own draft for publication. I was on the structure committee and I took that back to them. The rule was clarified quickly and there would be no action published other than the one we approved.

The report we wrote was approved unanimously by the committee and went to the Central Committee for action. There it was approved with five dissenting votes. Strangely enough it was received by both Arabs and Israelis with more enthusiasm than they had for the NCC statement. I personally could see little if any difference. I suppose that we were now more familiar with the problem and the words that we might use. We knew what would irritate and what would not. It is a commentary upon the problem and the people involved in it that the change of a single word can upset both sides. I do not need to dwell upon this, for Sadat and Begin have demonstrated this for all the world to see.

Later I had two more experiences with this question. At the Central Committee in 1969 we met in Canterbury, England. I was on the finance committee and in the meeting one day I received a cable from a Jewish friend in New York telling me of an action that was being presented in Central Committee and reporting a wording the Jewish committee did not like. I did not then know of the action, but when I saw it I knew what he meant. The wording was ambiguous. I pointed it out to an Arab friend on the committee and suggested he might want to change it. He saw the point but was not willing to change. It would look as though an Arab was backing down in public. I told him I would have to do it publicly if he was not going to do it. I did not have to. Another member saw it also and had it changed. But I was impressed by the fact that my Jewish friend knew more about the proposed wording than I did, and that my Arab friend was unwilling to back down in public when he knew he was wrong.

Later I was asked to edit a book on the Middle East and write one of the chapters. I consented to be the editor but refused to write a chapter. We had a committee to do it. But in the introduction to one of the chapters I wrote something like this: We will never solve this problem until all face the fact that each side has been terribly wronged and is trying to redeem what it has lost in making a settlement. The Holocaust has destroyed six million of the Jews. They now seek a guaranteed security from that happening again. The Arabs have lost people, land, and possessions as the Jews came in. They have suffered and they want it all back. Neither side can get all that it wants. Until each recognizes this and is willing to settle for less, we will never have a reasonable and lasting peace. Of course neither side liked what I wrote.

Chapter 12

A Moderator, a President, and Retirement

LIFE MOVES forward, sometimes rapidly, sometimes slowly. As early as 1958 some friends began to suggest that Pittsburgh Presbytery ought to nominate me for Moderator of the General Assembly. I discouraged them. Again in 1967 some friends in Pittsburgh Presbytery suggested it to me and I was still reluctant. However, in 1968 I concurred with them and they presented my name.

The Executive Committee of COEMAR had been consulted and had approved. One of them, Arthur Miller, who had been Moderator, gave me some good advice which I passed on to the Presbytery and which they used. They solicited the support of other Presbyteries and four or five of them joined with Pittsburgh in the nomination. It was before the day of public questioning of the nominees and the good nominating speeches made an impression. We were well ahead on the first ballot and won on the second.

The Office of the General Secretary in COEMAR had been functioning well and I was able to schedule my Moderator's duties so that I was in the offices of COEMAR for major meetings. Don Black, Ray Kearns, and Dan Pattison ran things while I was gone.

Preserving a Seminary

The Moderator's duties in General Council and in other committees of the church were familiar to me from observation and the burden was not too great. At the same time COEMAR profited from having its Secretary as Moderator and I got to see the whole church in a new way.

In addition to speaking from the floor on Vietnam and losing my point I participated in another action of the General Assembly. The Presbyterian Church U.S.A. had had Johnson C. Smith University and Theological Seminary in the South. The seminary was being neglected, not just because its students were black but because the university was not giving it adequate attention. The Council on Theological Education had had at least two studies made and now recommended to the Assembly that the seminary be closed and its remaining students be given scholarships to other seminaries, Presbyterian if possible.

Earlier in the year I had learned that the black Catawba Synod was utterly opposed to this solution and was sending a busload of people to the Assembly. They believed that scattering the black students would weaken their position in the church and, moreover, that few such students would return to the black churches in the South. I tended to agree with them from my own experience abroad.

The seemingly obvious solution was to merge the seminary with the Interdenominational Theological Center in Atlanta, which had adequate support and full accreditation. This had been suggested and had been turned down, but I thought it merited further consideration. I tried to get the two sides together outside the Assembly but could not fully persuade them. The blacks were not yet ready and the Council people really thought I was interfering in their business, which at points I was. Finally in the midst of a session, word was brought to me that they were ready to talk. I left the platform and we drew up a plan which I then presented. It called for funds to run the seminary another year while a committee studied whether or not the entity of the seminary could be preserved.

After the Assembly the Moderator usually has nine or ten committees to appoint. I gave more attention to two of them this time. One was on the seminary and the other the new one on "the Work of the Holy Spirit," which was to deal with our attitude toward the charismatic movement. The latter made new advances in the church's position and its report is still regarded as a good one, even outside our denomination.

The committee on the seminary had as its chairman the former president of Knoxville College, and as its able secretary Dr. Frank Wilson of Howard University (later of COEMAR's staff). I attended the first two meetings of this committee. At first the white members of the committee began giving answers to questions before the black members were finished discussing the issues. One member was a professor from the University of Pennsylvania. Finally Edler Hawkins leaned over, touched his arm, and said: "Will you keep quiet for a while? You don't know what is going on here." The man shut up, but came back to the next meeting. The committee took two years instead of one and finally moved the seminary to Atlanta with everyone reasonably satisfied. By all reports Johnson C. Smith Seminary is thriving within the context of the Interdenominational Theological Center in Atlanta.

The Council on Evangelism

My emphasis in speaking to the church as Moderator was to face the issues that we all must face in the church and the world and to face them within the context of a firm faith in Jesus Christ and confidence that the Spirit will lead us to solutions. I always tried to provide a time for questions. I learned to stop my speech before I was through, solicit questions, and sometimes add the rest of my speech at the end of the question period. Once in California a presbytery cooperated in scheduling me to meet with local sessions for some ten days in a row. There we often started with questions and faced them more informally. I recommend this. At least I learned more this way.

Out of this experience I became more and more convinced that the church needed leadership in evangelism. Sessions were asking for it and saying they were not getting it. As General Secretary of COEMAR I was a member of the Council on Evangelism. It was to meet in the spring and I asked for time on the docket. I told the Council what I had found as I traveled and urged them to formulate a more adequate program. Then they went round the circle in replying to me.

The first man said that he did not himself know how to speak to someone about his faith. Another agreed. Another said that the Council did not exist to lead the church in this but that it responded to specific requests when they came. Another theologically-minded person said that we must remember that there were times in history when Christians had to be silent. Their words would not be heard, but if they took their stand with the poor they would hear the gospel.

I had a chance to reply at the end. I said that we magnified the difficulty of witnessing. It was not a theological problem and we did not have to be prepared to argue with the people. We had only to witness to what we believed had happened to us because we had come to know God in Christ. I said also that I knew there were times in the Old Testament when the name of God was never mentioned but that was not after Jesus Christ had revealed His nature and His love. Our only need was to point to Jesus Christ. I said I also believed that we needed to take our stand with the poor. Often they cannot hear because we have not stood with them. But that did not preclude our speaking also about why we cared for them. As far as I know, I got nowhere with my plea.

Action on Poverty

The San Antonio General Assembly of 1969 was the Assembly where Jim Forman and the Chicanos spoke. The retiring Moderator is still chairman of the General Council during the Assembly, so that the question of what to do in the light of Forman's "Black Manifesto" came to us all while I was chairman.

Part of the answer was a committee of the Assembly to study ways of helping poor people participate in society, not through Forman's plan but in ways where we could best help. It was contemplated that this would call for new funds. COEMAR had a meeting in June that year and before the end of the meeting it was moved, seconded, and passed that the Commission charge the General Secretary with the task of seeing that overseas people were included in those to be helped with the funds from the new committee. Thus the trilogy of Race, War, and Poverty was completed in the concern of the church in the '60s and on into the '70s.

Uppsala, 1968

The year 1968 was destined to be one of the fullest years of our lives. We were just getting used to the idea of combining a Moderator's and General Secretary's schedules when, as Moderator, I participated with Gene Blake in the service that Don Campbell had planned for the dedication of the carillon at the

Stamford, Connecticut, Presbyterian Church. As we were robing, Gene said to me, "If you are not willing to accept a presidency of the World Council of Churches, you had better get ready to say no."

If there was anything in my life that came as a complete surprise it was this. I knew a committee had been selected to prepare nominations prior to the Fourth Assembly at Uppsala, which was to meet early in July. I also knew they would work on the presidents first, because of complications in meeting all requirements, but I never for one moment had even thought I might be nominated, or even considered. Gene told me they were approaching their final list and I was almost certain to be nominated. At that point there was nothing we could do about it. We could not turn down something we had not yet been asked to consider. COEMAR had nominated our delegation to the General Assembly. This time the committee had given attention to selecting delegates who could take the experience back into the church at the widest possible level. Kenneth Neigh, Bill Morrison, and myself had already been included along with Jim McCord, Art Mc Kay, Robert McAfee Brown, Bill Thompson, David Watermulder, Mr. Walter Greene, Mrs. Elaine Homrighouse, and four others, Alan Thomson of Indonesia among them. One place had been left for the Moderator, and since I already had a place, Edler Hawkins was included.

The Central Committee met on July 2, the Assembly opened on the 4th and came to a close on the 19th. The new Central Committee met the next morning and the new Executive Committee in the afternoon. The whole meeting took almost three weeks, but after all, there had not been an Assembly for almost seven years.

And what a seven years it had been! For one thing, we had grown in numbers. We had had 160 member churches at Evanston, 200 at New Delhi, and now we had 240. We expected to be excited as we met old friends. Now we also had the joy of meeting new friends. There were about 800 voting delegates, but when the categories of consultants, observers, guests, and press representatives were included we ran over 2,000 in all.

The variety extended beyond the superficial. Here we spanned the gap between Roman Catholic Bishop Willebrands and Billy Graham. The day when a meeting produces genuine consensus is over. We were now a diverse group, but we were committed to recognizing one another as Christians and being willing to listen to one another.

It was not only the increase in numbers and variety of people that made this meeting more complex than New Delhi, it was the increase in significant problems that the '60s had brought us. Rarely in all history had the church across the world been confronted with such a mass of problems, many of them related to one another. There was the civil rights problem and the race problem related to it. There was the problem of economic development, which can divide the world, including part of the United States. There was the problem of the Vietnam War, which so badly divided our nation itself and divided us from most of the rest of the world. There was the youth problem and the gap in generations, and we also had at least the beginning of the problem of women's rights. All of these, in one way or another, emerged at Uppsala. Most of these issues had been anticipated in the planning for the Assembly.

Because of his leadership in the United States and the respect accorded him throughout the world, Martin Luther King had been assigned the preaching of the opening sermon. But alas, an assassin's bullet took him from us. The choice to take his place was a good one, our friend Daniel T. Niles from Ceylon, who had preached the opening sermon at the First Assembly in Amsterdam in 1948, was now to preach in 1968. The theme of the Uppsala Assembly was his text, Rev. 21:5: "Behold, I Make All Things New." D. T. had one of the most brilliant minds in the whole of the world church and he did well this time. After describing the issues that together faced us, he ended by emphasizing the greatest need of all.

Should Jesus ask us now what we would have him do for us, what would we ask? Justice among men! Yes. Freedom for all from fear and want! Yes. Peace between peoples and reconciliation between individuals! Yes. The unity of the church and the renewal of its mission! Yes.

But, above all, would we not ask for that which is the direct need of the human heart, and which he alone can supply?

"Show us the Father, and we shall be satisfied" (John 14:8).

The opening speeches of the Assembly were by Blake and Visser 't Hooft. Blake's was the General Secretary's report. He had done well, coming in a bit late for the preparation of the

Assembly but very quickly getting on top of his job. There was no sense of interruption and there was a sense of movement.

Visser 't Hooft set the theme of the Assembly within the context of the history of the World Council. For many, the most significant statement was a sentence near the end, after he had summed up the material needs of a good share of the world. "It must become clear that church members who deny in fact their responsibility for the needy in any part of the world are just as much guilty of heresy as those who deny this or that article of the faith." This sentence was the one many remembered as setting the tone of the Fourth Assembly. The only comment I recorded was that of Jim McCord, who said that "the word should not be 'heresy' but 'schism.' "

Our friend Hendrikus Berkhof of the Netherlands opened the presentation of the theme of Section II (which dealt with "The Mission of the Church") with a paper on "The Finality of Jesus Christ." It was good and was followed by prepared comments from a Protestant, an Orthodox, and a Roman Catholic. We were soon in the midst of six sessions of Bible study. Two were in plenary session under the leadership of Hans-Ruedi Weber, and four were in our dormitories in small groups. Delegations were deliberately broken up so that one often lived with people he had never seen before. Some reacted by hiving off during the day to consort with old friends from home. Most accepted this as a chance to grow.

As usual I recorded my impression of the Communion service. It was unusual and good. It was in the cathedral, with the sermon by the archbishop, and the music was excellent. The Lutheran Church of Sweden did an unprecedented thing and invited all 2,000 of us to partake. The opening hymn spoke to our hearts: "All ye who hear, Now to his temple draw near, Serve him in glad adoration." As we went forward this verse seemed to me to be God's way of establishing our unity in Christ. As I have said before, the diversity here is greater than ever, both theological and confessional, and most of all on social and economic questions. But at the altar we are one. This Sacrament of broken body and shed blood—Christ's sacrifice with promise of forgiveness—is what binds us together across all our differences. Even those who felt they could not participate, and there were some, were there and joined with us in praising God for his gift in Jesus Christ.

In such Assemblies the substantial work is done in Sections, with reports to the Assembly later. I was in Section II, on the mission of the church. It was the most popular, with more than 300 people in it. D. T. Niles was the chairman of the drafting committee and was given help particularly by Newbigin and John Taylor, who had succeeded Canon Warren as Secretary of the Church Mission Society in England. A preliminary draft had been circulated and as a result we also had two other drafts, one from Germany and one from Scandinavia. The latter especially was close to a fundamentalist statement. It came from conservative missionary societies and was aimed at a confrontation with the original draft. None of these drafts survived. We wrote our own.

The result was not a very adequate document. We had both extremes in the Section—those who were gung-ho for social impact by itself and those who were for evangelism alone. We made some progress but we could not reconcile the differences. I wrote: "Few of us were satisfied. I may be prejudiced, but I think COEMAR did a better job in 1967 in its statement on purpose and objectives. I had a copy in my pocket, and I suggested some paragraphs; but in the time we had I did not convince them. This statement, like all statements at Uppsala, was approved in substance and recommended to the churches for study. This statement reveals rather clearly where we are— that is, the measure of clarity that we have and the extent of our confusion. We need to continue to talk to each other."

It should be noted that in Section II, as in all sections, all observers and advisers could be present and speak. This allowed for Roman Catholic participation but also for a variety of conservative evangelicals. This was usually done in good spirit. They could not vote but they were heard. I found that many of our Malone people were at Uppsala. We had two luncheons together and had a total of more than we could have gotten at Malone. They expressed enthusiasm for further talks. Leighton Ford, Billy Graham's brother-in-law and an evangelist in his own right, assured me that they were not there to tone down our social commitment but to assure themselves that evangelism was kept in its proper place.

In all the Sections, without exception, the issue of "economic development" came to the fore. No definitive recommendation was made but it was clear that the Central Committee would have to deal with it. We also assigned a committee to bring in a recommendation on racism. It did not succeed, although it worked into the night on the last possible day. I stayed with them until 1 A.M. and they continued for at least another half hour. (By the way, for most of us it was our first experience with a Swedish long day. At that time of year the sun furnished light until well after 10 P.M. and rose again at 2:30 A.M.)

On the last two days the Assembly gave time to adoption of reports, elections, and the final session in the Cathedral.

I'm sure that a delegate from outside Europe, attending his first Assembly, needs a staff course in procedures if he is to participate. This was my second Assembly and I had more confidence. I had presided at one of the sessions the last week and participated now in a hassle about the elections.

The nominations have to be carefully done. Those for the presidents are most complicated. There have been six presidents elected at every Assembly since the beginning. They are expected to represent both geographical and confessional constituencies. There is never more than one American president, for example, and never more than one Presbyterian from anywhere. They serve on the Central Committee and the Executive Committee. They do not replace anyone who might serve from the same denomination on the Central Committee.

The nominations are duplicated and distributed the day before the elections. For president those on the list were D. T. Niles, Ernest Payne, Alphaeus Zulu, Hanns Lilje, Archbishop Germanos, and myself. There was no discussion but there were two nominations added from the floor. This is difficult. The new nominee has to replace one on the list and represent the same constituencies. The first one did. She was a woman from Sweden and was a Lutheran and was intended to replace Lilje. The vote was 3 to 2 for Lilje. The second nomination was of an African woman who had American citizenship and who was classified as a Methodist. She was to replace me. A woman was presiding at the time and ruled that the nomination was out of order. It would replace Niles as well as Smith, which was true. We had known there might be pressure for a woman but the nominating committee had not chosen one. When Niles died in mid-term he was replaced by a Japanese woman, Dr. Cho, from ICU. At the next Assembly two women presidents were elected.

We had known that there was also unrest about the lack of blacks in the nominations from the United States for the Central Committee. There were 21 Americans; one was black.

But this one, as in previous years, was from one of two black churches. The list totally ignored the blacks in the mainline churches. This was not good enough now and the nominating committee had not sensed it. There had been a meeting of blacks on this and it produced nominations from the floor to replace some on the list. The first was Jean Fairfax of the United Church of Christ. Immediately the president of the United Church of Christ arose and tried to withdraw his name to make room for her. Then came the name of Edler Hawkins, and both Bill Thompson and Jim McCord tried to withdraw their names for Edler.

I had anticipated some of this, had asked the heads of United States delegations if they would agree for me to try to postpone the vote (it was already near the end of the day) and then meet with me that night so we could do this in an orderly fashion. They agreed, and I then had sent up to the platform my request to be heard, if I asked for it, that afternoon. The request also had to contain the motion I would make. At this point I rose and asked to speak. When I got to the platform, both Payne and Blake advised me not to speak; I would be defeated. I was welcomed by the Assembly; I had been elected a president only a few moments before. I said I hoped they would allow the United States delegation people to meet and sort this out. My motion carried.

Bill, Jim, and I went immediately to see Gene after the afternoon session. He advised that I did not have a seat to give up. Mine was not a United Presbyterian position by right. Also he wanted the strongest possible Central Committee and he thought we needed the Stated Clerk.

That night we met. It took some time but it was not too difficult, except at one point. Fairfax and the United Church of Christ were settled easily. The Episcopalians had a youth delegate who was nominated, and that was all right. We agreed with Gene that Bill Thompson should stay and that Jim McCord would make the motion the next morning. The Methodists had five seats; all but one of their candidates were bishops. They had a good black candidate who soon would be a bishop, but what bishop would they put off? Jim Mathews assumed responsibility for this, but by the next morning it hadn't happened. The one who ought to go off had gone home and they could not reach him. So a courageous Methodist layman nominated Roy Nichols to fill the absent bishop's place, and it all went through without a ripple. Representative blacks shared in these consultations, which focused on four denominations because the others had no black delegates, and only delegates were eligible for election.

There were wounds, of course, that can be survived. Roy Nichols became Bishop of Pittsburgh and a member of the Executive Committee of the World Council of Churches. Jean Fairfax became a member of the Combat Racism Committee and then was elected to the nominating committee for the General Secretary. Hawkins was on the Africa Committee and active in Inter-Church Aid. Jim McCord really was the hero. He offered to step down also from the Faith and Order Commission for a young black theologian, but the Assembly could and did elect them both. He also invited Edler Hawkins to become a professor at Princeton Seminary, which Hawkins subsequently did.

I was proud of our U.S. delegations. It was not just that we handled this crisis well and escaped a hassle on the floor that would have hurt us, but in other ways we demonstrated that amid the changes of the '60s we were sensitive and were learning. Europeans are theoretically committed to admit other races, but in practice they turn out sometimes to be different. They have not been hurting. We have been hurting and have been learning.

I have already reported, in the chapter on our relations to Roman Catholics, on our dinner for them at Uppsala. It was a tremendous evening and ten years later is often recalled with memories of individual friendships made that night. Let me add one thing. The Roman Catholic scholar who had spoken at the Assembly said flatly, "The World Council is not a Super Church." I take it he knows what a Super Church is.

Bill Thompson said I did one more thing at Uppsala that was important. The youth delegates numbered 125. They were sometimes militant in a paper they published, and they irritated Europeans more than they did us. Bob Brown and John Taylor were on a committee that worked with them. They had planned to demonstrate at the last worship service. They were persuaded to quote on placards the significant things they thought we had said and silently carry them into the worship service and stand behind the audience along the walls. The police would not let them do so without Blake's approval, and Blake's office would not let them approach Blake that last afternoon on the platform. Taylor came to me. I watched for my chance, caught Blake as he came down to the floor, and explained it. Taylor saw Blake and everything went off very well.

The closing service was in the cathedral. It was brief and without a sermon. We had already had too many speeches. We had Scripture readings in Hebrew, Swahili, Romanian, Greek, and Indonesian Bahasa. We had two choirs, one from the Russian delegation whose a cappella singing was "out of this world." (Metropolitan Nikodim is a baritone and my friend Kotliarov is a deep bass.) Dr. Visser 't Hooft came over after the Russians sang and said, "Could your American delegation sing like that?" The other choir sang a modern folksong from England, "Were you there . . .," and youth participants silently brought in placards with significant sentences from statements the Assembly had made. Then we made our commitment together in the words of this prayer:

God, our Father, you can make all things new.
We commit ourselves to you. Help us
    —to live for others since your love includes all men;
    —to seek those truths which we have not yet seen;
    —to obey your commands which we have heard but not yet
      obeyed;
    —to trust each other in the fellowship which you have given us;
and may we be renewed, through Jesus Christ,
your Son and our Lord. Amen.

Then we sang "Thine Is the Glory."

The service lasted less than an hour, but hundreds of people remained for almost that long outside the cathedral in the long dusk, talking, bidding good-by to old and new friends, and tasting and lingering over the fellowship we had experienced together as believers in Jesus Christ.

World Council Leadership

At the Central Committee meeting the day after the Assembly in Uppsala the nominations for officers and other members of the Executive Committee reflected the emphasis on integration and development.

M. M. Thomas of India was chairman, Pauline Webb of

England and Metropolitan Meliton of Greece were vice-chairmen. The six presidents were members also, and there were sixteen others: Bokeleale of Congo, Faune of the Philippines, Gottschald of Brazil, Josefson of Sweden, Lochman of Czechoslovakia, Marshall and Nichols of the United States, Nikodim of the Soviet Union, Reed of Canada, Rossel of Switzerland, Sabev of Bulgaria, Sarkissian of Lebanon, Simatupang of Indonesia, Tomkins of England, Weizsäcker of Germany, and Wesonga or Uganda.

Because of the six-year gap between Assemblies, the turnover in delegates was 65 percent at New Delhi and at least as great at Uppsala. The turnover is greater in the Central Committee and in its Executive Committee. Only nine out of the 25 in the Executive Committee had had experience on the Central Committee and five of these were now presidents, if one includes Visser 't Hooft, who was now the honorary president. Blake had emphasized to us that the continuity of the committee would have to come from the presidents in the first years of our service.

The idea of having six presidents is that the leadership can be representative and no one can be singled out as the head of the World Council of Churches. At all Central and Executive Committee meetings the presidents sit either on the platform or at a special place in the front. Their chairs have their names on them. They are sometimes charged with seeking procedural ways out of a thorny problem but ordinarily they do not serve on subcommittees. The presidents represent the World Council of Churches on formal occasions and they take counsel with the General Secretary. I attended almost every meeting from 1968 through 1972. Then Floy's health situation made travel usually impossible.

1969 Central Committee and the Program to Combat Racism

The WCC Assembly at Uppsala in 1968 left two major items of business to its Central Committee. Both racism and economic development had been discussed in the Assembly, but there had been no clear consensus about what should be done. There was emphatic support for actions of reference and there was expectation.

The World Council held a Consultation on Racism in London some time before the Central Committee met at Canterbury in the summer of 1969.

Having just come from our own General Assembly of 1969 in San Antonio and confrontation there with Jim Forman and later with him again at "475," some of us were prepared for Canterbury. But the other WCC people were hearing for the first time the thrust of the anger that sometimes motivates the protests against racism. They reported their reactions to us at Canterbury. One said: "I frankly confess to a profound personal reaction to the more unique aspects of the consultation—the blunt, bitter condemnation of racism and the unequivocal demand for concrete action to end it sounded by some of the participants and active observers." Another said: "No one could sit through these experiences without being forced to look anew at his own heart, his own sins of commission and omission as a churchman and a citizen."

The result was that the Central Committee established a Program to Combat Racism and contributed $200,000 from its reserves to start a fund for this program. The Program still continues and is supported by voluntary contributions. Sometimes it has been the center of outside criticism of a serious nature. The following is a personal experience that happened ten years before the program existed but which illustrates its operation.

After the Ghana IMC Conference in the winter of 1957–58, Winburn Thomas and I went on to visit the Cameroon and the Sudan for our first time. The Presbyterian Church in the Cameroon had just become independent from our church the year before, when Gene Blake as our Stated Clerk went out to celebrate the occasion. The French colonial government was already having to deal with rebels in the interior and was disturbed by the fact that Gene had chosen to preach on "Christian Freedom" at the celebration in Elat. The area of the work of the French Protestant missionaries as well as our area was in the interior where the rebels were.

Before we left the Cameroon, we called on the French High Commissioner. He was cordial but his military adviser questioned us sharply as to where we had visited, whom we had seen, and what we talked about. He asked me where we were going next and I told him Khartoum. He almost bristled at that.

We went to Khartoum by way of Chad and stayed with

missionaries there for three or four days. The second morning I was walking down one of the main streets and saw the sign of the Sudan Bible Society in one of the windows. I went in and met Rev. Prince Albert Hamilton, the Secretary of the Society. He was a black man from British Guiana, had been a British soldier, had married an Egyptian woman and become an Anglican clergyman. After we had talked a bit, I told my new friend that we had just come from the Cameroon. He then asked me if I would like to meet some Cameroon men who sometimes came to the Society to talk and sing hymns. I agreed and promised that Tommy and I would be back after lunch.

That afternoon we were introduced to five men from the Cameroon, all of them Christians. Two were Presbyterians from our church, one being a graduate of Cameroon Christian College. One was a Presbyterian from British Cameroon who had been a sergeant in the British Army. The other two were Roman Catholics, one having been a student for the priesthood. We soon learned that all five were part of the Cameroon government in exile, the balance of their executive committee being in Egypt.

We talked about what part Christians might play in government. I shared a book I had about the new government in Ghana and we all prayed together.

Our next stop was Geneva, and there I got a secretary and made a record of how I had gotten into this and all we had done. Some months later, after returning to New York, I received a letter from Dr. L. K. Anderson, our field representative in the Cameroon, telling me that the French government had asked the American consul in Yaoundé what I had been doing with those people in Khartoum. The French government had intercepted a letter from there to the rebels that told about our visit. I told Andy that the first reply to the American consul ought to be that it was none of his business, but that he could also give the consul a copy of my Geneva notes.

That was the last I heard, except for a conversation a year or so later at a luncheon in the White House. Cameroon was now free, and some members of its new Cabinet were to be guests of President Kennedy. The President invited a Roman Catholic, a Baptist, and myself to lunch to meet them. I sat beside one of the Cameroon Cabinet members and told him my story. He named three or four of the men that I had met and told me that they were now officials in the new government in Yaoundé.

The WCC Committee on the Program to Combat Racism dealt with situations like that, especially with continued relations and help in the form of medical and educational supplies. We had a strict rule that none of these supplies could be used for military purposes. From 1969 to 1975 I was a member of the Executive Committee of WCC, which had to approve all grants. For two years I served as a substitute member of the Combat Racism Committee itself. Once I traveled all the way from New York to Sofia primarily to stop a grant. I was successful, but I can well understand how a colonial government could count us among their enemies.

Montreux, 1970: Consultation on Economic Development

Jim Forman, in his insistence on "reparations" at San Antonio and then at "475," had linked the problem of race to economic development. This now became part of the preparation of some of us for the Consultation on Economic Development that WCC called in early 1970 in Montreux, Switzerland.

I had not attended the London Conference on Racism that preceded the Canterbury Central Committee meeting, but this time, in Montreux, I was a delegate from the Division of Overseas Ministries of the NCC. As a voting delegate I took my seat with everyone else, somewhat to the rear since my name was Smith. But because I was also a president of the World Council, on official occasions, such as the reception given by the mayor, I was a guest seated between the mayor and an archbishop.

Both as a missionary and as a COEMAR executive I had been partially prepared for Montreux. As early as 1935 I had said publicly that Americans needed to reduce their standard of living. Later Ernest Wykoff, a lay member of the Foreign Board, came back from a visit to India and quietly set up a small department in his store in Stroudsburg, Pennsylvania, to sell products from people that he had met on his trip. He had visions of expanding it but it went no farther.

In 1966 Eugene Adams of the COEMAR staff proposed that some of the "Unrestricted Reserves" of COEMAR be used as a fund for economic development overseas. This was realized when the chairman of COEMAR's Finance Committee proposed to COEMAR that we set aside one million dollars of our undesignated reserves to encourage development overseas. He hoped others would join us but they never did. However, the Emerging Economies Corporation (EEC) was formed in 1967 and we began operations.

At Uppsala, Don Black had presented the idea of an investment fund to the section which was discussing methods of economic assistance, but when I joined him in the plenary session neither of us made any impression on the group. It took eight or nine years before the World Council of Churches started such an investment operation.

However, during 1967 and 1968 a plan for such an investment fund was developed for minority groups in the United States by The United Presbyterian Church U.S.A., and 30 percent of the undesignated reserves of all agencies was set aside for this purpose. This was the Presbyterian Economic Development Corporation (PEDCO). It had the same dream that John Templeton had given us.

Our COEMAR project, the Emerging Economies Corporation (EEC), with its purpose of encouraging development overseas, was to be strictly business in its operations and to encourage small businesses to learn to operate in our economic system. We expected dividends of 5 percent on our investment. EEC has paid one dividend but lack of capital has hampered the operation. It now has joined with a secular corporation which is striving for the same ends. PEDCO has been less profitable in its operations but is becoming a businesslike corporation.

Parallel to PEDCO there had also developed a plan for raising funds for grants to groups seeking economic development, funds that would be raised for that purpose in the United Presbyterian Church. At the 1969 General Assembly a committee was appointed to prepare plans for such a campaign. We had just completed a fifty-million-dollar campaign for capital funds, both in the United States and overseas. It had been oversubscribed by more than 10 million dollars. Some dreamed of a similar campaign now for minority development. This was in the planning stage when Jim Forman confronted the Assembly in 1969 and demanded "reparations." We recognized his plight, assured him of our sympathy, and told him we were working on a plan through our own organizations for help for the needs that he was pointing to. When his confrontation at "475" became intolerable, we told him to leave and assured him that his continued presence was counterproductive for the efforts we were already making. He left only when we secured an injunction.

However, in the summer of 1969 COEMAR asked that the needs of development overseas be included in any plans for a campaign for development. This appeal went to the General Council and through it to the committee itself.

So I was partially prepared and had ample reason to be at Montreux.

Originally it was expected that there would be 80 delegates—40 from the West and 40 from the Third World. Actually we had 180 people there, only 100 delegates who worked in the subcommittees, but 80 more who were observers, press, etc. These could only attend the plenary sessions.

The WCC had also been involved in activity that led up to Montreux. At Saloniki in 1959, Christian responsibility in areas of rapid social change had been discussed, especially as this applied to Africa. Later, in the early '60s, after a survey of need among the nations that were gaining their freedom from colonialism, the WCC had had a special program for churches in these areas as they prepared to assume their responsibilities for the new life of the new nations. Clinton Marsh, a United Presbyterian minister, had been on loan to this WCC program for a number of years. Because of these things it was not surprising that preparation for Montreux was thoroughly done. The papers presented were evidence of the competence of their authors. Other consultants were available for advice.

We were divided into five sections of some 20 voting members each. They dealt with:

1. Process of development and objectives of projects
2. Policy and procedure for church-sponsored projects
3. Structure and organization
4. Technical services needed
5. Mobilization of funds

The discussions revealed that there was no question among us as to the urgency of the need and the responsibility of Christians. The decade of United Nations emphasis on Development was almost at an end and the gap between the rich nations and the poor nations was greater than when it started. Archbishop Helder Câmara put it this way: "We Christians are

20 percent of the world and own 80 percent of its wealth. We share responsibility for poverty and trouble in the world. The Roman Catholic Church and WCC could force the West to look at where we are before it is too late." We were also aware that what the churches can do is a very modest part of the whole. It will take government and business in major efforts, but we have a share, an important share, sometimes doing some things that others cannot do.

I was assigned to the third section, on Structure. Dr. Charles Sherman of Liberia, a former treasurer of his country and now the chairman of the Inter-Church Aid Division of the World Council, was in our group. It became evident that we were facing a serious issue and division of opinon on how we should go about it. Many who were engaged in relief and rehabilitation tended to believe that they were already involved in development. Others insisted this must be different. This is not charity or aid to the poor. This is offering them a chance to be free and take part in their own development. A structure that decides what is good for the poor without consulting and involving them is self-defeating.

The Churches' Participation in Development

It took us several sessions to discover that what Sherman and the others were talking about was something entirely different from what Church World Service and Inter-Church Aid was doing. Sherman called his own committee a "Donor's Club" with the power in the hands of those who gave the money. To have integrity the full power of decision must be shared. It made those of us who were in the agencies think afresh about our own motives. If we are Christians, we believe that God gave the resources of the earth for all people alike. We who have much were not thereby appointed his benevolent donors. We were appointed to talk together and find a way in which all could both work and receive a just share of these resources. To achieve this will be harder for all of us. We will have to find new attitudes and new practices to follow.

For a time this divided the group, both in the Section and later in the plenary. Old customs die hard. It took me two or three days to understand what was happening. When I did I took the side of the Third World. A German scholar and

Christian said, "The churches are too much concerned about motives for what they do and not enough about the effects of what they do." In other words, how do we look to the recipients when we are playing our part? At the time, this new look produced a kind of conversion experience in me. I soon found out this was also true with others. At the time I tended to offend my CWS and Inter-Church Aid friends.

The crux of the matter came in the structure we recommended. It must not be just the old structure. CWS and Inter-Church Aid could have overall management, but a semiautonomous commission must also be free to give guidance on process and attitude. Thus there came into existence the Commission on the Churches' Participation in Development (CCPD). At the end, Blake was there to help us fit the structure into the total WCC and also to assure himself and us that we could work together in this new fashion. The way donors organize themselves to help is a major element in the success of the operation.

The Consultation aimed high on fund-raising. They challenged the churches to give 2 percent of their annual income. They challenged individuals to do the same.

Their report was taken up two weeks later by the WCC Executive Committee; it was approved and sent to the churches. I was present at the Executive meeting, left early with the first copy of Gene Blake's letter to the churches, and gave it to Bill Thompson in a General Secretary's conference the next day after my return. He in turn gave it to the General Assembly committee, which was meeting that weekend.

The Self-Development Fund

With this documentation there was no longer any question about overseas being included in the plan for what the United Presbyterian Church was to call The Fund for the Self-Development of People. In COEMAR we prepared to back this up at the General Assembly with as much expertise as possible. Books were recommended for study and we emphasized what it was that Christians brought to this that made it different. Montreux had prepared us for this. The original report was good from a secular standpoint. The Third World people had insisted that the Christian context had to be written into it.

Archie Crouch and I had been working on an article for *Presbyterian Life* on evangelism and at the same time on a Significant Paper called "It Still Happens," which was also on evangelism. Now we set to work on another Significant Paper on development. It came out before General Assembly with the title, "Christians and Self-Development of People." This became Number 19 in the series of Significant Papers that COEMAR had published in pamphlet form during the 1960s.

The General Assembly committee recommended that funds for development be raised in connection with the One Great Hour of Sharing for Relief. I had questions about this, lest it confuse the two things. It has done so to a degree, but it has also furnished us a chance to explain the difference. Beginning in 1971 we have raised approximately $2,000,000 every year for this purpose.

The issue at General Assembly was never really in danger. Two Assemblies had already discussed this in principle. We were ready for it. National Missions and COEMAR joined together in supporting it. We had also joined in approving the form of the action.

The hassle at the Assembly came when the Assembly committee considering the report made an appeal to the General Council for some immediate funds to start the program. Approval in May 1970 would mean that the funds would be raised in the spring of 1971 and not really be available until late fall, a year and a half after approval. That also delayed any help we would be able to give to the World Council. The suggestion was that help be given immediately from "Undesignated Reserves."

Undesignated Reserves were not profits held over from previous years but were the legacies that the Board of National Missions and COEMAR received without designation. They were kept for a rainy day, and in each instance amounted to something less than $10,000,000. Neither of us resisted the suggestion that help be given from these reserves, but General Council voted against it. When the Council's report came to the Assembly, an amendment was made restoring the original request, and it was vigorously debated. The vote supporting the General Council's action was 3 to 2, and very clearly our ethnic minorities were defeated and they knew it. Both Kenny Neigh and I had anticipated this possibility and believed the General Council action was unwise. After the vote I asked to speak. I said the Assembly's vote got Ken and me off the hook; we now proposed to put ourselves back on the hook and would try to raise one and a quarter million dollars for the fund, to be used as it began. There was silence for a moment and then applause. Later two General Council officers chided us for overriding the General Council. The Stated Clerk and the Moderator immediately said we had saved the Assembly from much bitterness. Both of us got approval for advancing the money and the program started several months earlier than it otherwise could have. Also, the gift of $200,000 made to the WCC at the end of 1970 saved the Commission on the Churches' Participation in Development from possible disaster. In some mysterious way God was planning for us all to be more adequately involved in ministering to the world's poor.

Bob Bilheimer of the NCC had also been at Montreux and together we tried to get NCC involved. We reported early not only to the Division of Overseas Ministries but also to the Division of Home Missions. Later we got denominational leaders together, but only the Methodists cooperated. Gene Smith was now in the World Council's New York office, but during that last year I made speeches for the Self-Development Fund and one of them was at a Methodist Board meeting. Gene's successor, Tracey Jones, and I also shared memos from meetings with each other and circulated some of them to our staffs.

In the United Presbyterian Church the plan included forming presbytery committees across the country to help presbyteries not only in the raising of money but in encouraging and sponsoring projects in their own areas. Thus the church at the local level could involve itself and learn. We all needed this. At one presbytery where I spoke a young elder rose and said, "I do not want a poor person sitting on a committee that spends my money."

At the World Council level progress was slow but steady with some of the same problems arising. At Addis Ababa in January 1971 at a Central Committee meeting, an Inter-Church Aid staff man said to me: "We are doing well. When do you think we can merge this all with the other things we are doing?" I said, "Maybe we can talk about it at the next Assembly in '75." Then Bishop Thimme of Inter-Church Aid said publicly that they had been converted and had put more Third World people on their committee, and he thought they could now do development also. I waited until he was through and then replied: "Dr. Thimme, I know you and I are converted to this; that is not the problem. I know we are also not yet sanctified."

The Church as Stockholder

The involvement of the churches in the questions of race, war, and poverty led inevitably to the question of their own investments. Later this was cared for by responsible interdenominational and denominational committees, but at the beginning each agency in the United Presbyterian Church carried its own responsibility.

Eastman Kodak furnished the first case in which we were involved. A black community organization had been financed in part by the presbytery in Rochester, New York, with the help of the Board of National Missions. It had negotiated with Kodak concerning hiring practices and an agreement had been signed by the Kodak representative. Some days later Kodak rejected the agreement. National Missions conferred with Kodak but to little avail. COEMAR owned stock in Kodak and its executive committee authorized representation at the stockholders meeting in New Jersey where the protest would be brought. Don Black and Dan Pattison represented the Commission. By coincidence I was already to be present that day in Rochester, speaking at the presbytery meeting.

The protest was made at the stockholders meeting, and later the black community organization was recognized by Kodak. However, we experienced for the first time the difficulties of dealing with the established structure of a large business organization and its stockholders. We were also questioned at first about the legitimacy of a church organization being represented.

The next involvement arose from relations with South Africa and its loan fund, available from several New York banks. We held stock in both First National City Bank and Chase Manhattan Bank. Our first step was to talk with management, and in each case we saw top management, Walter Wriston and David Rockefeller. We got nowhere, although Rockefeller helped the Methodists and ourselves to meet one of the top businessmen in South Africa along with a Chase Manhattan vice-president.

In protesting against our being involved with apartheid practices, we used the illustration of James H. Robinson, a black United Presbyterian pastor who was the head of Operation Crossroads Africa and who was sent by the United States to a ceremony in Botswana with the status of an Ambassador. He was to change planes at Cape Town and the U.S. consul there met him at the airport. His next plane was delayed and he had to stay overnight. South Africa had not given him a visa and this posed a problem. The official at the airport solved it by promising that he could enter without record, stay overnight with the consul, and leave in the same way the next day. The consul immediately invited several American businessmen to have dinner with Dr. Robinson that evening. They all declined on the ground that to eat with a black man would endanger their business relations in South Africa. The South African businessman confirmed that this would be the case and said he thought declining the invitation was a wise move. The Chase Manhattan vice-president interrupted to say he would have advised their men to accept the invitation. We got no results but we had had a chance to register our protest at the highest levels.

Bishop Lloyd Wicke had been with me at the Chase Manhattan Bank and now we also went together to the stockholders meeting at the First National City Bank. Here we raised the question about the way the bank treated black employees in South Africa and its social responsibility to treat them as equals. The chairman of the board replied that the bank sought to exercise social responsibility in the United States, but in South Africa they were guests. "Our only business in South Africa is to make money for our stockholders." At this the stockholders applauded.

It was some years later that the loan fund was withdrawn and the banks established a policy of increased promotions and salaries for black employees.

About the same time there was a protest against Gulf Oil and its practices in Angola. Again we first approached management, this time on an interdenominational basis. The president and a public relations man flew to New York to see us. They said they had good relations with the government of Angola and that when they had visited the governor it appeared that he was supported by the people. A missionary of the United Church of Christ who was with us replied that he had heard the governor praise the Gulf Oil Company because their money was paying for the bullets which enabled them to put down the movement of blacks for freedom. Later there was danger that our approach to management would be confused with that of a very militant group which was preparing to attend the stockholders meeting. Joe Beeman of the Stated Clerk's Office and I visited the Gulf Oil management in Pittsburgh, and later a member of COEMAR and I attended the stockholders meeting. Because of the militant manner of others participating, we did not speak in the stockholders meeting but went to the platform afterward and presented a statement to the Directors. This resulted in an exchange of letters which indicated at least that we were being heard. Both meetings confirmed our first impressions that it took a lot of work and courage to confront management. No wonder many believe that stockholders meetings are rigged so that no criticism gets serious consideration. Actually at one of the meetings they did not count the votes of those who were there. They already had proxies supporting management from absent stockholders that gave them a good majority. However, not counting our votes was hardly a good way to assure us we were getting a fair hearing.

Subsequently the churches and others got better organized. Today they know how to present their protests through proper channels and get on the docket of a meeting. In many instances their protests have made a difference in the policy of the company involved. Only by making their voices heard in the meetings of companies where they own stock can the churches establish credibility among those who protest that they are being treated unfairly. As long as these channels are open, the churches ought not to use the weapon of selling their stock.

Successor Nominated

In the late 1960s the General Assembly had changed the retirement age of national agency employees from 70 to 65. However, for those who were already past 65, the agency was free to set the date after considering all the needs of the agency and the persons involved. My date was set for the end of December 1970, when I would be 67½. A committee was then appointed to search for a new General Secretary. Don Black was nominated and elected in the spring of 1970. He took a trip around the world to become up-to-date on our relationships, and took office on January 1, 1971. He had participated in COEMAR at the level of Associate General Secretary from its very beginning and was now a trusted leader in the church at home and abroad. Continuity with vision was being assured.

The Challenge of World Community

In 1965 I prepared with special care an address I made at Grosse Pointe, Michigan, and later at Englewood, New Jersey. In thrust it was not much different from others that I had made, but it was at once more comprehensive and more concise. I quoted William H. McNeill, the Chicago historian, in his book *The Rise of the West*, in which he describes the development across the long centuries by which various civilizations have stimulated one another in the direction of the *oikumene*, the realization of one human community. He documents the fact that this movement in history has been accelerated in recent decades, so that we are about to see the firm establishment of a world civilization based upon the industrial and technological advances that have come through the West. This new world community will have but one history; every major event anywhere in the world will be an event in the history of all people.

This new world civilization will be industrial, technological, and secular in character. The new nations reject the white man's control but they welcome Western education and technical know-how. Already universities and industrial communities are becoming international in character. Business knows its future depends upon the raw materials of the world and the markets of the world.

This new fact of world community confronts the Christian church with its demand for change. C. L. Sulzberger, in *The New York Times*, says: "The intellectual explosion which has begun in science and politics has come to the church." He carries it beyond the scientific world. New thinking must be done about mankind and the world, about the possibilities for both growth and destruction. Protestant, Orthodox, and Roman Catholic alike must prepare to meet the challenge.

The church in mission has lived for 150 years in a different and narrower world. Mission has been that which is done by

established churches for people less fortunate than themselves, at home and abroad. We have always been the
senders, they have always been the receivers of our benefi-
cence. This conception has outrun its usefulness. In no part
of the world are people waiting eagerly for someone in
another part of the world to tell them what to believe and
what to do, especially if the teller is of a dominant race.

The Christian church has not been completely unaware of
these challenges to change. Arend van Leeuwen, a Dutch
historian and theologian, in his book *Christianity in World
History* also follows the same thesis, that history moves
toward one world community. But he adds the fact that this
movement is of God. It is what God intended from the
beginning, and the influence of the revelation in Jesus Christ
has been the major fact in stimulating the development of
science and industry and spreading it throughout the world.
Therefore this change must be welcomed by the Christian
church as God's preparation of a greater opportunity. Sulzberger in his column quotes from the third chapter of
Revelation in this connection: "I have set before you an open
door, which no one is able to shut."

The church has been making preparations for this event.
The communities of believers established abroad are not
branches of our American church. They are Christian
churches in themselves, equal with us in the common task of
mission. We Americans no longer have a monopoly. The
churches we have established now share with us in the
challenge of this new world community. We all must share
our faith and we all are in need of stimulus from others. The
mission of the church is no longer the thrust of the Western
church out into the non-Western world. It is the whole thrust of
the whole church into the whole world—Asia, Africa, Latin
America—*and* pagan Europe and North America.

After I preached this sermon at Englewood I received a letter
from Bryant George, an executive of the Board of National
Missions and now an executive of the Ford Foundation. He had
been at the Englewood service and heard me. He now wrote,
"Given your personal activities in this past year, [and] my
knowledge of you, culminating in hearing that declaration
Sunday, I would say that the logical conclusion to be drawn
from that 'Re-formation of Mission' would be an organic

merger of the Board of National Missions and the Commission on Ecumenical Mission and Relations. It seems to me the logic of what you had to say was inescapable; the examples that you used to document this, and the theology, absolutely support it."

I shared the speech and Bryant's letter with four or five members of the COEMAR staff. Its conclusion was not a surprise to us. In the early 1960s I had thought that COEMAR and Christian Education had more in common, but had gradually changed my mind. As our conception of the world changed and we understood that the United States was only one part of that world, we began to see that we and the other churches of the world shared a common task, the sharing of our faith with the whole world, including the United States.

Later, National Missions and COEMAR appointed a joint committee whose business it was to look at areas of common concern and suggest ways of doing the work together. We already had been working as one in:

1. Leadership Development (joint office)
2. Urban and Industrial Ministry (joint office)
3. Office personnel
4. Coordinating Committee on Inter-American Affairs
5. Committee on Church and Race

We now began to look at possible merger of:

1. Travel Office
2. Medical Office and Advisory Medical Committee
3. Treasury—accounting processes; joint auditing firm, etc.
4. Legal Office
5. Funds development
6. Relations to United Presbyterian Women's organization

We set about improving our common relationship to:

1. Synods and presbyteries
2. Committee on Inter-Church Affairs
3. Communication and interpretation

And we examined together our:

1. Responsibility for relation to Jewish people
2. Activities in the field of evangelism

These were some of the steps that we considered, tried, and sometimes adopted as we faced the challenge of the world community that was emerging after the centuries of colonialism. We were beginning to accept it as a result of God's plan and to be thankful that we could face this emerging global community in company with all others of the world Christian community.

A Summing-Up

The last half of 1970 was a quiet period for me. Don Black was away touring the world in preparation for his service as General Secretary. I assumed many of his duties at "475," including the chairmanship of the Budget Committee. In some ways it was good to be back home, working at the nitty-gritty task of fitting resources and needs together.

The COEMAR budget-making process was not one in which decisions were made from the top down. We all shared in it. Once the limitations were set and we knew the dimensions within which we must operate, there was overall supervision but the final decisions came from the groups of people in the staff who would have to live with those decisions. In a real sense we were still a collegiate organization. And these decisions were hard. I remember that two or three different times in the process we had to come together as a whole and make sure that our initial distribution of the budget in its sections was just and fair.

On my last day in office after all were gone except Tommy (Winburn Thomas), who was waiting to go with me to our homes in Larchmont, I took the "General Secretary" designation off my office and put it on Don Black's office in place of "Associate General Secretary." Our offices were almost identical and he was going to stay in his old office with the new title. Oscar McCloud was to come into my office as the new Associate.

On our first day of retirement, January 1, 1971, we wrote our last "Dear Colleague" letter to missionaries, Commission members, staff, and synod and presbytery executives. Here are quotations from significant parts of it:

Dear Colleague:

It's seven thirty in the morning on the first day of the new year. Outside four or five inches of snow have fallen in the night and it is still snowing. Inside Floy and I are beginning the first day of our retirement; a new day dawning and new adventures ahead.

Forty-one years ago we were in language school in Japan. For twelve years our home was in Sapporo, Wakayama, and Tokyo. I personally had a "home" in Yokohama for the first six months of 1942. I did not choose it, but it proved to be a creative and rewarding experience.

For more than five years we were in Pittsburgh. For the last twenty-two and one-half years we've been in New York—at "156" with the Board of Foreign Missions, and then at "475" with the Commission on Ecumenical Mission and Relations. There are many things in these years also that we would not have chosen: the evacuation from Korea in 1950, and the "occupation" at "475" in 1969, for example. But these also are experiences from which we all have learned.

The year 1970 brought its own problems and challenges. We wrote you last in October as the pattern of the 1971 budget developed. The Commission meeting in November confirmed what the Executive Committee had anticipated. The budget for 1971 "holds the line." By taking another $1,500,000 from the fast-dwindling reserves of "unallocated legacies," assurance has been given that no more reductions in personnel need be made than those already planned. There are fifteen new appointments in the budget, but we would have needed seventy to replace those contemplating transfer or retirement during the year.

As anticipated, the Commission also authorized a special committee to work with staff in planning programs for the future within anticipated income. Don Black as the new General Secretary will be in touch with you about ways by which suggestions may be made. We have joined in welcoming him back from his trip, and pray God's blessing upon him as he begins his task today.

There have been endless discussions as to why there is this decline in giving to the General Mission Budget. Let me list in ascending order of importance what appear to me to be the major reasons:

1. *Decline in membership.* Percentagewise this is small, but it still is tens of thousands of people.
2. *Polarization.* The misunderstanding and discontent in some local churches with the General Assembly program has caused some withholding of funds. It is now possible for a congregation to designate its funds so as to guarantee that none of its money is spent on pro-

grams not approved by the congregation.

3. *Increased interest in local mission.* This is a good sign but it often results in less for General Mission.

4. *The Recession.* The national elections in November proved that the voters know we are having one. Members tend to restrict spending for all purposes, including the church. Even the Salvation Army had significant reductions in its giving at Christmastime.

5. *Inflation.* I'm convinced this is the single largest external factor. Even if we receive the same dollar income as three years ago, real income is reduced by 18 percent. The individual feels threatened and guards his own finances by giving the same or less to the church. The local congregation, presbytery, and synod are faced with inflated expenses and take a bigger bite before the money goes to national and international programs. The answer, of course, is in the Biblical practice of proportionate giving. But not many individuals, congregations, presbyteries, or synods follow that practice.

6. *A Crisis of Faith.* Here is the basic problem. If faith were present, the reasons above would not cripple the mission budget. Many United Presbyterians, along with other Christians in America, are in this crisis of faith. The lack of financial support is a symptom of a more serious disease.

We should have expected a great deal of this. We live in a period of phenomenal scientific and technological change. If man can go to the moon, he tends to believe he can solve all his problems if he puts his mind to the task of finding the right technical answer. More and more nominal Christians depend on what material progress can do for them. They no longer feel the same need for the church, much less believe they should share the Christian faith.

Often the church has made its own contribution to this failure by not seeking new ways of communicating with this new generation. It has also often failed to find flexible ways of bringing the Christian faith to bear upon such problems as war, poverty, and race, which our changing society has made critically urgent.

There are indications that the church has awakened to the need of communicating more effectively with this generation concerning the "Good News" in Jesus Christ. The church also is recognizing its natural identification with human need wherever it is found. There are also indications that the attitude toward the need for spiritual things has begun to change.

We need to remember that this isn't the first time the community of believers has been in a time of troubles; remember the family of Abraham which set out in faith for a land it did not know; the children of Jacob enslaved for 400 years in Egypt; the people of Israel wandering in the wilderness, and so troubled they wished they were back in Egypt as slaves; the remnant in exile far from the songs of Jerusalem; Jerusalem itself destroyed just 1,900 years ago and with it the mother church of the Christian faith; Rome destroyed by the Huns just as the Christian church had emerged as a significant factor in the Empire; and what a time of troubles the Reformation must have been! The mother church racked by division. The new churches struggling for their existence and often fighting among themselves.

And yet we look back on every one of these times as glorious periods in the life of the community. Then faith was deepened, courage was born, and new creative ideas emerged to challenge the future.

Those of us who serve in the mission of the church in the whole world, including the United States, can be encouraged by these things, knowing also that we have a particular contribution to make in this process by which God renews the life of the community of believers and sends them forth afresh as witnesses to the Good News.

Floy and I want to thank all of you for the many greetings and expressions of friendship that have come to us as we retire. The dinner and program at the time of the Commission meeting will always be remembered. I said to someone afterward that it had the warmth of a "stunt night" at a Mission meeting. The reply was, "Only more so." The letters and greetings at Christmastime and the two special books of letters will be constant reminders of your interest and concern. For me the greatest thing done for us was the staff's gift to Floy, as well as myself, of a pen and pencil set in recognition of the significant part she has played in all we have tried to do. We expect to live in Larchmont for the foreseeable future. We have two focuses of continuing interest. One is in the local community, where we want to be of greater service, and the other is in the World Council, where I serve as a president until the next Assembly in 1975.

We send greetings to all of you, and assure you that we will often think of you and pray for you. Ours is a great fellowship in the mission of Christ, and it continues through all of this life and beyond.

Sincerely,
Floy and John Smith

Index

321